VIP
VERY IMPORTANT PRINCESS

SUZANNE YM GALLAGHER

Tellwell Talent
www.tellwell.ca

ISBN
978-1-77370-834-8 (Hardcover)
978-1-77370-833-1 (Paperback)
978-1-77370-835-5 (eBook)

"This book is from the heart of a godly woman whose main desire is to encourage the next generation of women. And how desperately that is needed! Suzanne has done an excellent job of providing a 'sign post' which reads 'This is the way, walk ye in it.' I smiled, I cried, I was encouraged and I was challenged. I can't wait to buy this book for my teenage daughters!"

Kathy Fraser, mother, mentor and teacher

"VIP gently leads the reader to solutions so needed for the many tough places we find ourselves. The author, herself a born again school teacher, covers the often heart-wrenching, crisis-era of high school years through to career life. In continued personal testimony, Suzanne also shares how to cope with the ups and downs of courting, early marriage, and motherhood. You will enjoy and be helped, as you read about the real-life experiences Suzanne has walked through to wholeness. This book speaks of bible truth and very candid life encounters, walking the reader through despair in honest pursuit of hope and purpose. May I suggest we get on board with Suzanne's forty day journey and explore this great kingdom! Any girl or woman who gives her life to Christ is automatically a princess for she is a child of the King!"

Marian Agrey, cofounder of "The Father's House" in Morinville, Alberta

"There is an expression 'what leaves a heart reaches a heart'. In this interactive purpose planner, Suzanne freely and candidly shares her heart, discussing issues girls and young women are facing in these difficult, uncertain times. By sharing her personal journey and experiences, with honesty and transparency, Suzanne provides Christian youth with a gentle challenge to live their lives courageously from their real self, where Christ resides."

Pastor Crystal Terhorst, Educator, Speaker and Support Group Leader

"Written from the heart of a woman who has first-hand experience in life's journey of becoming a Princess Warrior."

Linda Starling, mentor, mother of a godly woman, and inspiration to me-Denise Rosaasen

ACKNOWLEDGEMENTS

With a heart of gratitude to God who has blessed me so much along this beautiful journey, thank-you. I give you all the glory.

To my steadfast parents, Ed and Laraine, who always taught me to walk the walk, not just talk the talk. They taught me most importantly, to love Jesus. Putting that love into action meant loving people where they were. Thank you for supporting me in everything I do, and anything I have ever done! Your unconditional love goes beyond what I deserve.

To my loyal husband, Sam, thank you for encouraging and loving me along the way. For working hard for our family so that I had the time to write this book, I thank you and have a deep-rooted respect for you. You inspire me daily with your undying love for our children; thank you for teaching them how to love their heavenly Father by showing them what an earthly Father's love should be.

To my daughter, Justice, I want to thank you for teaching me how to love without limits and for coming into my life when I needed you most. You are my beautiful rose. Always remember the meaning of your name, "mighty in battle, standing up for what is right." You are God's princess. You are God's mighty warrior. And most importantly, you are an overcomer!

To my son, Samuel, I want to thank you for your completing our family and for teaching me how to laugh. You truly are "an encourager, called by God, to do GREAT things!" You, too, are a mighty warrior prince in the kingdom of God.

Justice and Sammy, may you always know that you are strong, smart, kind and important; and that God has a purpose and a plan for your lives! Dream big!

I want to thank God for giving us baby Nathalie who inspired and confirmed the plans that were in my heart. Nathalie, you are the reason my spark turned into a flame. I pray you would know God's awesome plan for your life!

I want to honor and thank all the people at "The Father's House" in Morinville, Alberta, Canada, that helped to plant and nurture the seed of discipleship in me. Pastor Greg and Betty, you are true disciples leading by example! I praise God for both of you, and pray for his continued hand on your ministry!

Lastly, I also want to thank Beth Podgurny for her tireless efforts in editing and her willingness to be both honest and encouraging while remaining professional. Your "warrior" spirit inspires me!

DEDICATION

I dedicate this book to all young women who have yet to, or are in the process of; finding the treasure God has placed within every one of us. God longs for us to realize our role in his kingdom; as his daughters, a role that no other woman can fill, we are his glorious princesses!

As a good Father, he wants to see us use the gifts, talents, abilities that he has placed in us for his glory! May you come to see your role as a valiant princess in a kingdom that is out of this world and discover the true treasure within, while discovering your purpose at the same time!

In memory of some amazing people that inspired me during their time on earth, and continue to inspire me today: Denise Rosaasen, Lidia Sawchuk, Rachel Joy Scott, Diane L'Heureux, Lori Gagnon, Jesse Rotholz, and Diane Thompson.

In fond memory of some special students: Stuart McWhirter, Chantel Simon, Cam Petherbridge, Stephan Mueller, Matt St. Nicolaas, Nicole Poirier, Jr McLellan, Andrea Jacura, Gunner Christie, Jason Pelletier, and Braedon Schiele who had just begun to discover their treasure, but were taken from this world much too soon.

"But we have this treasure in jars of clay to show that this all-surpassing power is from God and not from us."

2nd Corinthians 4:7

YOUR MISSION:

KNOW GOD

FIND FREEDOM

DISCOVER PURPOSE

MAKE A DIFFERENCE

TABLE OF CONTENTS

Introduction – A Journey like No Other xi

KNOW GOD AND FIND FREEDOM

Pillar # 1 RISE Up Warrior Princess 1

    Day 1: You are here For "Such a Time as This!" 3

    Day 2: Take Action- It's Better than the Best Intention 9

    Day 3: Focus on the Unseen 15

    Day 4: Shine like Stars while Speaking Life 21

    Day 5: Prepare Your Body for Battle 27

    Day 6: Prepare Your Mind for Battle 35

    Day 7: Prepare Your Spirit for Battle 43

Pillar # 2 RUN the Race 49

    Day 8: Set Your Priorities Daily 53

    Day 9: Live with Christ's Priorities 61

    Day 10: Make God's Business a Priority 67

    Day 11: Keep the Finish Line in Focus 73

    Day 12: Make Kindness and Compassion Part of Your Day 79

    Day 13: Manage Your Gifts with Excellence 87

    Day 14: Get His Word in Your Heart 93

Pillar # 3 RADIATE Christ 99

    Day 15: Consecration is Necessary 105

    Day 16: You are Beyond Precious 113

    Day 17: You are Chosen 123

    Day 18: Seeing With the Eyes of Christ 129

    Day 19: Trust Your Father with All Things 137

    Day 20: Way beyond Me 143

    Day 21: The Character of Christ 149

Pillar # 4 REFLECT Intentionally **155**

    Day 22: Get Out of Your Tent so you can SEE the Stars 157

    Day 23: Come as You Are- Thankfulness is the Key 161

    Day 24: Replenish so You Can Pour Out 167

    Day 25: Reflection Leads to Revelation 175

    Day 26: Storms bring Rain Necessary for Growth 181

    Day 27: Drink From His Cup 187

    Day 28: Don't Wait For Tomorrow- Live for Today 193

Pillar # 5 RAISE Others Up **199**

    Day 29: The Prodigal 201

    Day 30: No one is too Far Gone 207

    Day 31: Remember When You were On Fire? 215

    Day 32: Inspire Others to go Deeper 221

    Day 33: We All Have Value 225

    Day 34: He Carries Our Burdens on His Shoulders 233

    Day 35: Jesus Our Humble King 239

DISCOVER PURPOSE AND MAKE A DIFFERENCE

REACH for Your Purpose- Erecting the 5 Pillars and Putting the Palace Together **245**

    Day 36: "WHO I AM" instead of "Who am I?" 249

    Day 37: To Whom Do I Belong? 255

    Day 38: "Who" or "What" is Leading You to your "WHY"? 261

    Day 39: True Warriors Are called to LEAD 267

    Day 40: Making It REAL & Integrating It Into Your Life 273

REDEEM the Time – Make the Most of Every Opportunity **279**

REAFFIRM Your Calling – Make A Difference **283**

NOTES **287**

A JOURNEY LIKE NO OTHER....

"I pray that you, being rooted and established in love, may have power, together with all the saints, to grasp how wide and long and high and deep is the love of Christ."

Ephesians 3:17-18

DISCOVERING HIDDEN TREASURE

Isn't the idea of finding hidden treasure exciting? What's more exciting is finding that treasure within us! So many young women today don't realize their value in Christ!

We are more valuable than the most precious gems that God has created for us to enjoy. Instead, we tend to see our flaws, our imperfections, our inadequacies....if only we could see ourselves as God sees us - perfect in every way!

It's interesting that North American culture sees a flaw as something that takes away from one's character. In Japan, flawed or broken objects are often repaired with gold; the flaw is seen as a unique piece of the object's history, which adds to its beauty!

"The Art of Kintsugi" (6:40 mins):
https://www.youtube.com/watch?v=TQW8t6w0Cy4

We need to see our flaws from this point of view! When we are broken, we tend to focus on our imperfections; we need to see the beauty that the gold brings out of those flaws. Your flaws should add to and enhance your character; giving us distinction and value.

The following video drives this point home of really embracing our flaws and seeing the beauty in them.

"STOP TRYING TO BE PERFECT" (3:44mins):
https://www.youtube.com/watch?v=LySC3v5geAc

This point of value was driven home, when I was sitting in a job interview for a teaching position, and was asked the question, "In one word, what do you see as the greatest challenge in your classroom today?"

I didn't have to think long, and responded with a word God placed in my heart- "devaluization".

Realizing I had probably just said a word that didn't appear in the English dictionary, the Principal and Vice Principal asked me to explain.

I said, "The biggest challenge is that our young people don't recognize they have value, therefore everything they do that is negative, in the classroom or not, flows out of the feeling of not having worth. If they are disrespectful, don't take pride in their work, dress inappropriately.....whatever the case may be, it all stems from the fact that they don't understand the inherent and intrinsic value of having worth."

My wish is that young people would understand that Jesus has given each one of us a purpose and plan for our life that no one else can fulfill. There is hope in Jesus and the plans he has for us, but unfortunately, the world tells our youth to "go with the flow" or "you're not guaranteed tomorrow, so do what feels good today", or "it's hopeless anyway, just live for the moment." Our world is this way because so many young people are finding their worth and identity in material things, relationships with the opposite sex; their job...the list goes on and on. These things are temporary and won't last. This is why they feel as though life has no purpose or meaning. Realizing that hope needs to be put in eternal things that will live on long after we are gone should be the focus.

That is the main reason I felt compelled to write this book. We need to realize the fragility of life. We are only here for a short time. I have deep wounds from former students that I have lost along the way and God has helped me to turn these tragedies into inspiration. He has given me a drive to want to do something for this generation. I will continue to make it a goal in my life to show young people to walk in purpose and know, beyond a shadow of a doubt, that they are here to do a specific job that only they can do.

What's In Store For You Over The Next 40 Days?

This book is a PURPOSE PLANNER. Each day's devotion gets you closer to discovering, planning, and LIVING OUT your purpose.

It will be a 40-day journey to discovering the treasure within you. Just as the Holy Spirit led Jesus into the wilderness for 40 days of testing, encounter, and renewal, you will also endure this over the next 40 days.

The days Jesus spent in the desert allowed him not only to be tested, but also to prepare for his mission on earth. I pray that this 40-day journey will also do the same for you- in order to become all God has called you to be.

This journey to become who you are called to be is one of choice. You need to choose to ACT. Go where no other young woman has gone before! You, and only you, are here for the purposes and plans God has for you. You are royalty. This journey will help you discover the treasure inside of you that makes "you" unique, and calls you to be a warrior princess for the next generation!

This journey may cause you to be uncomfortable, but God is more concerned about your character than your comfort. He loves you beyond what you could ever imagine! Nothing can separate you from his love (Romans 8:37-39). You may feel unloved, unwanted, or rejected by this world, but God's love is so great (1 John 3:1), that he promises never to leave you or forsake you (Joshua 1:5). Although people in this world will leave you and let you down, God will remain the only constant in your life (Hebrews 13:8).

My prayer is that this journey helps you discover the treasure God has placed within you. And through this discovery of your inner beauty and strength given to you by God, the pillars needed to build your palace of purpose will be built on a solid foundation! In turn, you can step confidently into your extraordinary "royal" position in God's kingdom, live out your calling, and continue to become a young woman of character to inspire others; full of beautiful flaws that add to your value and make you one of a kind!

Before you begin your journey, watch this clip reminding you of your gifts and your calling here on earth. Start today by living life like it's the only one you have!

"EVERYBODY DIES, BUT NOT EVERYBODY LIVES" (5:40 mins):
https://www.youtube.com/watch?v=ja-n5qUNRi8

Three Highlights At The End Of Each Chapter

Victorious Verse
Helps you focus on God's word and allows him to speak to your heart about what you have just read. Memorize the verse and get it in your heart. This will help you to hear God's voice and have victory in all areas of your life.

Mighty Melody
The song, (or songs), will wrap up your thoughts, allow you to meditate on what you have just read, and continue to build you up into the mighty warrior God sees in you.

Armour in Action (Call to War)
Taking what you have read and applying it to your everyday life is the key to becoming a warrior princess. Use the journal entries to challenge yourself and allow God to shape and mold you into the young woman He has designed you to be!

Instructions on how to get the most out of VIP:

1- Psalm 127:1 says, "Unless the Lord builds the house, its builders labour in vain." Therefore, as you begin to build your palace of purpose, ask God for HIS guidance, strength, and wisdom; he will help you as he is the master builder and craftsman; he created YOU didn't he?! You have five major pillars to erect that will enable you to build the palace suited just for you and your role in HIS kingdom. These "pillars" are listed in the table of contents and will appear at the beginning of each new section.

2- Not only does each pillar begin with a verb (rise up, run, radiate, reflect, and raise), but each pillar also has a week of daily devotions with action items attached. Spend 5-10 minutes a day reading the devotion, then spend time listening to the song and completing the action item. By completing the action item, it will allow you to spiritually build your palace! PLEASE write your thoughts and prayers in this book!! It will allow you to see your progression towards your final goal!

3- What is the final goal you ask? By the end of this book, you will be able to define your strengths, your purpose, know WHAT God is calling you to do, but more importantly WHY you are doing it!

4- Ultimately you can ACT on your purpose and calling in life, and fulfill your destiny as the daughter of the King of Kings! How exciting is that???!!

As the famous American essayist, lecturer, and poet, Ralph Waldo Emerson put it:
>Sow a **thought**, reap an **action**.
>Sow an **action**, reap a **habit**.
>Sow a **habit**, reap a **character**.
>Sow a **character**, reap a **destiny**.[1]

Watch this clip before you begin! Habits are important!

"Powerful Christian Motivational Video | SPEAK what YOU WANT into YOUR LIFE!" (13:29 mins): https://www.youtube.com/watch?v=FWQlaFZBXqQ

"ROYALTY IS MY IDENTITY.
SERVANTHOOD IS MY ASSIGNMENT.
INTIMACY WITH GOD IS MY LIFE SOURCE."[2]

BILL JOHNSON
(PASTOR, BETHEL CHURCH)

Payton and Zena

Introduction to Pillar **1**

RISE UP WARRIOR PRINCESS

Before we begin the first day, I want to share a powerful prophecy that was prayed over me by a mighty woman of faith, my friend Kathy Fraser, in 2008. I want you to put yourself in this prophecy and imagine it was written for you. Everywhere there is a blank, insert your name. I believe this prophecy is for all women. Run this race we call life with excellence! God is speaking this right from his heart:

_____, you are a beautiful young woman, but know also that I have placed within you an inner beauty. _____, as your physical beauty fades, your inner beauty will increase and it will not cease until the day you die. Those who have eyes to see will look upon you and see not only your outer beauty, but also your ever-increasing inner beauty.

This beauty comes from the overcoming love I've placed within you. This love will enable you to overcome your fears, your pains, your sorrows, your shortcomings....and every obstacle placed in your way. By this love, you will overcome your enemy. _____, your love for me and your love for others is an overcoming love.

_____, I have placed a weapon (the sword of the spirit) in your hand and I'm calling you to war. I declare to you today that you are my princess, my valiant warrior. Raise up your arm and hold high your weapon. You shall defend the defenceless, you shall protect the weak. By my love in you and through you, you shall cause others to become overcomers! From this day forward, you are called OVERCOMER!

Listen to the songs "Overcomer" by <u>Mandisa</u> and "Warrior" by <u>Hannah Kerr</u>. Whenever you feel OVERWHELMED, just play these songs to remind you that you are a WARRIOR for the kingdom of God and can OVERCOME anything in your path! With God's power within you, there is NOTHING that can stand in your way!

Look back at this prophecy and see your name written in the blanks. The name you have been given is powerful and can speak many things over you. If you don't know it already, look up the meaning of your name and write it on the lines below. Many times, there is also a "biblical" meaning for your name, and a Hebrew meaning. Look them up and get a sense of what your name truly means and the power behind your name.

Thank God that he can and WILL do mighty things in and through you because of the name you've been given!

_____

_____

"Greater is he that is in you, than he that is in the world." (1st John 4:4)

Watch the link on Lylah and her "overcoming". So cute, but yet so inspiring, as it is an analogy to life of overcoming obstacles. Enjoy while you cheer her on!

"Lylah Ninja Warrior in the Denver City Finals" (2:42 mins):
https://www.youtube.com/watch?v=wHvv2L7fMAo

Now begin your journey with a message of overcoming with faith and confidence in Jesus Christ!

"Faith and Confidence in God | Christian Video" (5:50 mins):
https://www.youtube.com/watch?v=v8oY3pY5HEc

There is a movie entitled *Overcomer*, (2019), that will motivate you to keep going despite the obstacles that are put in front of you. I encourage you to watch it and be the warrior God is calling you to be!

Day *1* RISE Up Warrior Princess

YOU ARE HERE FOR "SUCH A TIME AS THIS!"

"And who knows but that you have come to royal position for such a time as this?"
Esther 4:14

The book of Esther tells the story of a true hero. Esther was made queen by King Xerxes, and then had to save her people, the Jews, by approaching the king in the inner court without being summoned. She knew that approaching the king in this manner would most likely lead to her death, but she had courage and prayed for her strength to come from God in order to do what she needed to do.

"For Such a Time as This" (13:44 mins):
https://www.youtube.com/watch?v=Oo1A3sOvHyo

She fought for her people, and because of her actions, the Jews were saved. Had she shrunk back and allowed fear to paralyze her, she and her people may have been destroyed. With God, *all* things are possible! Where there is God, there is no fear!

"God is love. Whoever lives in love lives in God, and God in him. There is no fear in love. But perfect love casts out fear." (1st John 4:16b,18a)

Like Queen Esther, who faced her fears, you can too! Watch the following clip to remind you who you are in the face of fear:

"Put On Your Crown | Inspiring Christian Motivational Video" (14:20 mins):
https://www.youtube.com/watch?v=s4WSMeR1ZcY

You are here for a specific reason at this specific point in history. You have gifts and abilities that no one else on this earth has. You are in the town or city you are in because God has a plan for you there. God has put certain dreams and desires in your heart. Are these dreams and desires always going to be easy to achieve? More than likely, they will be quite the opposite.

In other words, Jesus knew it wouldn't be easy, but with his strength, you can do all things! (Philippians 4:13)

2nd Timothy 1:7(AKJV) says, "God has not given us the spirit of fear; but of power, and of love, and of a sound mind."

This is an interesting verse, because it helps us understand that fear is not a feeling, but a spirit. Therefore, break off that spirit in the name of Jesus if fear has come against you.

If fear is holding you back, watch this next clip. It is a powerful reminder that fear should NOT be a factor in your life!

"GOD'S PLAN FOR YOU | Understanding Your Purpose - Inspirational & Motivational Video" (10:02 mins):
https://www.youtube.com/watch?v=8fcLxYLJdCl

I LOVE how God always sees who we are BECOMING, not just who we currently ARE. He sees our future without fear in it, because his perfect love casts out fear.

The devil, on the other hand, uses fear against us.

Satan has used fear to paralyze Christians and keep us from our calling for thousands of years. We need to rise up and use what God has given us!

The first gift God gives us in 2nd Timothy is power from the Holy Spirit, which will always defeat fear.

Acts 1:8 states, "But you will receive power when the Holy Spirit comes on you; and you will be my witnesses..."

By being in communion with the Holy Spirit regularly, you will receive God's power to fight against the devil's schemes.

Love is the second gift God gives us, in 2nd Timothy 1:7.

As stated earlier, 1st John 4:16b says, "God is love. Whoever lives in love lives in God." Verse 18 goes on to say, "There is no fear in love. But perfect love drives out fear."

Therefore, if you have God in your life, and you are meeting with him continually, his perfect love will drive out fear. You do not have to fear the future or stepping out in faith, as long as you have God on your side!

The final portion of 2nd Timothy 1:7 states that he gives us the gift of a <u>sound mind</u>.

Jesus' mind had peace and purpose.

1st Corinthians 2:16 reinforces the fact that we have 'the mind of Christ'.

Christ's mind was 'sound', which means he exercised self-control and had true balance.

God has blessed you with this Christ-like mind and you need to use it to further his kingdom here on earth! Because you have <u>power,</u> <u>love</u>, and a <u>sound mind</u> from the Father, Son, and Holy Spirit (the trinity) you can stand firm when the enemy tries to say you aren't enough.

Fill in the blank....

Not _____enough. (skinny, smart, brave, holy, pretty, athletic, talented, etc.)

These lies of inadequacy must be put to rest. Instead, your imperfections add value and character. God knows all your flaws and loves you anyway.

Watch this video on the sad life of Whitney Houston. She never quite felt "good enough", and in the end, she paid the ultimate price with her life.

"Kevin Costner Was Whitney Houston's Real-Life Bodyguard" (6:03 mins):
https://www.youtube.com/watch?v=FsOZBvds8M4

With this previous story of this pop star who never felt "good enough", we can ask God for revelation on how he sees us. There is victory in God's perception of us!

"Tyler Perry: See Yourself as God Sees You | Praise on TBN" (8:58 mins):
https://www.youtube.com/watch?v=bDSlDDpjYdQ

"How God Sees You" (6:29 mins):
https://www.youtube.com/watch?v=CWB2lGRvlVY

In fact, in Psalm 139:14, we see that he knows everything about you. You are "fearfully and wonderfully made"! Who are we to say his creation is flawed?

The Psalm also says he is always with us.

"Where can I go from Your Spirit? Where can I flee from your presence? If I go up to the heavens, you are there; if I make my bed in the depths, you are there. If I rise on the wings of the dawn, if I settle on the far side of the sea, even there your hand will guide me; your right hand will hold me fast." (Psalm 139: 7-10)

With him by your side, you can have confidence to stand firm. There are at least 14 places in the bible where God tells us to "stand firm". I think he's trying to tell us something!

In order to see his plans fulfilled in your life, Paul tells us, "We won't be tossed and blown about by every wind of new teaching. We will not be influenced when people try to trick us with lies so clever they sound like the truth." (Ephesians 4:14 NLT)

Put on the "full armour of God, so that when the day of evil comes, you may be able to stand your ground, and after we have done everything, to stand. Stand firm then...." (Ephesians 6:13-14a)

Therefore, with the armour of God in place, and the God of the universe on your side, you are a true warrior for his kingdom. You are a soldier of the light and therefore, darkness has no place around you.

John 1:5 (ESV) confirms this. "The light shines in the darkness, and the darkness has not overcome it."

1st John 1:5 also says, "God is light; in him there is no darkness at all."

In fact, not only is there NO darkness in him, but "even the darkness will not be dark...the night will shine like the day, for darkness is as light to you." (Psalm 139:12)

If you truly want to see God's amazing plans unfold for your life, you must walk in His light.

Psalm 27:1 sums it up well- "The Lord is my light and my salvation, whom shall I fear? The Lord is the stronghold of my life; of whom shall I be afraid?"

A young man by the name of Inky Johnson knows all about God's plan for his life- listen to his story:

"Tragedy into Triumph- Inky Johnson Inspirational and Motivational Video" (9:53 mins): https://www.youtube.com/watch?v=KjJXB2Zkxgo

Inky's testimony proves that when you are up against something daunting in your life, he will grant you the strength and courage you need to fulfill what he has planned for you.

God did the same for the leader of the Israelites, Joshua.

In chapter one of Joshua, not only does he tell him he will never leave him or forsake him (Joshua 1:5), but he tells him at least four times in the same chapter to be strong and courageous. He promised to be with him wherever he went. (Joshua 1:9)

I'm sure Joshua was scared and nervous as he faced a huge task taking over as leader from such a wise man as Moses. Nevertheless, he stepped out in faith anyway, to accomplish the plans and dreams God had for him, and so can you! As God promised Joshua that he would be with him, he will also be with you mighty warrior princess!

"Before You Give Up, Watch This | Life Advice Will Change Your Future" (13:02 mins):
https://www.youtube.com/watch?v=e8P8mHm2NUo

As God walks with us, he will also show us our strengths. Do you know what your strengths are? A mighty warrior capitalizes on their strengths. In order to gain ground for the kingdom and walk in your purpose, you need to be confident in your strengths!

I pray that God speaks to your heart about where your strengths lie, so that you hear your calling to rise up and take your royal position!

Finally, watch as this former model heard God calling her heart to the mission field. She answered the call and rose up to her position in the Kingdom! This story illustrates that when you realize your strengths, you can trust God to do miraculous things in and through you as you follow HIS plan for your life!

"FROM MODEL TO MISSIONARY || My Christian Testimony" (9:09 mins):
https://www.youtube.com/watch?v=FEI42W2xlh0

Victorious Verse

"Finally, be strong in the Lord and in his mighty power. Put on the full armour of God so that you can take your stand...." Ephesians 6:10-11

Mighty Melody

"The Anthem" by Jesus Culture and "Fearless" by Jasmine Murray

Armour in Action

What is holding you back from being a mighty Princess Warrior? Write down your fears or insecurities and then speak to them in Jesus' name and tell them they have no power over you anymore! Write a prayer to God asking him to give you courage and strength to do what he's calling you to do!

Lastly, take the "**StrengthsFinder**" test found at: (there is a small fee required) https://www.gallupstrengthscenter.com/?gclid=CjOKCQiAkNfSBRCSARIsAL-u3X84yMGQ-ry367-2XwPbaNam2e7tMXP3nqbvZm9MjjcbMcUSIfMnNXQEaAtiwEALw_wcB

Write down your strengths in this notes section. Get to know your strengths well. Also, ask others around you what they think your strengths are. Add them to the list! Remember there is power in your strengths because those are the gifts that God has placed in you to make a difference!! Walk confidently in your strengths, and allow God to do mighty things through them!

Notes:

_____
_____
_____
_____
_____
_____
_____
_____
_____
_____
_____
_____
_____
_____
_____
_____
_____
_____
_____
_____

Day *2* RISE Up Warrior Princess

TAKE ACTION- IT'S BETTER THAN THE BEST INTENTION

"Stand firm...let nothing move you. Always give yourselves fully to the work of the Lord, because you know that your labour in the Lord is not in vain."

1st Corinthians 15:58

As referred to in Day 1, standing firm is so vital if you want to make a difference in the kingdom of God! Again, we see the message to "stand firm" in the book of 1st Corinthians.

The Apostle Paul says to let nothing move you and give yourself fully to God's work. In Chapter 16, he continues, "Be on your guard; stand firm in the faith; be men (and women) of courage; be strong." (1st Corinthians 16:13)

As women, sometimes we step back and tend to let things slide, or just think to ourselves that someone else will do what we are too uncomfortable to do. We are, too often, passive instead of assertive.

David said to Goliath, "You come against me with sword and spear and javelin, but I come against you in the name of the Lord Almighty." (1st Samuel 17:45a)

David had a peace that despite his big circumstances, his God was bigger!

Here is Pastor Louie Giglio's take on the story.

"Louie Giglio Overcomes Life's Giants" (9:14 mins):
http://www1.cbn.com/video/SUB258_LouieGiglio_071217/louie-giglio-overcomes-lifes-giants

Now, be inspired to face your own giants, like David!

"Facing Your Giants | God Still Does the Impossible - Inspirational & Motivational Video" (10:06 mins): https://www.youtube.com/watch?v=iLmHbYH1LiU

Imagine what may have happened if David hadn't stepped up to fight Goliath. If he had cowered and let someone else do it, he may never have become the 'man after God's own heart' for which he was known! He may never have written the Psalms and fulfilled the plan God had for his life! Instead, he knew from where his power came, and he trusted God to help him win an impossible fight.

As Kerry and Chris Shook put it in their book "One Month to Live" (2008, pg. 14), David had "ridiculous faith":

> "When you're operating on the basis of reason, all you can see is how big your giants are. If you're operating in faith, all you can see is how small your giants are compared to God.
> The one thing that separated David from the thousands who were there that day was 'ridiculous faith'. Let me humbly suggest that the only way you can slay the giants that stand between you and the life you were made for is 'ridiculous faith'."[1]

This song by John Waller speaks to the "crazy faith" David had! Listen and be moved!

"Crazy Faith" by John Waller (4:20 mins): https://www.youtube.com/watch?v=J3I9TVikxUE

David faced his giants because of this faith, and God was right beside him fighting that fight! This clip will encourage you to face the giants in your life!

"FACE YOUR FEAR WITH GOD ▶ Best Christian Motivational Video 2019" (11:23 mins): https://www.youtube.com/watch?v=jQWaT3dpXYU

Faith is what caused David, and many other characters in the bible, to have the courage to stand out, stand firm, take risks and live for God. I will conclude with Ruth who did exactly that.

Ruth was married to the son of a woman named Naomi. First, Naomi's husband died, and then her son (Ruth's husband) died as well. Naomi told her daughter-in-law to go back to her homeland so she could remarry and have a family, as she was still a young woman. Ruth stood firm and refused to leave her mother-in-law's side, and remained loyal and faithful to her saying she would go wherever she went, and stay wherever she stayed. (Ruth 1:16)

When Naomi realized Ruth wasn't going to leave her, they travelled to Bethlehem, where Ruth went into the fields and gleaned grain. Because of her assertiveness, she gained favour in the eyes of the landowner, Boaz, and eventually God gave Boaz to her in marriage. Boaz saw Ruth's faithfulness to Naomi, along with her hard work ethic, and he was moved.

His words display his admiration of her actions, "May the Lord repay you for what you have done. May you be richly rewarded (blessed) by the Lord, the God of Israel, under whose wings you have come to take refuge." (Ruth 2:12)

Again, you see how a person can make a choice to take action, and God uses it for his glory. Ruth took a step of faith and went with Naomi. Then, she willingly gleaned and gathered grain to provide for her mother-in-law and herself! If she hadn't done these things, she would have missed God's blessing and favour. She was proactive and God rewarded her!

Being proactive is a trait that God loves! Instead of reacting to what others do, take a step out of your comfort zone and watch God respond by meeting you halfway! He gives you strength to do what you cannot do on your own.

Being proactive in prayer is an excellent start! Watch this video on the power of a praying woman!

"Keep Praying Woman Of God | A Praying Woman Is Powerful!" (10:50 mins): https://www.youtube.com/watch?v=IYVZJwjgt2g

There is a movie called *War Room*, (2015), that has a victorious scene involving the main character "Elizabeth". She took charge and reminded satan that he had no power in her home. My prayer is that you will be blessed by this movie, should you choose to watch it.

Like Elizabeth, we can be proactive and come against the schemes of the enemy!

Proactive people listen to that still, small voice, which is the Holy Spirit working in them, and they don't follow the crowd. This actually involves going against what everyone else is doing, and carving your own path. It's like the salmon that spawn every season...in order to fulfill their purpose; they need to swim against the "flow". Many times as Christians, we need to do the same thing. Usually it is the more difficult path to take, but at the end, it is so much more rewarding.

Terry Crews and Father Gregory Boyle are examples of people who decided to be proactive and take action. Listen to their stories:

"I Wanted to Save My Mother | Terry Crews | Goalcast" (4:37 mins): https://www.youtube.com/watch?v=L79t3fPHvll

"One Of The Most Inspirational Speeches From Gangsters | Father Gregory Boyle | Goalcast" (6:03 mins): https://www.youtube.com/watch?v=zk--XN4ozr8

Just like Terry and Father Gregory, we all hope to hear those choice words from Jesus one day as we stand before him, "Well done good and faithful servant! You have been faithful with a few things; I will put you in charge of many things. Come and share your master's happiness!" (Matthew 25:23)

While the world says, 'go with the flow', 'do whatever feels good at the time', 'take the easy way out', or 'sit back and let someone else do the dirty work', God is saying step up and be courageous! Go against the flow and don't worry about what the world is doing! As Paul reminds us, "Do not conform any longer to the patterns of the world, but be transformed by the renewing of your mind. Then you will be able to test and approve what God's will is- his good, pleasing and perfect will." (Romans 12:2)

Too many times, Christians fall for the easy way out and go with what the world deems important, and we wonder why we find ourselves frustrated and confused. We are stuck in a never-ending battle, and our focus comes off Jesus and onto ourselves. We begin to lose sight of what really is important in the kingdom of God, and God's plans take a backseat to our own. We think our plans and purposes are good, but God's are beyond what we could ever hope for or imagine.

Help us God to keep our eyes on you and remember your words of encouragement, "So are my ways higher than your ways and my thoughts than your thoughts." (Isaiah 55:9)

Victorious Verse
"I keep my eyes always on the Lord. With him at my right hand, I will not be shaken." Psalm 16:8

Mighty Melody
"We Won't Be Shaken" by Building 429 and "Lose My Soul" by Kirk Franklin and Toby Mac

Armour in Action
Are there areas of your life where you can take action and be more proactive? Write down three situations where you can go "against the flow" and listen to God's voice and not the voice of the "crowd" or the "world".

Notes:

_____
_____
_____
_____
_____
_____
_____
_____
_____
_____
_____
_____
_____
_____
_____
_____
_____
_____
_____
_____
_____
_____
_____
_____
_____
_____
_____
_____
_____

Day *3* RISE Up Warrior Princess

FOCUS ON THE UNSEEN

"Finally,(brothers), whatever is true, whatever is noble, whatever is right, whatever is pure, whatever is lovely, whatever is admirable- if anything is excellent or praiseworthy- think about such things."

Philippians 4:8-9

Excellent warriors can see victory in the spiritual realm before it ever happens in the physical. They have their mind set on things that will help them to win the battle. Defeat is not an option.

Watch this clip entitled "Warrior" and be encouraged to see victory in every area of your life!

"Steven Curtis Chapman - Warrior (Lyric Video)" (4:31 mins): https://www.youtube.com/watch?v=rqrwLLE1azI

Now, listen to the song "Battle Belongs" by Phil Wickham! Be reminded of who is fighting the battle with you daily!

Phil Wickham - Battle Belongs (Official Music Video) (4:45 mins): https://www.youtube.com/watch?v=qtvQNzPHn-w

This can be you! Fix your eyes on Christ, he will draw closer to you and is able to give you victory through placing his peace, strength, and joy in your spirit!

Daniel was a wonderful example of this while he was in the lion's den. God protected him in the pit because his gaze was fixed on Jesus.

The king, who was distraught about putting Daniel there in the den in the first place, called out, "Has your God, whom you serve continually, been able to rescue you from the lions?" (Daniel 6:20)

Daniel replied, "O king live forever! My God sent his angel, and he shut the mouths of the lions. They have not hurt me, because I was found innocent in his sight." (Daniel 6:21-22)

The story then goes onto say, "When Daniel was lifted from the den, no wound was found on him, because he had trusted in his God." (Daniel 6:23a)

Those are powerful words! God will protect you, if you trust and put your faith in him, just as he did for Daniel! Simply keep your mind and gaze fixed on him!

There are also three other characters in the book of Daniel who were in a similar situation. They faced death, but decided to trust God and keep their eyes fixed on him in the midst of their circumstances. Shadrach, Meshach, and Abednego, were up against an evil king named Nebuchadnezzar. He wanted them to bow down to a statue of gold, and these three men refused, as they knew there was only one true God. Because of their stance against him, the king had them tied up and thrown into a blazing furnace. Even the soldiers who had taken the men up to the furnace had died because of the heat!

After the men had fallen into the furnace, the king was amazed, as he saw them walking around in the fire. When the king called on them, they came out of the fire, and he saw that their bodies weren't harmed.....not even one hair singed on their heads.

He was so amazed, Nebuchadnezzar proclaimed, "Praise be to the God of Shadrach, Meshach, and Abednego.....they trusted in him and defied the king's command and were willing to give up their lives rather than serve or worship any god except their own God." (Daniel 3:28)

Like Daniel, God has given you a fierceness that is holy and set apart. We can look upon Deborah in Chapters 4 and 5 of the book of Judges and see that she was wise, strong, cunning, courageous, beautiful, fearless, and victorious.

John and Stasi Eldridge (2005, pgs. 196-197) describe this one-of-a-kind prophetess that God used in a mighty battle:

> "Through her, (Deborah), God commanded the Israelites to go to war against Sisera and the Canaanite armies. The leader of the Israelite army, a man named Barak, would go to war only if Deborah went with them. He would not go if she did not. So Deborah went. 'But because of the way you are going about this,' said Deborah, 'the honor will not be yours, for the Lord will hand Sisera over to a woman' (Judges 4:9).
>
> The story of the battle is short. Led by Deborah, the Israelites were victorious. Their enemy Sisera, however, escaped and fled on foot to the tent of Jael, a wife and the 'most blessed of [the] tent-dwelling women' (5:24). While Israel's enemy slept in her tent, Jael took a tent peg and hammered it through his temple. He lay dead at her feet. Now, that is a fierce woman! Then, Deborah led Israel in a victory song":

'So may all your enemies perish, O LORD! But may they who love you be like the sun when it rises in its strength.' (Judges 5:31)[1]

Her focus allowed her to keep her eyes fixed on the Lord, and the enemy was just an afterthought!

The Apostle Paul was another amazing example of keeping his eyes fixed on Christ. Even while they were in prison, he and Silas were praying and singing hymns to God. (Acts 16:25-28) Paul had learned to be content in all circumstances. (Philippians 4:11) He had done a complete 180-degree turn in his life; went from being self-centered, to being Christ-centered.

Like Paul, you want your life to mean something, "I have fought the good fight, I have finished the race, I have kept the faith. Now there is in store for me the crown of righteousness." (2nd Timothy 4:7-8a)

In this first clip, you'll see Paul's conviction right to the bitter end; so powerful! Then, watch the video on what faith can do in YOUR life!

"I Have Kept the Faith- The Apostle Paul Endures to the End" (1:48 mins):
https://www.youtube.com/watch?v=yjlyUNAi7Oc

"Kutless, What Faith Can Do (lyrics!)" (3:51 mins):
https://www.youtube.com/watch?v=ur6Zznc407U

Paul considered "everything a loss compared to the surpassing greatness of knowing Christ Jesus my Lord." (Philippians 3:8) With his mind fixed on things that were true, noble, right, pure, lovely, admirable and praiseworthy, his testimony was beyond powerful!

I'm sure you've heard the saying 'have an open mind'. When you hear these clichés, you need to know God's word and how to respond! Like Paul, stay focussed on the things of God, remembering that we (you) have the mind of Christ." (1st Corinthians 2:16b) Otherwise, you could fall prey to deceit from outside sources.

You've probably also heard the saying 'if you don't stand for something, you'll fall for anything'. Especially in today's world, you must be bold and stand for what you value, while keeping your mind and eyes on the spiritual victory before the physical victory is won.

In the early months of 2020, there was a virus that brought fear into many hearts, including my own. Disaster seemed to be slowly striking around the world, and many people were left with much anxiety and they were scared of what the future would bring.

In the midst of that time, God inspired me to write the following poem as a reminder that we have the mind of Christ, and that our spiritual victory will come long before we see it in the physical realm. I pray you would be encouraged today!

TRUE FREEDOM

When Job lost everything he owned and all his children died,
He could have shaken his fist at God, and screamed and yelled and cried.

But instead, he tore his robe, shaved his head, and worshipped on his own accord;
He then cried, "Lord, you give and you take away, blessed be the name of the Lord!"

Like Job, when we are faced with fear, or faced with impending doom,
Do we speak of God's light and of his hope, or do we buy into the doubt and the gloom?

We are called to stand firm during these times of trouble and keep our eyes on HIM,
For our hope is not in this fallen world, so our faith should not grow dim!

Our light should shine much brighter, than it ever has before,
For we are HIS ambassadors, as we represent our King and our Lord!

So rise up, mighty warrior, you need to do what's right!
Your victory's already been won in heaven, so be courageous and fight the good fight!

The devil is prowling around as we speak wreaking havoc in hearts, minds, and souls,
He thinks he's got people right where he wants them, he thinks he's in control.

But we know he was defeated on that fateful day, when Christ gave up his life on that cross,
So devil go back where you came from, because your war's already been lost!

The book of Revelation tells us you've been overcome, by our testimonies and by the blood of the Lamb,
You have no power or clout in this hour, for our trust is in the great I AM!!

As we trust in HIM and not in the things of this world, and tell fear that he's a liar,
It's only then that we take our power back, and our spark turns into a raging FIRE!

A fire that cannot be quenched by any sickness, disease, or strife,
For it is for these things that Jesus died; it's why he willingly gave up his life.

So when you're tempted to let yourself go, and jump on this world's crazy train,
Keep your thoughts fixed on what is pure, honorable, right, and true, so his death may not be in vain!

Take captive every thought that comes, and make it obedient to Christ,
For we are called to love during these times of uncertainty, and to truly speak of God's light and his life!

Stop sitting in your idle ways, put all your false gods aside,
Pick up your sword of the spirit, and in HIM, you will abide.

Put on your helmet of salvation, and hold up your shield of faith,
Stand firm then with the belt of truth buckled tightly 'round your waist,

And finally, with the breastplate of righteousness in place, and your feet shod with the gospel of peace,
Paul tells us to be FEARLESS in spreading the gospel, and that our praying should never cease!

For when we pray we are liberated, from the fear that we can't see,
We are fighting the war in the spirit, and Christ's presence can set others free!

So in solidarity we battle together, as we let true freedom ring,
And in these dark and troubled times, may we bring glory and honor to our King!

You are a MIGHTY WOMAN OF GOD. Watch this video and be ready to move for God!

"Start Living On A Different Level | One Of The Best Christian Motivational Videos" (16:00 mins)
https://www.youtube.com/watch?v=0srzOadjFTc

Victorious Verse

"Let us run with perseverance the race marked out for us, fixing our eyes on Jesus, the author and perfecter of our faith. Who for the joy set before him, endured the cross." Hebrews 12:1-2

Watch the video:
"Run the Race- The Faith in Christ that Perseveres" (2:48 mins):
https://www.youtube.com/watch?v=Nhk_5c6H-yc

Mighty Melody

"Fix My Eyes on You" by For King and Country and "Turn Your Eyes upon Jesus" by Hillsong

Armour in Action

Like Daniel, what are some of the "lions" in your life that take your eyes off Christ? Make a list of these distractions in your life and pray that God would give you the strength to keep your eyes on him and keep your priorities where they should be.

Notes:

_____
_____
_____
_____
_____
_____
_____
_____
_____
_____
_____
_____
_____
_____
_____
_____
_____
_____
_____
_____
_____
_____

Day *4* RISE Up Warrior Princess

SHINE LIKE STARS WHILE SPEAKING LIFE

"Do everything without complaining or arguing, so that you may become blameless and pure, children of God without fault in a crooked and depraved generation, in which you shine like stars in the universe as you hold out the word of life."

Philippians 2:14-16

Jesus said, "I am the way and the truth and the life." (John 14:6a)

He doesn't just give life, he IS life itself.

When we shine like stars for HIM, we can bring the life of Jesus to others! Start off today's devotion by listening to these songs, as they will pump you up to SHINE!

"Skillet - Stars - (with lyrics) (2016)" (3:41 mins):
https://www.youtube.com/watch?v=s5uxB6gzWUY

"Owl City - Shooting Star [Official Lyric Video]' (4:06 mins):
https://www.youtube.com/watch?v=K7KMRBoqQUg

Jesus also said, "I am the vine; you are the branches. If you remain in me and I in him, he will bear much fruit; apart from me you can do nothing." (John 15:5)

I remember an analogy of this concept using a beautiful plant growing in my garden. The colors were radiant pink and stark white- a striking stargazer lily. Wanting to bring the beauty indoors, I cut off a gorgeous flower and brought it into my kitchen. The moment it was cut, the flower was dead. This is just like us, when we are cut off from our heavenly Father who gives us life. We may look pretty for a little while, but eventually we will die (spiritually) because we are not connected to the vine.

There was a critical time in my life when I felt cut off from Jesus. I had lost all hope after a failed marriage, and really felt like I had hit rock bottom. Not only did I feel like I let God down, but I felt like a failure in my parent's eyes, whom I had tried hard to please and make proud my whole life. As I contemplated taking my life, Jesus came into my bedroom and brought HIS light, and breathed HIS LIFE into me. He spoke of his love for me through a devotional book I had, and he told me to hand my life over to him and give him control. I was flooded with emotion and humbled that the God of the universe would show his love for me in such a brilliant way. He showed me that I was his masterpiece. (Ephesians 2:10 NLT)

From that point on, I realized that he died for me so I could live for him. I handed my life over to him and wanted to live every day wholeheartedly for Christ. I knew he had great purposes for my life, no matter what my circumstances were. Instead of letting the circumstances hold me back and tell me it was hopeless, I chose LIFE that night! Within the next year, I quit my job, entered discipleship school, and God was using my life while on mission work in Mexico. What an awesome God we serve!

You have that option when darkness knocks on your door. You can choose life or death; it is really about being self-centered or Christ-centered. It is all about making a conscious choice.

A young man by the name of Jake Bailey was faced with physical death when he was diagnosed with cancer. Let his message speak to your heart.

"How to Live a Life of Gratitude- Jake Bailey- Goalcast" (4:33 mins):
https://www.youtube.com/watch?v=EiWD_aEARic

Here is Luke's testimony as well.

"Luke Hahn's Testimony: God Had to Strip Me of Everything" (20:31 mins):
https://www.youtube.com/watch?v=t7B3KMbpMXo

Sometimes, it takes something drastic in our lives in order for us to REALLY live!

Some, like Jake or Luke, face physical death, while others may face emotional and spiritual death. Many times, when we are going through a valley in our life, our hearts can become like stone. The heart is where Christ resides, so it is very important that we protect it from becoming cold and hard. We can't lose sight of what God is doing! Allow HIM to put his healing balm on your heart so you can be pliable in the potter's hands. Only then will your heart be ready for all that he has in store!

Psalm 27:8 (NLT): "My heart has heard you say, 'Come and talk with me.' And my heart responds 'Lord, I am coming.' "

This song is a beautiful reminder of surrendering our hearts to God:

"Casting Crowns - Here's My Heart (Live)" (6:46 mins):
https://www.youtube.com/watch?v=qkSBmRAVXNc

It is tougher to guard, rather than follow your heart, but it is worth it!

Therefore, you must listen carefully to his words in order to bear fruit in your life and in the lives of those around you. Speak life into all situations! When the world says 'No Way', you say 'YAHWEH'!

Jesus tells us in the book of Matthew that the wide road, or easy way that most people take, usually leads to destruction, but "narrow the road that leads to life, and only a few find it." (Matthew 7:13-14)

Christ took the more difficult, narrow road, and it was FAR from easy. Because he was human, he had a point in his walk leading up to his death on the cross where he asked his Father to help him and take the cup from him. (Luke 22:42) He was sweating drops of blood as he agonized over his fate of dying on a cross; he felt as though it was too much, and he became overwhelmed. Nevertheless, he is Jesus, and he knew his Father's will needed to be done above his own. What is extremely comforting to know is that as soon as Jesus turned his will over to his Father, the next verse states that an angel came and strengthened him. (Luke 22:43)

I believe that God will do the same for you when you find yourself overwhelmed. When you begin to see his will and give your life over to him, he sends a supernatural strength that will help you get through whatever you are up against.

When the world seems to be closing in on you, remember, "The world and its desires pass away, but he who does the will of God lives forever." (1st John 2:17)

I witnessed this firsthand when I rededicated my life to him that night in my bedroom when I felt like the world was a hopeless place. I should have spoken God's promises over my life instead of letting my feelings of weakness and helplessness try to overcome me!

Interestingly enough, after the encounter with God, I felt renewed and strengthened. I cried out to him, and began to feel stronger than I had felt in a very long time. I believe I had an encounter involving the supernatural strength of angels, and that God wanted to display his power through me.

God loves to hear his children cry out to him! When we do, we are claiming life, abundance, and prosperity over situations instead of death and poverty. Speaking his word and truth over our lives becomes easier the more we do it! In spite of darkness, despair, and death, we speak life, and thus have victory over death, just like Christ!

A quote by author Beau Taplin sums it up nicely, "Perhaps the butterfly is proof that you can go through a great deal of darkness yet become something beautiful."[1]

In Ephesians, Paul speaks of this death and darkness in which we often find ourselves.

He states, "But because of his great love for us, God, who is rich in mercy, made us alive with Christ even when we were dead in transgressions (sins)." (Ephesians 2:4-5)

He freely gave us life, while we were still sinners! Thank-you, Jesus!

Again in Romans, "God demonstrates his own love for us in this: While we were still sinners, Christ died for us." (Romans 5:8)

God understands that darkness will come, and so he sent his son to die for it all. What an amazing God we serve!

Further along in Romans, Paul states that we need to "offer yourselves to God, as those who've been brought from death to life; and offer the parts of your body to him as instruments of righteousness." (Romans 6:13)

This is key to your mission here on earth, as you leave your old ways and put on Christ, as he IS life. Only then, can you fully offer yourself to him, to be used for his glory here on earth, and fulfill your purpose!

Therefore, when I refer to the words 'speak life', it means to stay positive and speak his promises over ALL situations. When you continue to do this despite the trials you are going through, your will becomes secondary, and his will becomes primary in your life. Jesus is the only one that can bring you from death into life! When you understand this concept, you can begin to fully serve God and bring him all the glory he deserves!

End today's devotion with these two videos. They are a refreshing reminder to "speak life"!

"A MUST WATCH:THESE THREE WORDS FROM GOD WOULD CHANGE YOUR LIFE FOREVER" (16:50 mins):
https://www.youtube.com/watch?v=HMiVQiwcyhk

(**This clip was referenced earlier in the book, but bears repeating**)

"Powerful Christian Motivational Video | SPEAK what YOU WANT into YOUR LIFE!" (13:29 mins):
https://www.youtube.com/watch?v=FWQIaFZBXqQ

"IN EVERY ENCOUNTER, WE EITHER GIVE LIFE OR WE DRAIN IT; THERE IS NO NEUTRAL EXCHANGE."[12]

BRENNAN MANNING

Victorious Verse
"In a warped and crooked generation, you will shine like stars in the sky as you hold firmly to the word of life." Philippians 2:15b-16a

Mighty Melody
"Speak Life" by Toby Mac, "Resurrection Power" by Chris Tomlin and "Resurrecting" by Aaron Shust

Armour in Action
What are some areas of my life that I need to surrender to God so he can "resurrect" those parts of me? How am I bringing him glory and already speaking life in daily situations? Think of at least two examples.

Notes:

Day *5* RISE Up Warrior Princess

PREPARE YOUR BODY FOR BATTLE

"You are not your own; you were bought at a price. Therefore honour God with your body."

1st Corinthians 6:20

The bible says, "You yourselves are God's temple and that God's Spirit lives in you." (1st Corinthians 3:16) Your body does not belong to you.

This is in direct opposition to the world around us. Women abort their babies because it is 'their' body and they are free to make this choice. Women abuse their bodies with drugs and alcohol; because after all, you only live once, do what feels good in the moment. If women can't find happiness in their marriage, they find it somewhere else. So many lies we choose to believe! In a world that tells us so many different things, how do we know what is truth and what isn't?

Truth has become a subjective reality that is different for everyone. There seems to be no standard anymore, which is so dangerous. The lines between right and wrong have become blurred, truth is relative, and we no longer have common sense.

Jesus said, "I am the way and the TRUTH and the life. No one comes to the Father except through me." (John 14:6)

In order to find out what is important to God, you need to read his word. He tells you that Christ died and paid the ultimate price, therefore you need to honour him and his word when it comes to your body. When you really think about it, we all abuse our bodies in different ways and fail to treat it as the temple of God!

To some degree, we are saying 'Jesus, your sacrifice wasn't enough. I'm going to live my life my way and treat my body in whatever way feels good to me.' We overeat or eat unhealthy, we smoke, watch movies that subject our minds to all kinds of evil, we stay in relationships that we shouldn't, which is hard on our hearts. It all contributes to our well-being.

I remember a time in my life when my physical well-being took priority over everything else in my life. It became an idol in my life. I was treating my body like a temple, but it was for all the wrong reasons. I wanted to feel love and at a low point in my life, I thought looking and dressing a certain way would bring me what I longed for. Physically, I was in the best shape of my life, but I wasn't doing it to honour God, I was doing it for selfish reasons. God understands where we are and he longs for us to get to the next level. He met me during that phase of my life and challenged me to start living for him.

Over time, I saw that my intentions were not right. Therefore God was able to teach me to honour my body through dressing appropriately and being physically healthy, which in turn, brought HONOUR to HIM, not bring attention to myself. I was learning the truth of the scripture "He must increase, but I must decrease." (John 3:30 ESV)

This verse brought the true meaning of modesty into my heart.

As Jessica Rey, an American actress and designer put it, "Modesty isn't about hiding your body, it is about revealing your dignity."[1]

This quote is echoed in the following clip.

"What Everyone Gets Wrong About Modesty" (1:56 mins): https://www.youtube.com/watch?v=Do_2uxkaBPM

Paul put it like this in his letter in 1st Timothy (1:9-10a), "....women dress modestly with decency and propriety, not with braided hair or gold or pearls or expensive clothes, but with good deeds."

I believe he was telling us that our focus should be on our heart. Should we look presentable and take care of our outer appearance? Most definitely! We are ambassadors for Christ! It just shouldn't come before making our hearts presentable to him first. Honour God with your heart and physical body, and you will be richly rewarded!

Unfortunately, there are many ways we dishonour God by abusing our bodies; some examples may be not eating properly, or we may not get enough exercise or sleep. Nevertheless, God warns us "there is a way that seems right to a man, but in the end it leads to death." (Proverbs 14:12)

In addition, Paul states in Romans "the wages of sin is death." (Romans 6:23) It may not be a physical death, but it may be an emotional or psychological death. Death can present itself many ways in our lives, and is definitely imminent in the spiritual battle we face.

Daily we are struggling in a world where there is death all around us. We try to reach out to hurting people, we try to bring acceptance and love to those who are suffering or lonely....we are the hands and feet of Christ. Many times, our words are accepted, but there are times we are shunned and people do not want to accept what we have to offer. Our hands and feet take a spiritual beating, just as Christ's physically did.

From touching the blind, lame and mute, to healing a paralytic man, Jesus' hands were always bringing forth life for others. His feet also brought life by bringing him to many places where he could perform his miracles and preach to many people. In the end, both his hands and feet were, not only spiritually, but physically pierced and crushed by this world. However, because our God is alive, he triumphed over this world and his hands and feet are now reflected in us, if we let him be Lord and Saviour of our lives.

As a woman, I feel that the gift God has placed in us as nurturers is indeed a blessing, but we need to learn to have balance. We are the hands and feet of Christ, and satan wants nothing more than to take us out of that role and keep us busy "doing" instead of just "being".

Max Lucado (Christian author and preacher) states, "You are valuable because you EXIST, not because of what you DO or what you HAVE DONE, but simply because you ARE."[2]

The story of Martha and Mary in Luke 10:38-42, is a classic example of how we as women get distracted with "doing" in this life and forgo just "being" with Christ and letting him show us the purposes and plans, Christ has for us. We are striving when we don't need to be, and therefore become caught up in the noise and static, instead of tuning into our Father's soft, gentle voice.

Luke 10:40 actually states, "Martha was 'distracted' by all the preparations that had to be made." Mary, on the other hand, was sitting at Jesus' feet and listening to what he was saying. Too many times, we are Martha; serving others instead of listening to what God is calling us to do.

Jesus stated, "Mary has chosen what is better, and it will not be taken away from her." (Luke 10:42)

I believe that Jesus is saying that Mary is hearing God's truths for her life and gleaning his wisdom, therefore the devil cannot steal her peace from her, as she knows she has value in just "being", not in "doing".

There definitely has to be a balance between the "Martha" and "Mary" characteristics.

"Martha or Mary- Who Should You Be?" (4:12mins):
https://www.youtube.com/watch?v=BvjHcUPo3c8

Balance and making sure our identity is in Christ are vitally important!

Too many times, we define ourselves by what we do in school or at our jobs. Then, down the road when we are wives and mothers, we define ourselves by what we do for our kids, husbands, and the world in general. We get lost in the mix and we wonder why we've lost our peace, or feel unfulfilled. Our thoughts seem caught up in the lies that we can never do or be enough for those we love now, or in our careers or marriages in the future.

When our focus comes off of God, and onto ourselves, we will start feeling these feelings of inadequacy. I love how Nicole Johnson describes how God sees the work we are doing, and that is what matters.

"The Invisible Woman (Preview) by Nicole Johnson" (5:46 mins):
https://www.youtube.com/watch?v=9YU0aNAHXP0

As women, we need to rest in the fact that what we are "doing", we are "doing" for HIM, not for anyone else!

Many times, we are overwhelmed with guilt that we aren't pretty enough, skinny enough, holy enough, "doing" enough and this guilt again robs us of our peace. We forget that God gave us his hands and feet and we need to sit at his feet as Mary did and take him by the hand and listen to his wisdom and not the wisdom of the world around us, which tells us to strive for perfection.

There is a woman in the book of Proverbs who seems like this perfect version of what the world tells us we should be. She is talked about in Proverbs 31:10-31 and seems to have all her ducks in a row all the time. She keeps up with taking care of her husband and family and wins their praises, and she is the supermom or super wife we all believe exists somewhere.

However, as I meditated on this scripture, I see that she isn't perfect at all; she still struggles with all the things that every woman struggles with, but she too, aims to keep Christ at the center.

Her hands and arms are mentioned at least 5 times in the scripture itself and I believe that God wants to illustrate that our hands are sacred and we need to fill up with him before we can pour out to others. We need to throw away the idea of being flawless, and instead, have our confidence in Christ and long to be more like him daily.

As it says in the following song, the only thing that makes us "flawless" is the cross of Jesus Christ.

"Flawless by MercyMe lyric video" (4:18 mins):
https://www.youtube.com/watch?v=_h5Y4l0_Rs4

"We who worship by the Spirit of God, who glory in Christ Jesus... put no confidence in the flesh." (Philippians 3:3)

I remember getting a revelation of this idea of being the perfect woman. God showed me the difference between the noun and the verb form of "perfect".

The noun '**pur** –fikt' is defined as "entirely without any flaws, defects, or shortcomings", whereas the verb 'per- **fekt**' is defined as "to improve or make better."[3]

In other words, we are not meant to be the noun form of the word, but instead the verb! The action of being refined is what God wants! Instead of striving for the worldly perfection that can never be attained, he wants us to be always improving, moving forward, forgetting the past, reaching for his calling and purposes in our lives! Paul in his letter to the Philippians drives this concept home:

> "Not that I have already obtained all this, or have already become perfect, but I press on to take hold of that which Christ Jesus took hold of me... I do not consider myself yet to have taken hold of it. But one thing I do: Forgetting what is behind and straining toward what is ahead, I press on toward the goal to win the prize for which God has called me heavenward in Christ Jesus. All of us who are mature should take such a view of things. And if on some point you think differently, that too God will make clear to you. Only let us live up to what we have already attained." (Philippians 3:12-16)

I love this scripture; it reminds us that God will always reveal to us what we seek. However, we can only seek him by sitting at his feet. We can then fill up our hearts to be able to minister and take care of those he has placed in our lives to love. Just as Christ filled himself up, so he could pour out by spending time with his father on a regular basis, we need to follow his example.

The Proverbs 31 woman does not obsess about her outward appearance, but instead focuses on her heart being right with God and getting meaning and her sense of value from her heavenly Father. I'm sure she struggles with balance as much as we do, but this scripture just encourages us to keep coming back to him and asking him to bless our hands and feet to do his will every day.

Like Christ whose hands and feet were crushed and bruised by this world, our hands, and feet take a beating every day with all the tasks that need to be done. The list some days can seem a mile long.

Your list may look something like this: doing homework, working part-time, babysitting, getting good grades....it can seem overwhelming! Whereas, the list for a wife and mother may look more like this; your hands are busy cleaning the house, washing dishes, folding laundry, or making supper. And it continues with changing diapers, giving hugs and kisses, soothing a crying child, bathing children, rubbing lotion on their little fingers and toes, turning the pages of a book as a bedtime story is read, embracing your husband, baking for someone in need. A woman's work seems to never end. Our feet are taking us to all these tasks and help us to walk around getting all the errands done we do during the day. If we don't submit our hands and feet to Christ on a daily basis, they can lose their sacredness and just become bruised, beaten, and performing aimless tasks that take us further and further from God's purposes for our lives.

Sitting at the feet of your Saviour brings you peace because it orders your day, provides you with perspective, and allows you to prioritize. God needs to be first in your life because he gave you life. Without his wisdom, you fall to worldly wisdom and your hands and feet become useless for the kingdom of God.

It's not complicated....God loves you for who you are, not for what you do. He longs for you to be Mary and choose what is better. Then your hands and feet will be blessed to do the work that God has for you, rather than the work of distraction and meaningless tasks that take away your peace and tranquility.

It is then and only then, that you will be healthy enough to pour out to others, and serve like Martha did.

My prayer for you today is that you submit yourself to Christ and stop this mirage of perfectionism and be thankful for who you are and all that he is calling you to be. God we give you our hands and feet and ask that you protect them to do your will and help us reflect your glory to all those we journey with on this walk of life.

I'd like to end this day's devotion with a poem that I wrote to remind us to "be still" like Mary and glean from our Saviour, before we set out to serve like Martha!

BE STILL

"Be still my soul", why is it so hard to do?
Because our identity is in doing, not being. And of true rest, we have no clue.

All our lives we've been programmed...even as little girls we are taught,
Being Martha is where it's at, and in our own battle we are caught.

The battle between resting and being still in our skin.
Taking time to pause and reflect, and search deep within.

Always warring against us- struggling to get ahead and succeed.
To please others before God and ourselves as we rush around doing "good deeds"

Instead of buying into society's distraction and lies,
We need to open his word and let it be our guide.

He tells us to be still, to be quiet, be calm.
Turn off the outside world as he applies his spiritual balm.

He promises to lead us beside quiet waters, he makes us lie down in green pastures,
restoring the souls of his precious daughters.

He prepares a table for us In the presence of our enemies, he anoints our heads with oil and we're followed by his unending goodness and mercy.

He reminds us to wait patiently for him as we quiet our souls,
And as we learn to trust him more and more, we know he'll never let us go.

So help us, Lord, to listen to you.
THY will be done, as our hearts are renewed.

Placing our lives in your hands will help us slowdown in this race,
As we spend time with you, truly seeking your face.

And as we bask in your presence, and feel the depth of your love,
Help us see that your sacrifice was more than enough.

Victorious Verse

"Your beauty should not come from outward adornment, such as braided hair and the wearing of gold jewellery and fine clothes. Instead, it should be that of your inner self, the unfading beauty of a gentle and quiet spirit, which is of great worth in God's sight." 1st Peter 3:3-4

Mighty Melody

"Live Like You're Loved" by Hawk Nelson and "If She Only Knew" by Micah Tyler

Armour in Action

Think of some times in your life when you were Mary, remembering your worth and value was in "being" a daughter of the King, not in "doing". When you sat at the feet of Jesus and allowed yourself to glean wisdom from your Saviour. Has there ever been a time when you allowed others to serve you or graciously accepted help with something in your life? If so, thank God for those times right now. Pray that God would help you to have balance; to begin with being Mary, so you can serve like Martha.

Notes:

_____
_____
_____
_____
_____
_____
_____
_____
_____
_____
_____
_____
_____
_____
_____
_____
_____
_____
_____
_____
_____
_____
_____
_____

Day *6 RISE* Up Warrior Princess

PREPARE YOUR MIND FOR BATTLE

"Jesus replied, 'Love the Lord your God will all your heart and with all your soul and with all your mind.' "

Matthew 22:37

You can literally be as strong as an ox, but if your mind is weak, you will live a mediocre, instead of victorious, life with Christ. One way to strengthen your mind is to meditate on his word.

Psalm 1 illustrates this perfectly when David says, "Blessed is the man who does not walk in the counsel of the wicked...but his delight is in the law of the Lord, and on his law he meditates day and night. He is like a tree planted by streams of water, which yields its fruit in season and whose leaf does not wither. Whatever he does prospers." (Psalm 1:1a-3)

If I could bear fruit in every season of my life, and whatever I put my hand to prospered, I would want to live a victorious life like that! Fruit such as "love, joy, peace, patience, kindness, goodness, faithfulness, gentleness and self-control" (Galatians 5:22) illustrate we are living an overcoming life.

Your mind has the power of life or death in any situation. You can be going through a difficult time, but as long as you "take captive every thought to make it obedient to Christ" (2nd Corinthians 10:5), you will have peace in that situation.

Steven Furtick explains peace as part of the journey, not a destination that you will arrive at some day; he refers to it as the path "of" peace, not the path "to" peace.

"Don't Wait For Peace | Steven Furtick" (8:53 mins):
https://www.youtube.com/watch?v=2ID5UvuHRzU

Peace isn't a place you arrive at one day; not only is it a fruit of the spirit, it is a choice in the midst of circumstances. You get to choose peace! Isn't that awesome? Jesus is with you in the boat during the storms of life! The "Prince of Peace" (Isaiah 9:6) never leaves your side; all you have to do is keep your mind right and keep it centered on Christ. God will handle the rest!

How do you take your thoughts and make them obedient to Christ? First, we need to start with a definition of the term obedient. It is defined as being submissive to someone else's will.

Just as Christ said, "Not my will but yours be done" (Luke 22:42b), you need to lay down your will and your life and surrender it to God. Then, you can start speaking his promises over your life and circumstances. So many times, we look at our situation as BIG and our God as small. Instead, you need to tell your small problem to our BIG GOD!

I remember a time in my life when fear and anxiety seemed like such a giant compared to God.

Spending time reflecting on why I was feeling this overwhelming anxiety, I realized that the root of anxiety is fear itself. I researched, and found that anxiety is 'fear gone wrong'. Because of these underlying fears, I dealt with different situations in my life by using anxiety as an outlet. I finally cried out to God and talked to my husband about how I was feeling, which was a huge step towards facing the fears I had buried for so long. Then God spoke to me about this anxiety and it was a powerful revelation for me:

> "Who AM I?" I asked today,
> God said, "You are my child, and you've lost your way."
>
> "You are ravaged by anxiety, realizing one important thing;
> Your life is truly not your own, and I have a new song for you to sing!
>
> I'm calling you to be my friend, to walk with me every day.
> To be my disciple so we can change the world, quit sitting in your idle ways!
>
> You think you have seen the hand of God, but you ain't seen nothin' yet!
> You will see even greater things than this, when you follow me, there are no regrets!
>
> So get off your high horse and put your false gods away, and come and meet with me.
> There's so much depending on your discipline, the souls of the lost, including your own family.
>
> The battle is raging around you, you're getting weaker by the minute,
> How can you fight and defend the ones you love, when your mind's not even in it?
>
> I'm calling you to war today, so be brave and do what's right!
> Pick up your weapon mighty warrior, and be ready to fight the good fight!"
>
> "I feel too depleted Lord, I am frail and I am weak.
> Help me to find the strength I need, that I so desperately seek.

I've been running on fumes for far too long,
My body and mind aren't right, there's something really wrong.

Give me the wisdom, Lord, to help myself,
Give me a vision into which I can delve.

Take away my distractions, help me focus on you.
I'm drowning in a sea of anxiety, and I don't know what to do.

Anxiety is defined as 'fear gone wrong',
Help me, Lord, to overcome this fear, and have the peace for which I long.

You are the source of wisdom, so God hear my anxious plea,
I've come to the end of my weary self, this is not who I was meant to be.

Help me put my faith in you, so you can be glorified in my life.
Break off this spirit of fear in my heart, I'm tired of fighting this fight.

2nd Timothy states that I have power, love, and a sound mind,
So why does this fear have such a grip on me, I'm really in a terrible bind.

Your word says to take authority, cast fear into the pit where it belongs,
I want to quiet this chaos in my head, I want to sing a peaceful song.

Help me, Lord to start somewhere, renew my mind day by day.
In turn, help me "rebuild" my temple into a place I desire to stay.

A place of wholeness and healing, where debilitating anxiety is gone,
Fear has no place in my fragile heart....devil, I'm no longer your pawn!

So fill me with your peace, O Father; please be my light and my guide,
May I remember that I never walk alone, for you'll never leave my side.

Help me call upon your precious name, give me your strength and grace when it's tough.
Take away my guilt and shame, and the lies that I'm not enough.

For you showed me on the cross when you died for me, the battle was won in your name.
I need to stop this dangerous dance with the devil, stop joining in his evil games.

Because with you I'm an overcomer, you see me as I long to be.
So I'll keep rising up against the enemy, knowing I already have victory!

Quoting your word when the fear creeps in, knowing there's power in Jesus' name,
The warrior in me is awakened, I will never be the same!"

Don't allow the lies of the enemy to take root in your heart. Fear and guilt can consume you, and cause you to lose your 'kingdom' focus.

Remember, when you focus on the "threat", you will experience fear, but when you focus on "JESUS", you will experience faith! The following videos are inspiring when it comes to overcoming fear in our lives.

"DO NOT FEAR | Trust God's Plan - Inspirational & Motivational Video" (9:30 mins):
https://www.youtube.com/watch?v=CZ9FaLhOkWo

"It's Time to FACE Your Fears // Carter Conlon" (24:10 mins):
https://www.youtube.com/watch?v=R6PIZnwOlTk

You can only realize your potential when you stop looking at your circumstance, and start focussing on the opportunities God has placed in front of you. With God, you CAN overcome your fears!

God told me to start speaking his promise of peace over the anxiety and fear in my life. He gave me this scripture in Philippians:

"Rejoice in the Lord always. I will say it again: Rejoice! Let your gentleness be evident to all. The Lord is near. Do not be anxious about anything, but in everything, by prayer and petition, with thanksgiving, present your requests to God. And the peace of God, which transcends all understanding, will guard your hearts and minds in Christ Jesus." (Philippians 4:4-7)

I memorized this verse and kept it in my heart. In the midst of my anxiety, I was choosing peace because I knew this is what God promised. The anxiety was very real to me, but his promises held power over it.

I had a pastor pray over me a few months after God had spoken this verse over me. He broke off the spirit of fear, which was the root of my anxiety, and reminded me that I was a powerful warrior for the kingdom of God! I left that service feeling as if I could take on the world! I realized that FEAR could either mean "Forget Everything and Run" or "Face Everything and Rise", and I wanted victory, so I chose the latter.

The anxiety didn't disappear overnight, and there are times when the devil uses my fears and insecurities to bring me back to that place of feeling defeated and weak, but that is when I need to stand firm and remind him that he has no power in my life! I remember driving home after that church service and seeing a license plate coming towards me that read 'NO FEAR'. God was reminding me of his promises that never change! The attacks from the enemy will always come, especially if we are advancing for the kingdom of God, but if we keep our minds right and focused on HIM, we can be victorious!

Our minds are powerful, and when combined with others who are like-minded, we most certainly are unstoppable! When we are accountable to each other, and are all committed to the same goals, God can do astounding things!

When I was single, I owned a home in a small town. I surrounded myself with young women who were like-minded in their walk with Christ from our church. They rented rooms in my home and they were all about 10 years younger than I was, so it was rewarding that I could speak into their life about many experiences I had walked through. We were all committed to the same goals, and we all kept each other accountable when it came to dating or other struggles we faced as young women on a daily basis.

This was a time in my life where God was able to use me as a mentor, yet these younger women taught me so much in my prayer life and about surrendering my life to God and trusting that he would take care of me. They softened my heart in many ways. I believe we needed each other at that point in our lives; therefore, God put us together under one roof to encourage and inspire each other. It is amazing how God can really cause you to grow if you keep people with the same mind-set around you.

As I witnessed the growth in these young women, I reflected and wrote them a letter to let them know how proud I was of them. Here is an excerpt from it:

> "I sit here and I am in awe of the amazing women of God you are becoming....I look at you all and I see the promise of a young life being lived purely and solely for God. You all inspire me daily as I watch how your actions speak to others. Your love for Jesus is shown constantly in the lives of those around you. You are awesome, valiant warriors for the kingdom of God, and God is, and will continue, to use you all mightily!

> I don't think you know how much of a blessing you all are to me...in the last few years, I became introverted in order to protect myself from being hurt again, therefore, I was not living the life God called me to live.....having all of you here reminding me that there is goodness and hope, has ignited a new fire within me. I know God has placed you in this house for a reason...not only will we teach each other valuable things, but we will grow in intimate relationship with Christ, as he reveals the purposes and plans he has for our lives!"

Surrounding yourself with negative women will bring you to a place of discouragement, anxiety, and discontentment. However, being around positive, Christ-minded women can build you up, cause you to grow, and be encouraged to follow God's plans for your life.

"Who's on YOUR team? #besomebody." (2:34 mins):
https://www.youtube.com/watch?v=Rm4OT_DraUs

As we live in a world that constantly wants to belittle, berate, and bewilder us, we can fight back by having a "team" of people behind us who are willing to be positive and keep our minds right. We all have a choice of whom we call our friends. If they are life giving and build us up, these are the people we want on our side, cheering us on in the game of life!

Here is a good link about who you should include in your inner circle:

"Not Everyone Deserves To Be Close To You" (11:58 mins):
https://www.youtube.com/watch?v=agAmHLnOhjo

Victorious Verse
"You have the mind of Christ." 1st Corinthians 2:16

Mighty Melody
"Voice of Truth" by Casting Crowns and "Fear is a Liar" by Zach Williams

Armour in Action:
Who are the people in your life that are like-minded, encouraging, and lift you up? Take the time today to call them and thank them for being an encouragement in your life. Maybe even do a random act of kindness for each of them. Write them a card or take them for a coffee. It just may be the boost they need!

Finally, tell satan he has no place in your life. You have victory over all his lies. Don't let fear be a factor for you!

Notes:

Day *7* RISE Up Warrior Princess

PREPARE YOUR SPIRIT FOR BATTLE

"The spirit is willing, but the flesh is weak."

Matthew 26:41b

Jesus asked - Father take this cup from me, but then submits to his Father's will when he says "may your will be done." (Matthew 26:42)

In his spirit - Jesus knew he had to go to the cross and lay down his life for us, but his flesh was fighting what needed to be done.

Jesus surrendered his life even though his flesh wanted to run the other way. We all need to learn from him about courage and being steadfast.

When Jesus died, he left you with the Holy Spirit to be your guide. When you are at peace during storms in your life, it is evidence that the spirit is leading you, because peace is a fruit that is very visible to others.

There will be times in your life when your spirit is willing, but your flesh fights back. Many times this may paralyze you, causing you to question God's will and plan.

Watch the "Skit Guys" and their explanation of God's will.

"What Is God's WIll?" (4:42mins):
https://www.youtube.com/watch?v=5n7ip-VzrtY

Point well made that God's will is much easier than we make it. We tend to overanalyze things and we start listening to our flesh instead of the Holy Spirit, and then wonder why we are way off course.

It is like a boat that goes only one degree off its course. Eventually, when the captain looks at the map, he will see that over time, the ship is quite far from its initial destination. When you stray just slightly in your life, you find yourself in a much different place than what God intended. Even when your flesh is fighting every ounce of your Spirit, you need to stand on God's promises and his word and proclaim victory and freedom in your life.

For example, when I was pregnant with our daughter, my husband and I were told she might have genetic abnormalities. An amniocentesis was recommended, which tests for certain genetic problems, and if we found that there were issues, we could choose to terminate the pregnancy. We both knew that no matter what would come, we would not terminate the pregnancy, but we were still afraid and confused as to what the situation would bring.

God provided us with wise counsel from a woman in our church named Beth. She had walked through the same thing a few years earlier with her pregnancy. She stood on God's promises and had victory in her situation, so that gave me confidence to stand firm as well, instead of being paralyzed by my fear. Along with other Christians who supported and gave us strength, our Pastor Greg and his wife Betty also gave us sound advice. They told us to sit and write out God's promises instead of focussing on what the doctors were trying to tell us. We began to speak life and power over our daughter by quoting God's word.

The world/our flesh says:	**God's promises/the Holy Spirit says:**
-your child is at risk of being abnormal	-"You created my inmost being; you knit me together in my mother's womb. I praise you because I am fearfully and wonderfully made." Psalm 139:13-14
-it is not a human being; you can terminate it if you need to	-"Before I formed you in the womb I knew you, before you were born I set you apart." Jeremiah 1:5
-you should worry and be anxious	-"The Lord turn his face toward you and give you peace." Numbers 6:26 -"Rejoice in the Lord always, again I say rejoice...do not be anxious about anything, but in prayer and petition, with thanksgiving, present your requests to God, and the peace of God which transcends all understanding, will guard your heart and mind in Christ Jesus." Philippians 4:4-7
-you should fear the future	-"For God did not give us a spirit of fear, but of power, love, and a sound mind." 2nd Timothy 1:7
-focus on yourself and your suffering	-"Have mercy on me, my God, have mercy on me, for in you I take refuge. I will take refuge in the shadow of your wings until the disaster has passed." Psalm 57:1 -"He himself gives all men life and breath and everything else." Acts 17:25b
-this world is where we should put our faith/hope	-"In him we live and move, and have our being...we are his offspring." Acts 17:28 -"Why are you so downcast, O my soul? Why are you so disturbed within me? Put your hope in God, for I will yet praise him, my Saviour and my God." Psalm 42:5

After quoting these verses over our circumstances, we felt God's power working, and it taught us how to trust him more. Our daughter was born on September 9, 2013 with no complications and was a beautiful, healthy baby girl. We felt so blessed to have taken a step of faith during our time of need, and in turn, God helped us to be spirit led, instead of worrying and led by our fears.

In the book of Galatians, Paul says, "Since we live by the Spirit, let us keep in step with the Spirit." (Galatians 5:25). Walking in the spirit means to listen to the Holy Spirit and have victory in our lives because of our faith, trust, and hope in the unseen. We aren't always able to see around the next corner as we journey through this life. That is why allowing the Holy Spirit to guide us is wise. That still, small voice nudges you towards the will of God for your life. It helps us navigate in the storms of life!

Rise up in the midst of the storm young warrior princess! Be encouraged by this next clip that not only is God beside you and walking THROUGH the storm with you, but be reminded that you need to keep your eyes on the PROMISE, not the problem! Don't be afraid of the situation, or circumstance! By faith, let Jesus deal with the circumstance and witness HIS power working in and through it!

"TRUSTING JESUS IN THE STORM (Afraid of the Wrong Thing) ||Powerful Inspirational/Motivational Video" (9:30 mins):
https://www.youtube.com/watch?v=n_39W9wk8zE

The disciples had Jesus with them in the storms of life. In Mark 4, we see how Jesus was totally at peace during a physical storm on the water. The waves were breaking over the boat, and it was nearly sinking. The disciples were very afraid, and found Jesus sleeping on a cushion in the midst of this chaos.

They woke him, thinking they were going to drown, but Jesus calmed the storm with just three words, "Quiet! Be still!" (Mark 4:39) Our example is Christ, once again, in the storms; he is at peace, knowing his Father is in control.

You can have God's power on your side at all times if you choose to be led by the Spirit. When you have Almighty God's power, no battle is too big! There will always be a struggle between the flesh and the Spirit, but you must continue to overcome this struggle by preparing your spirit daily. You prepare your spirit by reading God's word, claiming his promises for your life, and in turn, living in freedom and in victory!

You may have times where you end up following your flesh, but you need to ask for forgiveness and keep going in the battle of life! The more you follow the Spirit, the stronger you get in your walk, and the more God can use you in the lives of those around you! The further you get on your journey with Christ, the more you will want to choose the Spirit over the flesh, as you seek to become more and more like Jesus.

A spirit-led life will be so bountiful, that the branches of your tree will be bent and touching the ground with beautiful, juicy, ripe fruit! In addition, not only will there be an abundance of fruit, but also it will be sweeter than any earthly fruit you have ever known!

When others see you peaceful in a difficult situation and trusting in God, it is a testimony to God's power and how it can change lives! It also shows them that you can be free in the midst of a time where worry and anxiety could take up so much of your energy. In your struggle, there is power in God's peace, and your struggle is a setup for something bigger, which will lead you to freedom in an area of your life where you see shackles and chains and hopelessness.

Watch Steven Furtick and get inspired at how God will use your struggle as a setup for something BIG.

"Your Struggle Is A Setup- Pastor Steven Furtick" (13:00mins): https://www.youtube.com/watch?v=KseeN9-u8GE

Sometimes, the best question in the midst of your struggle is not, "Jesus, can you change these things around me?" But instead, "What are you doing in me and changing in me as I'm walking through these things around me?"

End today's devotion with this testimony from Peter Sage. His story of how he used his struggle to help others and grow is truly humbling!

"How to Become Your Best When Life Gives You Its Worst | Peter Sage | TEDxKlagenfurt" (16:15 mins): https://www.youtube.com/watch?v=I4svF7J6MWg

Victorious Verse
"Where the Spirit of the Lord is, there is freedom." 2nd Corinthians 3:17

Mighty Melody
"Freedom Reigns" by Jason Upton and "Death Was Arrested" by Aaron Shust

Armour in Action
Is there an area in your life now in which you are being led by the flesh? Are you worrying or anxious?

Remember that either WORRY or WORSHIP can come out of your mouth, not both. You have a choice. Choose wisely.

When we worship our King, there is no room for worry! Praise you Jesus!

"Matt Redman - 10,000 Reasons (Bless the Lord)" (4:21 mins):
https://www.youtube.com/watch?v=XtwIT8JjddM

Have you lost your peace or joy? Write down a list of at least three things the flesh is telling you, and on the other side, list three promises of God that will allow you to be led by the Spirit. Watch your outlook change in the middle of your circumstance as you gain power in seeing that your struggle is a setup for the mighty purposes God has for your life!

Notes:

_____
_____
_____
_____
_____
_____
_____
_____
_____
_____
_____
_____
_____
_____
_____
_____
_____
_____
_____
_____
_____
_____

Introduction to Pillar 2

RUN THE RACE

To be an effective athlete and run a race with excellence, you must incorporate healthy habits. Forming a new habit is a process, not an event. When you have healthy habits, you will be fulfilled and on track. You can move towards your destiny with efficiency and purpose. Some of the research says that it takes 21 days to form a new habit, but it actually, on average, takes closer to 66 days. Obviously, this number can vary depending on the behaviour, the person, and the circumstances. Remember, if you mess up, it's OK! Progress, not perfection is the key!

Dr. Stephen Covey wrote a book in 1989 called "The Seven Habits of Highly Effective People." Here is a brief synopsis of these habits in video form:

"THE 7 HABITS OF HIGHLY EFFECTIVE PEOPLE BY STEPHEN COVEY- ANIMATED BOOK REVIEW" (6:42mins):
https://www.youtube.com/watch?v=ktlTxC4QG8g

Also, former US Navy Admiral, William H. McRaven, speaks to this idea of habits in his address to a graduating class.

"Make your bed" (2:27mins):
https://www.youtube.com/watch?v=0iaGn8pqQQE

In other words, if you are faithful with little things, God will give you GREAT and MIGHTY things (Matthew 25:23). Be encouraged today that the little things matter and will lead you closer to all God has for you!

Moreover, this Pastor speaks about being obedient, even in the face of looking "stupid", and therefore reaping the rewards of being successful in the kingdom of God.

"Achieving Success (In A Surprising Way) | Pastor Steven Furtick" (11:04mins):
https://www.youtube.com/watch?v=1UBJy_Y_zS0

May you get a revelation of godly "success", while working in a steadfast manner on your habits to get there!

Remember that gaining godly habits in your life is proof of you taking action in spite of what may be standing in front of you.

In Day 6, we touched on obstacles or "fears" that could stand in your way. I want to remind you that "running the race" requires us to take action and make these healthy habits a reality.

Sometimes, fear causes us to become paralyzed. Our inaction actually breeds more doubt and fear, whereas ACTION will breed courage and confidence. As American writer and lecturer Dale Carnegie put it, "If you want to conquer fear, don't sit and think about it, go out and get busy."[1]

American entrepreneur Marie Forleo goes on to say that, "Spending too much time trying to defeat or eliminate your fear will only keep you stuck. Don't get seduced into thinking some magical day will arrive when you no longer feel afraid and then you'll be ready to act. That's not how it works...... ACTION metabolizes fear; the fastest way out of our fear is THROUGH IT."[2]

Interestingly enough, there is an actual term for fear of failure or fear of not being good enough. It is penned "atychiphobia"(atikuhfohbeeuh).[3] I have struggled with these fears off and on for many years. While fear is very real, if you seek God's face in the midst of your fear, he will give you revelation on how to defeat it. Part of taking action is speaking his word and his promises over your life.

I had read this specific verse from the book of 1st John many times, but for some reason, God revealed it to me in a whole new way which was monumental for me in my walk as I continued to struggle with high anxiety resulting from fears I was holding onto in my life.

The words seemed to jump out at me and come right off of the page.

"God is LOVE......there is no fear in love, but perfect LOVE casts out fear" (1 John 4:16b,18)

Therefore if I really rest in his love and acceptance of WHO I am, (a daughter of the King), instead of who I've been striving to be for so long, fear begins to dissipate. God IS LOVE, and if HIS love casts out fear, I need to rest in that if I want to have victory over this anxiety. Watch how Leah reminds us of this:

"What is love? The baby Leah say,"God!" God is love." (3:43 mins)
https://www.youtube.com/watch?v=59l852NhmEY

This song has really ministered to me and helped me to stand in the love of Christ when fear begins to get a foothold in my spirit:

"Stand In Your Love - Josh Baldwin | Live From Heaven Come 2018" (6:44 mins):
https://www.youtube.com/watch?v=oFizRY8w0-I

Another verse that has really been a go-to for me in this battle against fear is in the book of Joshua. God doesn't just tell us or suggest to us, but instead, COMMANDS us not to be afraid:

> "Have I not commanded you? Be strong and courageous. Do not be terrified; do not be discouraged, for the Lord your God will be WITH you wherever you GO." Joshua 1:9

Here are some other worship songs that can help when fear begins to creep in:

"Whom Shall I Fear [The God of Angel Armies] By Chris Tomlin with Lyrics" (4:28 mins):
https://www.youtube.com/watch?v=R0gu0nOaFsI

"The Afters - I Will Fear No More (Official Lyric Video)" (3:24 mins):
https://www.youtube.com/watch?v=wMmmbJlWhtk

"Building 429 - Fear No More (Official Lyric Video)" (3:12 mins):
https://www.youtube.com/watch?v=3cJFAGw3OaQ

"Chris Tomlin - Fear Not *Lyrics*" (4:00 mins):
https://www.youtube.com/watch?v=ppfwXKqDkPs

So, when looking at the end of the verse from Joshua 1:9, we are once again reminded that we need to MOVE and take action. And when you move, he is with you "wherever you GO." When you begin to make your way through your fear, instead of waiting for it to leave, you begin to realize that having courage isn't the absence of fear, but instead, it is realizing that there is something else on the other side of that fear that is far more important. And most likely, that fear was keeping you from God's purpose and will for your life.

Take the examples of Abraham, Noah, or Mary. All of them had to step out and take action, in spite of, or in the face of, fear, and in turn, they were blessed beyond measure.

Abraham was blessed with "descendants as numerous as the stars in the sky and as countless as the sand on the seashore." (Hebrews 11:12) Noah AND his sons were blessed (Genesis 1:9) because of Noah stepping out in faith! Finally, Mary's actions resulted in her giving birth to the King of Kings! "I am the Lord's servant....may it be to me as you have said." (Luke 1:38)

Therefore, you can see that obedience in the face of fear leads to the blessing of the Lord. If you meet God in your fear or unbelief, he will show his power in and through you!

By taking action, you can FEAR LESS, and if you fear LESS, you can become fearless! And when you are fearless, you become LIMITLESS.

Lay down your fears, and focus on God!

"FAITH OVER FEAR | Focus on God - Inspirational & Motivational Video" (10:54 mins): https://www.youtube.com/watch?v=E9YXqxuB2z4

Go ahead, princess warrior, take the first step, begin to embrace healthy habits, and boldly RUN the RACE fiercely pursuing all that God has for you!

"Be FEARLESS in the pursuit of what sets your soul on fire."[4] Jennifer Lee

Finally, Skillet reminds us to be FEARLESS, and BOLD in this powerful song! Be blessed, cherished daughter of the King as you passionately pursue your purpose!

'Skillet - "Lions" [Official Lyric Video]' (3:23 mins): https://www.youtube.com/watch?v=DzjfNI2XEBs

Day *8* RUN *the Race*

SET YOUR PRIORITIES DAILY

"What good is it for a man to gain the whole world, and yet lose or forfeit his soul?"
Luke 9:25

Jesus knew how to set his priorities, "seek first the kingdom of God and his righteousness." (Matthew 6:33)

He always spent time with his Father, and made sure their relationship was first.

This priority remained intact throughout his time on earth, because there was a specific purpose for his life, and he didn't have any time to waste. In that regard, he knew he had to stay focussed to fulfill God's will.

Usually, in our lives the urgent things take the place of the important. For example, work or school deadlines take the place of important connection time with God or the people you love. If you don't schedule time in your day to sit and talk to God, or have a sit down suppertime to bond and connect with your family, it probably won't happen.

There is a demonstration that illustrates this very well. If you fill a jar with large stones, you can then pour smaller stones in the jar and they will fall between the larger ones. The jar may look full, but you can then pour sand between the smaller stones and fill the jar to the brim. Once again, to glance at the jar, it looks full, but water can be poured in and it will trickle down between the sand particles and NOW the jar is full! Each material put into the jar represents your priorities. If you put the important things in your life in first, there will always be time for the little things that come up!

Most of us would say that the most important things in our lives would be the people and relationships we build along the way.

The following poem by Linda Ellis (1996)[1] brings this concept home:

The Dash

I read of a man who stood to speak at the funeral of a friend.
He referred to the dates on the tombstone from the beginning...to the end.

He noted that first came the date of birth and spoke the following date with tears.
but he said what mattered most of all was the dash between those years.

For that dash represents all the time that they spent alive on earth.
And now only those who loved them know what that little line is worth.

For it matters not, how much we own, the cars...the house...the cash.
What matters is how we live and love and how we spend our dash.

So, think about this long and hard. Are there things you'd like to change?
For you never know how much time is left that can still be rearranged.

If we could just slow down enough to consider what's true and real,
and always try to understand the way other people feel.

And be less quick to anger, and show appreciation more,
and love the people in our lives like we've never loved before.

If we treat each other with respect and more often wear a smile,
remembering that this special dash might only last a little while.

So, when your eulogy is being read, with your life's actions to rehash...
would you be proud of the things they say about how you spent YOUR dash?

This poem is a powerful reminder that we are only here for a short time. I read that the average person lives for 27,375 days (which is around 75 years). When looking at that number, it doesn't seem very long.

Watch this clip on a soldier facing his mortality. It will change your life.

"Major Jeff Struecker - Liberty University Convocation" (33:20 mins):
https://www.youtube.com/watch?v=Yy7yoNr9d6E

Jeff was willing to die, knowing he was doing God's will following his plan for his life.

If we want to fulfill God's plan in our lives and feel fulfillment, we must spend our time wisely, as we live each day for him! Moreover, in order to live for him, we must seek his face! "For it is time to seek the Lord." (Hosea 10:12)

When we seek him, it humbles us and allows us to see with eyes of the kingdom of God, which places priority on people and relationships instead of things.

The world tells us in order to be successful, we must gain possessions and money, but at the end of our lives, these things mean nothing; it is a big lie. Relationships are most important, and sadly, many people don't realize until it's too late.

The love of money many times takes precedence over relationships. Paul gives us a sober reminder of this in 1st Timothy (6:7,9-10):

> "For we brought nothing into the world, and we can take nothing out of it....People who want to get rich fall into temptation and a trap and into many foolish and harmful desires that plunge men into ruin and destruction. For the love of money is the root of all kinds of evil. Some people, eager for money, have wandered from the faith and pierced themselves with many griefs."

Bill Connor, the father of a daughter who drowned at the tender age of 20 years old, reminds us of the value of life. His quote at the end of this clip saying none of our earthly items matter, all that matters is life itself, is a sobering reminder. Watch this and be moved to tears!

"A father cycled 1,400 miles for a cause" (2:58 mins):
https://www.youtube.com/watch?v=Bwn2BeGAkfw

We also see evidence of this very thing with an unknown person who supposedly was very successful in the world's eyes. While many have said that Apple co-founder, Steve Jobs, said these words on his death bed, the authenticity of this claim has been disputed. Whether he said it or not, it is a grave reminder to pursue the things of God, which are the eternal things. The things of the world in the end, truly mean nothing:

> "I reached the pinnacle of success in the business world. In others' eyes, my life is an epitome of success. However, aside from work, I have little joy. In the end, wealth is only a fact of life that I'm accustomed to. At this moment, lying on the sick bed and recalling my whole life, I realize that all the recognition and wealth that I took so much pride in, have paled and become meaningless in the face of impending death. ..Non-stop pursuing of wealth will only turn a person into a twisted being, just like me...The wealth I have won in my life I cannot bring with me. What I can bring is only the memories precipitated by love."[2]

We can learn much from this person who had so much wealth, but in the end, it meant nothing at all. Our priorities certainly need to be set for us to feel peace in our final moments.

This young man's speech conveys this very message about setting your priorities and making relationships the most important priority in your life.

"Brutally Honest Valedictorian Regrets Being Top of the Class" (8:03 mins):
https://www.youtube.com/watch?v=T76FdtKreNQ

To help you maintain your priorities, God should always come first. When you start your day with him, everything else falls into place. Relationships with your parents or a spouse, if you decide to get married, then your siblings and extended family would be your next priority. Your job should never come before relationships. If it is affecting relationships, then you must take action, as this will be a detriment to the people you love. You are setting yourself up for failure when you become an adult and you have formed a habit of putting your job before your spouse and children. Lastly, always remember that you must also set aside time for yourself to connect with others and to enjoy life. Renewal and reflection are a necessity for a healthy mind and body. This is essential to learn now, because it will be imperative that you take time for yourself when you have a family to look after in the future.

A day timer is a great idea to help you stay on track. This is what I use and have an acronym that I follow every day. It helps me to set my mind on what is important, and keep a balance in my life. When we are organized, there is a sense of peace.

Even God loves order! "God is not a God of disorder, but of peace." (1st Corinthians 14:33)

When you are at peace, everything seems to go a lot smoother- and writing things down helps you to prioritize. This acronym works for me:

B   Body Care- this is care of my physical body- exercise, eating

A   Achievements- all of the things I need to get done that day- my "to do" list

C   Connect- God time and people I need to connect with

E   Enjoyment- things I enjoy doing- schedule time for them during my week- i.e. playing drums, reading, etc.

I write this acronym daily in my calendar, and put my list underneath the letter that corresponds to it. I find that if I write things down, they get done, and if I don't, they get done when I get around to it, which means I'm not using my time wisely.

Always be aware, whether it is the day-to-day activities, or your life goals, what you want NOW will always try to trump what you want MOST. If you stay focused and stick to your main priorities and goals, you will be well on your way to achieving success for the kingdom of God instead of worldly success which means nothing!

Finally, I have included a copy of the affirmations I say over myself daily. When you continually speak your identity over yourself, it helps you to keep your priorities where they need to be, and helps you maintain a kingdom focus!

MY IDENTITY DOESN'T COME FROM WHAT "I DO". My identity comes from WHO "I AM" IN CHRIST!

WHO AM I?

I AM "GODFIDENT", MEANING MY CONFIDENCE IS, FIRST AND FOREMOST, IN GOD. (JEREMIAH 17:7) I WILL NOT WORRY OR BE ANXIOUS ABOUT ANYTHING; WITH THANKSGIVING I WILL PRAISE HIM, AND HE WILL GRANT ME HIS PEACE! (PHILIPPIANS 4:6-7)

I AM BOLDLY (HEBREWS 4:16) WALKING IN PURPOSE BECAUSE "HE HAS NOT GIVEN ME A SPIRIT OF FEAR, BUT OF POWER, LOVE, AND A SOUND MIND!" (2 TIMOTHY 1:7)

I AM SIGNIFICANT AND DEARLY LOVED BY GOD, (COLOSSIANS 3:12) THEREFORE, I AM FREE FROM FEAR AND ANXIETY BECAUSE "GOD IS LOVE….. THERE IS NO FEAR IN LOVE; BUT PERFECT LOVE CASTS OUT ALL FEAR." (1 JOHN 4:16, 18)

I AM A CHILD OF GOD, (GALATIANS 3:26) THEREFORE, I AM "MORE THAN A CONQUEROR!" (ROMANS 8:37) I HAVE VICTORY IN MY LIFE THROUGH CHRIST! (1 CORINTHIANS 15:57, REVELATION 21:7)

I AM AN AMBASSADOR FOR CHRIST. (2 CORINTHIANS 5:20) I AM SET APART, (1 PETER 1:16) AND I AM CREATED IN HIS IMAGE, (GENESIS 1:27) FOR HIS GLORY. (ISAIAH 43:7)

WHO AM I?

I AM THE DAUGHTER OF A KING, (GALATIANS 4:6-7) WHICH MAKES ME A VIP (VERY IMPORTANT PRINCESS).

I AM ROYALTY, (1 PETER 2:9) I HAVE DESTINY, (JEREMIAH 29:11) I HAVE BEEN SET FREE, (GALATIANS 5:1) AND I'M GOING TO CHANGE HISTORY. (JEREMIAH 29:11)

WHO AM I?

I AM BEAUTIFUL, (ECCLESIASTES 3:11, SONG OF SOLOMON 4) I AM HIS MASTERPIECE, (EPHESIANS 2:10) AND I AM FEARFULLY AND WONDERFULLY MADE! (PSALM 139:14)

I AM A FEARLESS WOMAN WHO HAS BEEN BOUGHT AT A PRICE (1 CORINTHIANS 6:20), THEREFORE I HAVE NO ROOM FOR FEELINGS OF UNWORTHINESS BECAUSE MY BODY IS A TEMPLE WHERE THE HOLY SPIRIT RESIDES. (1 CORINTHIANS 6:19)

I AM AN OVERCOMER BECAUSE CHRIST IS AN OVERCOMER (JOHN 16:33). I CAN COURAGEOUSLY WALK IN MY CALLING BECAUSE HE GIVES ME MY STRENGTH, (PHILIPPIANS 4:13) AND MY TIME ON EARTH IS LIMITED. (PSALM 39:4-5)

WHO AM I?

I AM A WOMAN WHOSE HEART, MIND, AND SPIRIT ARE TRANSFORMED AND RENEWED FROM THE INSIDE OUT. (ROMANS 12:2)

I AM CLAD WITH HIS ARMOUR FROM THE TOP OF MY HEAD TO THE TIPS OF MY TOES. (EPHESIANS 6:10-18)

I AM A WARRIOR, (DEUTERONOMY 20:1-4, PSALM 144:1-2) BECAUSE GOD IS A WARRIOR, (EXODUS 15:3) AND I AM HERE TO FIGHT FOR HIS KINGDOM! I DON'T NEED TO BE DISCOURAGED OR AFRAID, FOR HE IS WITH ME WHEREVER I GO! (JOSHUA 1:9)

WHO AM I?

I AM A HUMBLE SERVANT OF CHRIST AND I'M NOT TRYING TO WIN THE APPROVAL OF PEOPLE. (GALATIANS 1:10)

I AM SUZANNE YYONNE MARGUERITE GALLAGHER. MY "WHAT" IS TEACHING, DRUMMING, AND ENCOURAGING PEOPLE. MY "WHY" IS TO INSPIRE YOUTH TO WALK IN PURPOSE. LOOK OUT DEVIL, YESTERDAY WAS NOT YOUR DAY, TODAY DEFINITELY ISN'T, AND TOMORROW DOESN'T LOOK GOOD EITHER; YOU WILL BE DEFEATED BY THE BLOOD OF THE LAMB AND THE WORD OF MY TESTIMONY! (REVELATION 12:11)

Victorious Verse

"God is not a God of disorder, but of peace." 1ˢᵗ Corinthians 14:33

Mighty Melody

"Don't Blink" by <u>Kenny Chesney</u> and "100 Years" by <u>Five For Fighting</u>

Armour in Action

Who is one person in your life that you need to make a priority? Call this person and tell them you want to connect with them this coming week. Schedule a time to sit down, talk with them, and share your heart. For you, this person could be Jesus! Make sure you are regularly meeting with him!

Another action item is to calculate how many days you have left on this earth if you were to live to 75. Here is an example:

> If you are 15, multiply your age X 365 = 5475, then add approximately how many days you have been that age. For example, if you turned 15 in July and it is December, 5 more months in days (5 X 30) is approximately 150 days. So, 5475 + 150 = 5625 days.

> If you have been alive for 5628 days already, subtract this value from 27,375, therefore you would have 21,744 days remaining if you were to live to the average age of 75.

> Sure puts it into perspective doesn't it. Unfortunately, not one of us knows how long we have. Some have only a few minutes and die shortly after birth, some die when they are infants or toddlers, some die as young teenagers or young adults......you never really know how much time you have. So living with some sense of urgency is one of the keys to living your life on purpose.

One last way to give your life perspective and realize the impact you have on others is found in Josh's story here.

"This is How 936 Marbles can Change Someone's Life | Josh Shipp | Goalcast" (5:36mins): <u>https://www.youtube.com/watch?v=FrV9oO0BOtk</u>

And finally, "be a Mr. Jensen" reminds us of how one moment can change a life forever!

"Inspirational Video- Be a Mr. Jensen- MUST WATCH!!" (3:12 mins): <u>https://www.youtube.com/watch?v=4p5286T_kn0</u>

Notes:

Day *9* *RUN the Race*

LIVE WITH CHRIST'S PRIORITIES

"There is a time for everything, and a season for every activity under heaven."

Ecclesiastes 3:1

When you are healthy in all areas of your life, you can show others how to live a life of victory too! In order to have "mountaintop" experiences though, you must also walk through some serious valleys in life. Valleys are indeed difficult, but it is in these valleys where you have the most growth!

A pastor once put it like this. He told me to envision a mountain range. As I closed my eyes and thought, he asked me what I saw in the valleys. I told him I saw lush, green foliage and a lot of life! He then said, well what do you see on the mountaintops? In my mind, I saw a barren, desolate, wind-swept landscape up in the clouds.

He said that this is a picture of our spiritual journey. The valleys are the low times in our lives, but this is where God can cultivate growth in us, and we spring forth from these experiences full of life and wisdom. The mountaintops are the times in our lives when we feel as though we are on top of the world, or "on cloud nine". These times are wonderful, but there is very little fruit or growth that happens. We need the valleys in order to produce the fruit that God longs for us to have.

God's word says in Psalm 23, "Even though I walk through the valley of the shadow of death, I will fear no evil, for you are with me; your rod and your staff, they comfort me." (Psalm 23:4)

He is always with us, and we walk through the valleys with him right by our side.

God has said, "Never will I leave you; never will I forsake you. So we say with confidence, 'The Lord is my helper; I will not be afraid. What can man do to me?'" (Hebrews 13:5-6)

We have all gone through different seasons in our lives when we struggle in the valleys. We feel as though we are just surviving. From "survival mode", we can reach a time of stability.

Stability is the time you can analyze and assess your situation. Stability can then lead to success, where you are making strides to better your life and set your priorities where they should be. Lastly, you can get to a level of significance. This is when you can help others.

Tim Tebow, athlete and motivational speaker, shares a sobering story reminding us that success and significance are two very different things; what is going to define your life?

"LIVE A LIFE OF FULFILLMENT - Live For Jesus | Tim Tebow - Motivational & Inspirational Speech" (4:43 mins):
https://www.youtube.com/watch?v=orj8KaD5JZo

Here is what John Maxwell, author, pastor and motivational speaker had to say about success and significance:

"John C Maxwell on SIGNIFICANCE (Success Magazine Oct '11)" (1:50 mins):
https://www.youtube.com/watch?v=Zhs3sX_0uyM

The following story of two dogs, (Miley and Frankie), is so touching and beautifully illustrates this progression from survival to significance. This real life encounter correlates with how our Savior brings us out of our "mess", cleans us up, and gives us the strength we need to move from survival, to stability, and then to success. And because of the pain and suffering that we walked through when our Savior found us in our brokenness, we can truly empathize with others walking through challenging times. Finally, our hope should be to reach the stage of significance where our pain is the pathway to our purpose, which can catapult us into making a difference in the lives of others!

"NEW VIDEO: Saving Miley: a MUST SEE rescue + a video update ONE year later!!! Please share." (5:19 mins):
https://www.youtube.com/watch?v=guXVL-mMcbI

God promises that he will turn ALL things for good, "In all things God works for the good of those who love him, who have been called according to his purpose." (Romans 8:28)

Therefore, if God can use the valleys of your life to help others, you must be willing to be molded and fashioned as his beautiful pottery; vessels that He can fill to overflowing in order to pour into others who are hurting.

"We are the clay, you are the potter; we are all the work of your hand." (Isaiah 64:8)

That way, you are full of life-giving water that can quench a dry and thirsty world. By remaining full of God's pure and refreshing water, you can maintain healthy habits so that you not only better yourself, but also in turn, can benefit others.

There is a Christian actor that is living by example and giving back. Watch this clip on Mark Wahlberg:

"From Prison to Faith- Mark Wahlberg Motivational & Inspirational Video" (4:32mins): https://www.youtube.com/watch?v=17960ovlxsc

Jesus is ultimately our example of being a role model and benefiting others. He embodied one who lived by healthy habits. He made sure relationships were of utmost importance in his life.

In a book by Christopher Maricle (2007)[1] titled "The Jesus Priorities", he tells us how Jesus prioritized relationships.

Maricle tells us that building a relationship with God involves the priorities of "praying" and "seeking God's will". He goes on to say that the remaining priorities of "healing, loving, spreading the word, building up treasure in heaven, accepting children as precious, and living with humility" describe our relationship with people. Notice how all these priorities of Jesus begin with verbs-, which are action words. Jesus just didn't SAY these things were important, he SHOWED us by acting on them and living them out. This is one of the reasons all the pillars in your palace begin with verbs as well. Just like Christ, verbs prompt us to move and get things done!

You need to do the same thing as Christ when it comes to priorities and healthy habits in your life. What good are they to you or to others if they are just words on paper? You must live your priorities out, so that others may follow.

Jesus said it very well in the Sermon on the Mount, "Let your light shine before men, that they may see your good deeds and praise your Father in heaven." (Matthew 5:16)

In other words, your actions will speak much louder than words in eternity. They will cause others to act and follow in your footsteps, which will bring them into a deeper relationship with God and with each other.

When you get into deeper relationship with others, it allows you to be vulnerable and allows others to truly see your heart, which is the opposite of how the world sees it.

The world wants you to be proud and not accept help. The world wants people to be jealous of each other, instead of being humble and learning from one another. Comparison steals your peace and joy as you stay hidden behind the fences and walls that you build, so you won't be judged or ridiculed. Learn to trust each other and allow them to pray for and heal you.

The world wants you to "keep up with the Joneses", no matter what the cost, instead of being happy for others and for their blessings and in turn, being content with what God has given you. The world says to hold onto your possessions so no one takes them from you, instead of knowing that God owns everything you have and trusting that he has enabled you to manage all he has given you.

So many times the world tells us one thing, and God tells us another. As you get closer to God, his Holy Spirit will guide and show you what you need to say or do in your relationships with others.

In addition, as you listen more to the Holy Spirit, the priorities that Jesus had will become easier to incorporate into your life.

A brief description of Maricle's "Jesus Priorities" (2007)[1] helps us truly get a grasp on what Jesus deemed as important.

THE JESUS PRIORITIES

Priority 1 – **HEAL**
Say yes to strangers, ask God to help you see with your heart, do what is in your heart, stay deeply connected to compassionate acts

Priority 2 – **LOVE**
Forgive without limits, show mercy in all situations, and express your love for God by loving others unconditionally. (But also remember that loving yourself involves setting healthy boundaries)

Priority 3 – **PRAY**
Pray alone, pray simple prayers, pray with others, pray earnestly and fervently.

Priority 4 – **SPREAD THE WORD**
Share Christ's mission with others, challenge yourself and others to live out the gospel, invite everyone to God's banquet table.

Priority 5 – **BUILD UP TREASURE IN HEAVEN**
Maintain a mentality of abundance, detach yourself from possessions, act justly in all things, remember God is the owner and we are managers

Priority 6 – **SEEK GOD'S WILL**
Rely on the example of Jesus and focus daily on God's will for your life, maintain a sense of urgency by seeking to be in a state of grace, see all tasks as acts of love, like the apostle Paul, see sacrifice as gain.

Priority 7 – **ACCEPT CHILDREN AS PRECIOUS**
Protect and welcome children, seek to be like children in thought and deed.

Priority 8 – **LIVE WITH HUMILITY**
Rely on God's mercy, not your own merit, lay down your pride and ego, assume the lowest place

These priorities seem like a tall order for most, but remember that God is not looking for perfection, but progression.

You've heard it said, "I'm not where I want to be, but thank God I'm not where I used to be!"

Living a life full of the priorities of Christ is definitely progressive, and as you become closer to Jesus and walk with him, it gets easier and easier to live as he did. It is just like when you hang out with a close friend, you start to become like them in many ways. Their values become your values. Having a friend like Jesus is a win-win situation.

He encourages you to live a fruitful life full of love, joy, peace, patience, gentleness, goodness, kindness, faithfulness, and self-control. (Galatians 5:22) When the spirit is leading you, this fruit will be evident in your everyday life.

He laid down his life for you, so you could spend eternity with him. He is such a caring and loving shepherd, "The good shepherd lays down his life for the sheep." (John 10:11)

He walks with you throughout life; whatever it brings, and never leaves you. What more could you ask for in a friend?

Victorious Verse
"Even though I walk through the valley of the shadow of death, I will fear no evil, for you are with me." Psalm 23:4

Mighty Melody
"You Redeem" by Aaron Shust, "You Never Let Go" by Matt Redman, and "Nothing I Hold Onto" by Bethel

Armour in Action
What priorities of Jesus do you struggle with? Write down two priorities that are challenging for you, and pray for God to help you make them priorities in your life. Write down two ways that you will incorporate these priorities this week. Trust God to continue the work he started in you.....he is making something beautiful out of you!

Notes:

_____
_____
_____
_____
_____
_____
_____
_____
_____
_____
_____
_____
_____
_____
_____
_____

Day *10* RUN *the* Race

MAKE GOD'S BUSINESS A PRIORITY

"The thief comes only to steal and kill and destroy; I have come that they may have life, and have it to the full."

John 10:10

The noun form of the word busy is "busyness" which is defined as "meaningless activity or pursuit".[1]

Isn't this definition interesting? What is important? What will bring us joy, fulfillment, and peace; your busyness or God's business?

The devil has all kinds of ways to get you off track and distract from the life God wants for you. You can choose to busy yourself with mindless activity, or you can focus intentionally on what God's plan is and live a full life!

I often think of it this way – are we being "busy" or being about God's "business". It really is a simple, daily, conscious choice. How often have you heard yourself or others say these words... "I'm just too busy...."

This is a constant struggle in our society today.

In the book of Ecclesiastes, King Solomon defines everything as meaningless...wisdom, pleasures, toil....they are simply a chasing after the wind which is pointless. (Ecclesiastes 1:14)

He was alluding to the fact that all the things we do apart from God are meaningless. When we are too busy, we are performing this "chasing after the wind"; we are not listening to his voice.

Listen to what these athletes had to say about their faith.

"Faith beyond the game" (10:46mins):
https://www.youtube.com/watch?v=8wQH-u9ShXk

"10 Professional Athletes who are standing up for Jesus Christ" (3:30mins)
https://www.youtube.com/watch?v=CnSYWHwSYos

"Athletes for Christ - Glorify God with your talents (Celebrities for Christ)" (2:46 mins):
https://www.youtube.com/watch?v=-iDjsRJqTyM

If their sport were "everything", they would be chasing after the wind, but these athletes have found their "purpose" in their "passion".

Tim Tebow's story also echoes this steadfast faith.

"Tim Tebow - John 3:16" (7:45 mins):
https://www.youtube.com/watch?v=SFQZtrDSObA

God's business has purpose and gives us passion for all we do. Without purpose, we are running around with no sense of direction. Urgent things take the place of important things and we don't prioritize properly. God is in the business of order, not chaos.

You need to set him as the foundation and constantly revisit your need for him. Then he will help to order your steps. "A man's steps are directed by the Lord." (Proverbs 20:24)

If God is numbering your steps, you'll never be too busy to do the work he has given you to do. Upon reflection of the word busy in the Bible, I found it interesting what God had to say.

In 1st Kings, Elijah began to taunt the people who were calling upon Baal to light the sacrifice on fire.

Elijah made fun of them saying, "Shout louder! Surely, he is a god! Perhaps he is deep in thought, or busy, or traveling." (1st Kings 18:27)

Elijah was saying that "Baal" was too busy, and when we are busy, we miss the important. He was insinuating that Baal should have shown his power against Almighty God, but Baal obviously was too busy and maybe doing unimportant things at the time instead of listening to his followers.

This proved Baal was a false god and gave God a chance to show his power and might! God showed up in a BIG way- lighting the sacrifice on fire even after it had been doused with water not once, twice, but THREE times over! He is always there...he doesn't miss the important areas of our lives!

As we read further in 1st Kings, we see a prophet who was supposed to guard a captive in the thick of battle, or so he said, and while the prophet was busy, the man disappeared. (1st Kings 20:39-40)

When you are busy, as this prophet was, you miss what God has for you.

In the book of Isaiah, it states, "For my thoughts are not your thoughts, neither are your ways my ways," declares the Lord. "As the heavens are higher than the earth, so are my ways higher your ways and my thoughts than your thoughts." (Isaiah 55:8-9)

This passage reminds us that our ways are not always best. God's business is where our focus should be. Many times, I believe we think our way is best which leads us back to the busyness of the world and meaningless activity, rather than being about his business.

Another biblical example of busyness is in the book of Haggai. God is talking about building his house in which he will be honoured. Everyone was so busy building their own house, they neglected God's house. (Haggai 1:7-10)

This illustrates, when you focus on your own "busyness", God is pushed aside. You may fail to go to church on Sunday because of your busyness, therefore losing that time of fellowship with believers who can encourage you and help you grow. You miss the gifts he has waiting for you at his house!

The final biblical example of busyness God revealed to me is the infamous story of Martha and Mary, (that we talked about in Day 5), found in Luke's gospel. It states that when Jesus arrived at the home of Martha she was "distracted" and instead of sitting at the feet of Jesus as her sister Mary did, she was complaining about how much she was doing and how little her sister was doing! (Luke 10:38-42)

Worldly "busyness" causes you to compare yourself to others and get angry with those around you that you feel should be doing more.

Life is not about comparison to others, but more about realizing our purpose and direction as we spend time with our heavenly father. When we are comparing ourselves to others, we are missing this precious time with God.

In 1968, Kent Keith, American writer and leader, came up with the "Paradoxical Commandments".[2] Mother Teresa revised them, which shows the paradox of loving people even though they don't deserve it.

DO IT ANYWAY

> People are often unreasonable, irrational, and self-centered; forgive them anyway.
> If you are kind, people may accuse you of selfish, ulterior motives; be kind anyway.
> If you are successful, you win some false friends and some true enemies; succeed anyway.
> If you are honest and frank, people may cheat you; be honest and frank anyway.
> What you spend years building, someone could destroy overnight; build anyway.
> If you find serenity and happiness, they may be jealous; be happy anyway.
> The good you do today, people will often forget tomorrow; do good anyway.

Give the world the best you have, and it may never be enough; give the world the best you have anyway.
You see, in the final analysis, it is between you and God;
It was never between you and them anyway.

Stop comparing yourself to others as Martha did. Go about your days forgiving, being kind, succeeding, being honest, building, being happy, doing well, and giving the best you have....don't worry about the next person. Theodore Roosevelt, a former US president, summed it up like this, "Comparison is the thief of joy."[3]

When you are living your life intentionally and on purpose, peace and joy will be evident and you won't have time to compare and judge others.

Watch this clip and see the harm that judgemental Christians can make on our hurting world. Graham has a very raw reaction and really calls out Christians in their judgements of others.

"Don't Judge a Book By Its Cover" (6:02mins):
https://www.youtube.com/watch?v=HYODSbNeNkQ

I agree with Graham in that Jesus came to seek and save the lost, not to judge them.

This next clip is real and raw, just like the last one, and calls judgemental Christians out:

"Church Pew Bar Stool - A CALL FOR LOVE" (3:55 mins):
https://www.youtube.com/watch?v=1APw1Ux9w4M

There are all kinds of reality shows that illustrate this same concept of judging a book by its cover. Here, a young man is judged by his appearance, even before he opens his mouth.

"Opera duo Charlotte & Jonathan - Britain's Got Talent 2012 audition - UK version" (7:30 mins):
https://www.youtube.com/watch?v=ZsNlcr4frs4

"Do not judge and you will not be judged. Do not condemn, and you will not be condemned. Forgive, and you will be forgiven. Give and it will be given to you. A good measure, pressed down, shaken together and running over, will be poured into your lap. For with the measure you use, it will be measured to you." (Luke 6:37-38)

This passage shows that when you live your life first for God and focus on what he has for you, you will be blessed beyond measure.

Do as Mary did, sit at the feet of Jesus and in the words of a famous hymn, "Turn Your Eyes upon Jesus", by Helen Lemmel (1922)[4]:

"Turn your eyes upon Jesus...look full in his wonderful face.....and the things of earth will grow strangely dim, in the light of his glory and grace."

God wants you to realize life is a journey with you and him, walking side-by-side. Those around you should be there to encourage you and be encouraged by you, not compared to.

When we surround ourselves with the right people, our priorities tend to be in the right place, or else we have people that will hold us accountable if they aren't. Then when we say we are "busy", we can have someone call us on our "busyness" and help to remind us about what's important.

Challenge yourself the next time you say the words, "I'm too busy" and really ask yourself if your actions are leading you closer to or farther away from God. Is your busyness helping or hindering the relationships with those around you?

If you stop and rest beside still waters and lie in God's green pastures, you may be surprised to see what God has waiting for you around the bend.....and you won't be too busy to find out!

Victorious Verse

"Am I now trying to win the approval of human beings, or of God? Or am I trying to please people? If I were still trying to please people, I would not be a servant of Christ." Galatians 1:10

The gospel tells us that we are secure in Christ, our security does not come from the approval to others. Watch this pastor explain:

"Approval in Christ" (3:34mins):
https://www.youtube.com/watch?v=vXWR_Cc8CPQ

Mighty Melody

"Only You" by Phillips, Craig, and Dean and "Everything" by Lifehouse

Armour in Action

Ask God to show you if you are distracting yourself with the "busyness" of the world and comparing yourself to others. Ask him to show you his "business" and all that he has for you, while you seek his approval, not the approval of man. Are you a people pleaser? Are you fighting battles that don't need to be fought? Ask him to help you say no to things that he may not be calling you to do during this season of your life. Pray that you may have a godly balance in your life.

Notes:

_____
_____
_____
_____
_____
_____
_____
_____
_____
_____
_____
_____
_____
_____
_____
_____
_____
_____
_____
_____
_____

Day *11* RUN *the Race*

KEEP THE FINISH LINE IN FOCUS

"I consider my life worth nothing to me, if only I may finish the race and complete the task the Lord Jesus has given me."

Acts 20:24

Nick Vujicic is a world-renowned motivational speaker. He is an amazing individual who has written books, travels the world, has a beautiful wife, children, and loves the Lord. It sounds perfect. Nevertheless, he was born with no arms and no legs.

I've listened to him speak many times and there is one quote that has stuck with me, "It's doesn't matter how you start, what really matters is how you finish."

Watch the following video titled:

"With God You are Limitless- Nick Vujicic Inspirational & Motivational Videos" (7:40mins): https://www.youtube.com/watch?v=57fUwOwjKhE

It is so raw and real when he spoke about being a young boy, and he felt like taking his own life because he felt so alone, as though God had forgotten him. I'm sure many of us have felt this way at some point in our lives. We feel as though God left us in our pain and we are saddened that we had to carry our burdens on our own. Little did we know, Jesus was with us all the while, actually carrying us when we couldn't stand on our own two feet.

The famous "Footprints" poem originally written by Mary Stevenson (1936), and modified by Carolyn Carty (1963)[1] depicts this perfectly:

FOOTPRINTS

One night a man had a dream. He dreamed He was walking along the beach with the LORD.

Across the sky flashed scenes from His life.

For each scene, He noticed two sets of footprints in the sand. One belonging to Him and the other to the LORD.

When the last scene of His life flashed before Him, he looked back at the footprints in the sand. He noticed that many times along the path of His life there was only one set of footprints. He also noticed that it happened at the very lowest and saddest times of His life.

This really bothered Him and He questioned the LORD about it.

"LORD, you said that once I decided to follow you, you'd walk with me all the way. But I have noticed that during the most troublesome times in my life there is only one set of footprints. I don't understand why when I needed you most you would leave me."

The LORD replied, "My precious, precious child, I Love you and I would never leave you! During your times of trial and suffering when you see only one set of footprints, it was then that I carried you."

God loves to help. When you recognize your need for him and realize that he can carry your burdens, you can rest with assurance that he's holding onto you and won't let go; especially during difficult times.

"'Come to me, all you who are weary and burdened, and I will give you rest. Take my yoke upon you and learn from me, for I am gentle and humble in heart, and you will find rest for your souls. For my yoke is easy and my burden is light.'" (Matthew 11:28-29)

It is so comforting to know you can rest and regain your strength when he is carrying you. It is during these times that he shows his mighty power in your life, "'My grace is sufficient for you, for my power is made perfect in weakness.'" (2nd Corinthians 12:9a)

The analogy of a Father carrying his son was lived out in 1992 at the Olympic Summer Games in Barcelona. A runner from Great Britain by the name of Derek Redmond was a favourite to win the 400m race. He began the race without incident, but about halfway through; he collapsed holding the back of his leg. He had torn his hamstring, but while the crowd looked on in that moment, they saw him stand and begin to hobble towards the finish line. As he limped, a man fought through security to get to the track. That man was his father. He wrapped his arms around him and began to help. As they neared the finish line, Derek finished the race by himself as his father looked on with the crowd giving him a standing ovation. What a beautiful picture of a father's love!

When you are hurt and making your way to the finish line, God comes along side, helps, and carries you. He is your source of strength in your weakness.

Derek Redmond's father shows this compassion and love of a father in the following clip:

"Derek Redmond- You raise me up" (3:18mins):
https://www.youtube.com/watch?v=7VfSbMh9gqU

Like Derek, your part in the whole scenario is to keep your eyes fixed on the finish line. This allows you not only to keep things in perspective, but also to reach goals that you set your sights on. If you do your job, God can do his- cheering you on from the sidelines like a proud father, and coming to help or carry you if needed. If you are constantly looking at your pain or unfair situation, you will miss the finish line completely because you focus on the small things, and lose sight of the bigger picture.

Watch the video "No Excuses Motivation" (1:01mins):
https://www.youtube.com/watch?v=mEHQ9tzJpYA

While there may be times when we wallow in our self-pity for a while, there are also times to pick ourselves up, dust ourselves off, and keep reaching for that end goal....no excuses!

Setting attainable goals for your physical, psychological, and spiritual well-being is very important! Even while working towards these goals, you will have challenges. If you are struggling, you may need an outlet such as a counsellor, pastor, or prayer warriors to lift you up and keep you accountable.

Accountability is a very important key to being an over comer. We all struggle with certain areas in our lives, and if we have people that will help us in our times of weakness, and keep us in check, it most certainly helps us to become victorious and reach the finish line!

In Genesis 25:32-34, it shows how Esau lost sight of the finish line and became so focused on the here and now, that he did something he would regret for the rest of his life; he gave away his birthright for a bowl of stew!

We can learn from Esau and remember to surround ourselves with people that are going to support and challenge us. This is so important in the race of life!

"Two are better than one, because they have a good return for their work: If one falls down, his friend can help him up." (Ecclesiastes 4:9-10)

It really is amazing how God puts certain people on your path at specific times to motivate and encourage you to be all you can be! Who are the people in your life that motivate and encourage you?

These next two stories are so uplifting! They show the power of encouragement. Be blessed by the beautiful message of hope!

"What I Learned from My Mother's Boyfriend | E.J. Carrion | Goalcast" (5:50 mins): https://www.youtube.com/watch?v=vXpNffsRinE

"Pastor Dr Ron Archer testifies, 'I was born a trick baby' " (7:46 mins): https://www.youtube.com/watch?v=HfKS6vCC4FA

The positive people we surround ourselves with will help us find our passions, and achieve our dreams! Their words and actions can help us when we can't help ourselves. These people are vastly important to our destiny!

TD Jakes, American bishop, author, and filmmaker, describes the first group in your "inner circle" as your confidants.[2] They will support you no matter WHAT! You can confide in them- you can trust them with anything. Who are your confidants?

Next, there are constituents. They are the ones who support your cause, they are not necessarily there because of you- the attraction is the mission itself! Constituents will come and go- they are the scaffolding- it is needed to build, but then it goes when the building is done. They are there for a season. Who are your constituents? Remember that the motives of the confidant and constituent are completely different.

Lastly, who are your comrades? They will fight for what you are against, but they are not your friend- they have no loyalty to you whatsoever. Never confide in a comrade, because they will use it to destroy you!

KNOW the difference between the three- confidant, constituent, and comrade; ask the Holy Spirit for wisdom about these people in your life.

On the other hand, are there people in your life that always drag you down? Maybe you need to let some of those people go for a season to allow the positive people to come in! That is something only you can decide, but ask the Holy Spirit to help you discern the people you should be hanging out with.

Ask yourself, "Who do I want in my inner circle?" Your inner circle is a reflection of what is going on inside you. If you have people around you that are on the same path and are committed to making it to the finish line with excellence just as much as you are, you are indeed blessed!

As a young girl, I remember running races in school track meets. Moreover, in the midst of the race, I remember family, friends, and teachers who helped me train along the sidelines rooting for me as I fixed myself on the finish line.

I'm sure Olympians feel that support on a much larger scale when they see fans waving their country's flag and thousands of people clapping and cheering for them.

This is analogous to our spiritual journey. We "are surrounded by a great cloud of witnesses" (Hebrews 12:1) that spur us on to the finish line!

So keep your eyes on the prize, and be thankful for all the people supporting you along the way! They are what keep you going when you need it most, and of course, our Saviour is there to help you every step of the way! What a friend we have in Jesus!

Victorious Verse

"If either of them falls down, one can help the other up. But pity anyone who falls and has no one to help them up." Ecclesiastes 4:10

Mighty Melody

"Friends Are Friends Forever" by Michael W. Smith, "I'll Be Your Friend" by Amy Grant, and "What a Friend We Have in Jesus" by Matt Maher

Armour in Action

Who are the people in your life cheering you on from the sidelines as you reach for the finish line? Or maybe they are running beside you! Have you thanked them for encouraging you lately? Write their names down and write how they have influenced your life. Write a prayer of thanksgiving to God for placing these people on your path.

This week, make an effort to say thank-you to at least three people who are your "spiritual cheer-leaders". If you feel led to, write them a card or note or give them a heartfelt gift; whatever God puts on your heart.

Notes:

_____

_____

_____

_____

_____

_____

_____

_____

_____

_____

_____

_____

_____

_____

_____

_____

_____

_____

_____

_____

_____

_____

_____

Day *12* RUN the Race

MAKE KINDNESS AND COMPASSION PART OF YOUR DAY

"God's kindness leads you toward repentance."

Romans 2:4

How many people draw closer to God through fire and brimstone sermons and judgemental Christians? I'd venture to say very few, if any. Our main way to reach others is through relationship and showing the heart of God, which is through kindness and mercy. That's probably why random acts of kindness make the giver and the receiver feel so good! It is showing people God's heart of compassion!

Zach Williams' song prompts us to be more like Christ as we walk through our everyday lives.

"Zach Williams - Less Like Me (Official Music Video)" (3:40 mins):
https://www.youtube.com/watch?v=fkYL1b7MCEw

There are many stories of kindness and compassion in the bible. However, the following story of the Good Samaritan in the book of Luke has always stuck with me. We find a badly beaten man who was left on the road to die. What happens next is truly sad, yet heart-warming at the same time. We see the indifference of two men contrasted with the mercy of another. Such a beautiful ending to a story that began so horribly:

> "'A man was going down from Jerusalem to Jericho, when he fell into the hands of robbers. They stripped him of his clothes, beat him, and went away, leaving him half-dead. A priest happened to be going down the same road, and when he saw the man, he passed by on the other side. So too, a Levite, when he came to the place and saw him, passed by on the other side. But a Samaritan, as he traveled, came where the man was; and when he saw him, he took pity on him. He went to him and bandaged his wounds, pouring on oil and wine. Then he put the man on his own donkey, took him to an inn and took care of him.'" (Luke 10:30-34)

What's incredible is that the man who was injured was Jewish. Jews and Samaritans were archenemies! Therefore, for a Samaritan to stop and help was unbelievable! This story teaches us that when we lay our differences aside, we can love one another like Jesus did in a lost and broken world.

Here is a re-enactment of the story:

"The Good Samaritan" (2:55mins):
https://www.youtube.com/watch?v=YYjurJyJN7g

This is how the hurting will come to know Christ; through our display of kindness and compassion.

For example, I remember when I was travelling in the country of Thailand. As I sat waiting for a ship, I noticed a man who was wearing a shirt that was soaked with dried blood. His face was also full of dried blood, and his lips were mangled; it looked like he had some kind of disease like leprosy. He was crying and people were keeping their distance. I went over and began talking to him. He told me he was beaten up the night before, and in a foreign country, he didn't know where to go to get medical attention. He was alone and very scared. I sat with him on the ferry over to the other island while everyone else kept their distance and stared. I don't know what ended up happening to the young man, as we parted ways after the ship ride, but I believe I was put in his path to show him that he was not alone. I showed compassion by listening and sitting with him. My experience, even years later, remains etched in my memory, because it taught me that when we are willing, God can use us to show his heart to others.

Another much more powerful example of unconditional love is a young woman by the name of Rachel Joy Scott who also understood this concept of loving others like Jesus did. Unfortunately, she was the first murder victim in the Columbine High School shooting in Littleton, Colorado on April 20th, 1999.

Rachel, mocked for her faith in Christ, was shot while eating lunch with her friend. Ironically, many of her diaries that were found after she died at the tender age of 17, showed a love for God and others unlike many young people her age. She had a passion for reaching the hurting and lost. The following essay written by her sums this up so well. She was a young woman wise beyond her years!

MY ETHICS, MY CODES OF LIFE

Ethics vary with environment, circumstances, and culture. In my own life, ethics play a major role. Whether it was the way I was raised, the experiences I've had, or just my outlook on the world and the way things should be. My biggest aspects of ethics include being honest, compassionate, and looking for the best and beauty in everyone.

I've been told repeatedly that I trust people too easily, but I find that when I put my faith and trust in people when others would not dare to, they almost never betray me. I would hope that people would put that same faith in me. Trust and honesty is an investment you put in people; if you build enough trust in them and show yourself to be honest, they will do the same in you. I value honesty so much, and it is an expectation I have of myself. I will put honesty before the risk of humiliation, before selfishness, and before anything less worthy of the Gospel truth. Even in being honest and trustworthy, I do not come off cold and heartless. Compassion and honesty go hand in hand, if enough of each is put into every situation. I admire those who trust and are trustworthy.

Compassion is the greatest form of love humans have to offer. According to Webster's Dictionary, compassion means a feeling of sympathy for another's misfortune. My definition of compassion is forgiving, loving, helping, leading, and showing mercy for others. I have this theory that if one person can go out of their way to show compassion, then it will start a chain reaction of the same. People will never know how far a little kindness can go.

It wasn't until recently that I learned that the first, the second, and the third impressions can be deceitful of what kind of person someone is. For example, imagine you had just met someone, and you speak with them three times on brief everyday conversations. They come off as harsh, rude, stubborn, and an ignorant person. You base your judgment on just these three encounters. Let me ask you something... did you ever ask them what their goal in life is, what kind of past they came from, did they experience love, did they experience hurt, did you look into their soul and not just their appearance? Until you know them and not just their "type," you have no right to shun them. You have not looked for their beauty, their good. You have not seen the light in their eyes. Look hard enough and you always find a light, and you can even help it grow, if you don't walk away from those three impressions first.

I know that my codes of life may be different from yours, but how do you know that trust, compassion, and beauty will not make this world a better place to be in and this life a better one to live? My codes may seem like a fantasy that can never be reached, but test them for yourself, and see the kind of effect they have in the lives of people around you. You just may start a chain reaction.

Rachel Joy Scott (1999)[1]

In a world that is closed off, where our fences are literally so high that it cuts us off physically and emotionally from our neighbours, where we wear masks pretending everything is ok, where we feel like we can't trust anyone, where a person's word or a handshake means very little; we need to step out and make an effort to be kind. Before you know it, it will turn into a habit, something that is second nature!

This is why random acts of kindness are so powerful. It means doing something random for a person with the knowledge that you probably won't get anything in return. Something happens outside ourselves, and we don't know how far that simple act will go. It will change your life and the life of another. Let's think long and hard about whether we are taking the time to show others God's heart.

As Rachel states, "You just may start a chain reaction."

Read the following story about kindness by John Schlatter, (1998), it changed a life, and SAVED a life[2]:

One day, when I was a freshman in high school, I saw a kid from my class was walking home from school. His name was Kyle. It looked like he was carrying all of his books. I thought to myself, "Why would anyone bring home all his books on a Friday? He must really be a nerd."

I had quite a weekend planned (parties and a football game with my friend's tomorrow afternoon), so I shrugged my shoulders and went on. As I was walking, I saw a bunch of kids running toward him. They ran at him, knocking all his books out of his arms, and tripping him so he landed in the dirt. His glasses went flying, and I saw them land in the grass about ten feet from him. He looked up and I saw this terrible sadness in his eyes. My heart went out to him. So, I jogged over to him and as he crawled around looking for his glasses, I saw a tear in his eye. As I handed the glasses to him, I said, "Those guys are jerks. They really should get lives." He looked at me and said, "Hey thanks!" There was a big smile on his face. It was one of those smiles that showed real gratitude.

I helped him pick up his books, and asked him where he lived. As it turned out, he lived near me, so I asked him why I had never seen him before. He said he had gone to private school before now. I would have never hung out with a private school kid before. We talked all the way home, and I carried some of his books. He turned out to be a pretty cool kid. I asked him if he wanted to hang out with my friends. He said yes.

We hung out all weekend and the more I got to know Kyle, the more I liked him, and my friends thought the same of him. Monday morning came, and there was Kyle with the huge stack of books again. I stopped him and said, "Boy, you are going to really build some serious muscles with this pile of books every day!" He just laughed and handed me half the books.

Over the next four years, Kyle and I became best friends. When we were seniors, we began to think about college. Kyle decided on Georgetown, and I was going to Duke. I knew that we would always be friends, that the miles would never be a problem. He was going to be a doctor, and I was going for business on a basketball scholarship.

Kyle was valedictorian of our class. I teased him all the time about being a nerd. He had to prepare a speech for graduation. I was so glad it wasn't me having to get up there and speak. Graduation day, I saw Kyle. He looked great. He was one of those guys that really found himself during high school. He looked great in glasses, and he had become popular and the girls loved him. He had more dates than I had! Sometimes I was jealous. Today was one of those days. I could see that he was nervous about his speech. So, I slapped him on the back and said "Buddy, you'll be great!" He looked at me with one of those looks (the really grateful one) and smiled. "Thanks," he said.

As he started his speech, he cleared his throat, and began. "Graduation is a time to thank those who helped you make it through those tough years. Your parents, your teachers, your siblings, maybe a coach...but mostly your friends... I am here to tell all of you that being a friend to someone is the best gift you can give them. I am going to tell you a story." I just looked at my friend with disbelief as he told the story of the first day we met.

He had planned to kill himself over the weekend. He talked of how he had cleaned out his locker so his Mom wouldn't have to do it later and was carrying his stuff home. He looked hard at me and gave me a little smile. "Thankfully, I was saved. My friend saved me from doing the unspeakable..." I heard the gasp go through the crowd as this handsome, popular guy told us all about his weakest moment. I saw his Mom and Dad looking at me and smiling that same grateful smile. Not until that moment did I realize its depth.

Never underestimate the power of your actions. With one small gesture, you can change a person's life. For better or for worse. God puts us all in each other's lives to impact one another in some way. Look for God in others.

Here is a video version of the story:

"Story Of Kyle – An Inspiring Reading" (3:58 mins):
https://www.youtube.com/watch?v=463GNnt8_0Y

When we look for God in others, we will see his heart come alive! His love for his children is so deep that we cannot even comprehend it!

Step back and analyze if you really are living with the heart of God. In the "love" chapter, 1st Corinthians chapter 13, it really speaks to where you are with your relationships.

Substitute your name where the underlined word "love" would appear.

"Love is patient, love is kind. Love does not envy, love does not boast, love is not proud. Love is not rude, love is not self-seeking, love is not easily angered, love keeps no record of wrongs. Love does not delight in evil, but rejoices in the truth. <u>Love</u> always protects, always trusts, always perseveres. <u>Love</u> never fails." (1st Corinthians 13:4-8)

When you look at the scripture like this, it really brings it home and makes God's word personal, and holds you accountable to how you are treating others. You become real with God and with yourself.

When you do this exercise, you can ask God for forgiveness and start the next day with a clean slate. God never asks for perfection, just progression!

Keep the chain of love, kindness, and compassion alive! In the words of Rachel Joy Scott, "People will never know how far a little kindness can go."

Finally, watch this clip about a family who did something unbelievable, and in turn, received kindness in full force. It will definitely warm your heart!

"FOX5 Surprise Squad: Couple Adopts Dying Neighbor's 3 Kids, Comes Home, Finds House Different" (10:09mins):
https://www.youtube.com/watch?v=DqxCfg1WRpk

Victorious Verse
"A kind hearted woman gains respect." Proverbs 11:16
"It is God's kindness that leads you to repentance." Romans 2:4

Mighty Melody
Watch this video in memory of Rachel Joy Scott. See the young woman with so much courage; who truly lived for her King! The video is set to the song:
"This is Your Time" by Michael W Smith (written for victim of Columbine school shooting)

"Rachel Joy Scott - This Is Your Time" (4:30mins):
https://www.youtube.com/watch?v=6SUHyVmOxl0

Armour in Action
Write out the love verse with your name in it, and memorize it this week. Also, consciously do at least three random acts of kindness for people you don't know. It could be as small as holding a door open with a smile, or buying someone his or her coffee. Whatever God puts on your heart to do, be a light to all you meet!

Watch the movie "I'm not Ashamed" (2016), which is the inspiring story of Rachel Joy Scott. See how she lived unashamedly for Christ!

Notes:

_____
_____
_____
_____
_____
_____
_____
_____
_____
_____
_____
_____
_____
_____
_____
_____
_____
_____
_____
_____
_____
_____

Day *13* RUN *the* Race

MANAGE YOUR GIFTS WITH EXCELLENCE

"Each man has his own gift from God; one has this gift, another has that."

1st Corinthians 7:7

God has entrusted and blessed each of us with material possessions, gifts, and abilities. Our gift back to him is what we do with them.

Speaking of gifts, when we tithe, (or give a portion of our money to God every month), we are giving back to our heavenly Father. At one point, I struggled with tithing, but my wise pastor at the time, Pastor Greg Fraser, once explained to me, "Suzanne, ultimately, God owns everything you have. You are simply the manager."

This was a revelation! I always thought my money and possessions were "mine", but then I realized that God gave me the abilities and gifts to do my job, and the pay check was just the result of what he had given to me...so I was just giving back to him what was already his in the first place! I began to understand the concept of being a good manager in all areas of my life, including my finances.

Life is a constant battle to maintain balance. We need encouragement from others, as well as wisdom from God to be a good manager. When we think of the word "manager", we think of a person in charge of people or "things". That is what we do every day! We manage our time, our possessions, our talents, and our money. If we understand that God owns all we have, it is easy to manage these things with excellence because we want to make him proud and bring his name glory!

The story in the bible that has always taught me to manage with excellence is the parable of the talents found in the book of Matthew. The master entrusted each servant with a different amount, depending on what the master knew they could handle:

> "It will be like a man going on a journey, who called his servants and entrusted his
> property to them. To one he gave five talents of money, to another two talents, and

to another one talent, each according to his ability. Then he went on his journey. The man who had received the five talents went at once and put his money to work and gained five more. So also, the one with the two talents gained two more. But the man who had received one talent went off, dug a hole in the ground and hid his master's money." (Matthew 25:14-18)

Therefore, this story is an analogy of your Christian life. When gifted with certain abilities from God, you need to give back to God your absolute best.

The Skit Guys do a wonderful job of telling this story through the idea of not wasting the precious gifts and time God has given us.

"Don't Waste Your Life" (9:32mins):
https://www.youtube.com/watch?v=ilnn_3PN1VE

Jordan Peterson also has a way of making us think about the time we have on this earth, and if we are really living it to our full potential.

"How Many Hours Do You Waste? | Jordan Peterson | Goalcast" (4:53 mins):
https://www.youtube.com/watch?v=trUpZbAzNDY

Are you squandering what God has given you? Are you wasting your "talents"? If you answered yes, today is a new day, so start living on purpose today! The biblical story itself continues and the best is yet to come!

The key part of this story is when the master returns from his journey:

> "After a long time the master of those servants returned and settled accounts with them. The man who had received the five talents brought the other five. 'Master,' he said, 'you entrusted me with five talents. See, I have gained five more.' His master replied, 'Well done, good and faithful servant! You have been faithful with a few things; I will put you in charge of many things. Come and share in your master's happiness!'" (Matthew 25:19-21)

Therefore, when God sees that you are using your talents and ability to bring him glory, and you are faithful with your finances, he gives you more to manage! He will always challenge you to go to the next level, calling you to live a life of excellence for him!

The book of Proverbs, which is the book of wisdom, says it like this: "A man's (woman's) gift opens doors for him (her) and brings him (her) before great men." (Proverbs 18:16)

What an awesome promise we have about the gifts we have been given!

There are many real-life stories of people living a life of excellence for God. One is a Christian surfer from Hawaii by the name of Bethany Hamilton. Her gift was athletic ability. She began surfing at a very young age, and winning competitions not too long after. When she was 13, a tiger shark attacked her and she lost her left arm. Instead of her experience hindering her, she chose to step out and continue to be a good steward of her gifts. Not only does she still surf and win competitions, but also writes books, goes around the world doing speaking engagements, and inspires young girls to live healthy physical and spiritual lives. What an inspiration to managing your gifts with excellence! After her ordeal with the shark, she turned what could have been a very negative time into something very positive, and God saw her faithfulness and rewarded her with many responsibilities she never had before.

Here is a young woman using her gifts with excellence!

"Bethany Hamilton short documentary by - This Iz My Story" (7:19mins): https://www.youtube.com/watch?v=ePFKksDOXkQ

Bethany chose to rise up and shine. God longs for us to step out of the shadows and shine for HIM!

This quote by Marianne Williamson (*A Return to Love*, 1992, pg.190-191)[1] sums up this idea of using our gifts to shine for his glory:

> "Our deepest fear is not that we are inadequate. Our deepest fear is that we are powerful beyond measure. It is our light, not our darkness that most frightens us. We ask ourselves, who am I to be brilliant, gorgeous, talented, and fabulous? Actually, who are you not to be? You are a child of God. Your playing small does not serve the world. There is nothing enlightened about shrinking so that other people will not feel insecure around you. We are all meant to shine, as children do. We were born to make manifest the glory of God that is within us. It is not just in some of us; it is in everyone. And as we let our own light shine, we unconsciously give others permission to do the same. As we are liberated from our own fear, our presence automatically liberates others."

Motivational speaker, Nkechi Nwafor, is a woman who endorses this beautiful, yet powerful, quote by Marianne Williamson. She reiterates that we were all meant to shine our light and use our gifts for his glory:

"Does Mispronouncing Your Name Matter? | Nkechi Nwafor Robinson" (6:44 mins): https://www.youtube.com/watch?v=M6ddGpZ6EGQ

Jesus put it like this, "I have brought you glory on earth by completing the work you gave me to do." (John 17:4)

Therefore, when you know that you MATTER, you will manage your gifts with excellence, and others will be inspired to follow suit. As a result, God will get all the glory he deserves! God blesses your faithfulness, and you receive even more talents to manage.

What a sweet day it will be when you lay your crowns at his feet!

As part of a vision given by Jesus to John in the book of Revelation, the 24 elders fell at his feet and worshipped him:

> "The twenty-four elders fall down before him who sits on the throne, and worship him who lives forever and ever. They lay their crowns before the throne and say: 'You are worthy, our Lord and God, to receive glory and honour and power." (Revelation 4:10-11a)

When you follow these actions of the elders and fall before him, you will humbly lay your crowns at the feet of your Saviour, and your reward will be eternity with Jesus! What an awesome God we serve!

Victorious Verse

"Well done, good and faithful servant! You have been faithful with a few things; I will put you in charge of many things." Matthew 25:23

Mighty Melody

"Well Done" by The Afters, "We Fall Down" by Kutless and "I Can Only Imagine" by Mercy Me

Armour in Action

What are some gifts God has given you to manage? Are you musical, athletic, artistic, encouraging to others, are you a great leader or teacher? Think of at least three gifts God has blessed you with. Write them down and ask yourself how you could make the most of them. Plan to do at least one thing today that will give glory to God from using your gifts with excellence!

There is a movie titled *Soul Surfer* (2011), about Bethany Hamilton focussing on her teen life and accident, and a documentary titled *Unstoppable* (2018) which is about her life since the accident and how she juggles being a Mom. Watch them and see how she gains her strength and courage from Christ!

Notes:

_____
_____
_____
_____
_____
_____
_____
_____
_____
_____
_____
_____
_____
_____
_____
_____
_____
_____
_____
_____
_____
_____
_____
_____

Day *14* RUN the Race

GET HIS WORD IN YOUR HEART

"For the word of God is living and active. Sharper than any double-edged sword, it penetrates even to dividing soul and spirit, joints and marrow; it judges the thoughts and attitudes of the heart."

Hebrews 4:12

Memorizing God's word can be difficult at times. Sometimes, it can be monotonous, sometimes we are too busy, or a certain passage just doesn't make sense to us. The old adage, 'If you fail to plan, plan to fail' definitely applies here. If you don't plan to spend time with God, you usually won't find time to do so.

Picture a place that you feel most comfortable. Maybe it's on your beanbag chair, maybe it's on your bed, maybe it's right in front of your fireplace in a cozy chair, maybe it is outside on your favourite bench watching the sunrise or sunset. You need to think of God as a good friend who waits for you to come to that place and spend time with him.

He loves you so much, he longs to "woo" you and establish a deep connection with you on a daily basis. Just like with the special people in your life, it takes effort to maintain a healthy relationship.

When you have healthy relationships and balance, you feel confident knowing that Christ is the center and everything flows from him. He gives you supernatural strength and power through his word that you can't get anywhere else.

As a young woman, you need to make sure your value and self-worth is based on his promises and what HE says about you. Do not base your value on what others think.

The artist Lauren Daigle had a revelation of this when she wrote a recent song. Here is the story of how the song "You Say" came to be.

'Lauren Daigle - The Story Behind "You Say"' (4:08 mins):
https://www.youtube.com/watch?v=XPDmjNXt_K4

And here is the song itself. Let it speak to your soul.

"Lauren Daigle - You Say (Lyric Video)" (4:29 mins):
https://www.youtube.com/watch?v=N8WK9HmF53w

This song is a powerful reminder that our identity is in Christ, and not of what others think of us! There is a quote by Zig Ziglar, author and motivational speaker, (2013) that goes like this:[1]

> "Your value does not decrease based on someone's inability to see your worth.
> Never let someone else's opinion of you become your reality."

Because human beings are imperfect, we will always make mistakes, and say the wrong things. If we base our value or make our love conditional on what others say or do, we will be disappointed. God's love is the only love that is unconditional and nothing we can do will make him love us less.

We see this unconditional love in the book of Romans. A love almost incomprehensible!

> "Neither death nor life, neither angels nor demons, neither the present nor the future,
> nor any powers, neither height nor depth, nor anything else in all creation, will be able
> to separate us from the love of God that is in Christ Jesus our Lord." (Romans 8:38-39)

The following is a love letter from God ....he expresses his thoughts towards us, and allows us to gain more of an understanding of how much he values each one of us. It's truly overwhelming that his thoughts towards us are as numerous as the grains of sand on the seashore! (Psalm 139:17-18) This is a beautiful reminder of his undying devotion to us.[2]

MY CHILD

You may not know me, but I know everything about you. Psalm 139:1 I know when you sit down and when you rise up. Psalm 139:2 I am familiar with all your ways. Psalm 139:3 Even the very hairs on your head are numbered. Matthew 10:29-31 For you were made in my image. Genesis 1:27 In me you live and move and have your being. Acts 17:28 For you are my offspring. Acts 17:28 I knew you even before you were conceived. Jeremiah 1:4-5 I chose you when I planned creation. Ephesians 1:11-12 You were not a mistake, for all your days are written in my book. Psalm 139:15-16 I determined the exact time of your birth and where you would live. Acts 17:26 You are fearfully and wonderfully made. Psalm 139:14 I knit you together in your mother's womb. Psalm 139:13 And brought you forth on the day you were born. Psalm 71:6 I have been misrepresented by those who don't know me. John 8:41-44 I am not distant and angry, but am the complete expression of love. 1 John 4:16

And it is my desire to lavish my love on you. <u>1 John 3:1</u> Simply because you are my child and I am your Father. <u>1 John 3:1</u> I offer you more than your earthly father ever could. <u>Matthew 7:11</u> For I am the perfect father. <u>Matthew 5:48</u> Every good gift that you receive comes from my hand. <u>James 1:17</u> For I am your provider and I meet all your needs. <u>Matthew 6:31-33</u> My plan for your future has always been filled with hope. <u>Jeremiah 29:11</u> Because I love you with an everlasting love. <u>Jeremiah 31:3</u> My thoughts toward you are countless as the sand on the seashore. <u>Psalms 139:17-18</u> And I rejoice over you with singing. <u>Zephaniah 3:17</u> I will never stop doing good to you. <u>Jeremiah 32:40</u> For you are my treasured possession. <u>Exodus 19:5</u> I desire to establish you with all my heart and all my soul. <u>Jeremiah 32:41</u> And I want to show you great and marvellous things. <u>Jeremiah 33:3</u> If you seek me with all your heart, you will find me. <u>Deuteronomy 4:29</u> Delight in me and I will give you the desires of your heart. <u>Psalm 37:4</u> For it is I who gave you those desires. <u>Philippians 2:13</u> I am able to do more for you than you could possibly imagine. <u>Ephesians 3:20</u> For I am your greatest encourager. <u>2 Thessalonians 2:16-17</u> I am also the Father who comforts you in all your troubles. <u>2 Corinthians 1:3-4</u> When you are broken-hearted, I am close to you. <u>Psalm 34:18</u> As a shepherd carries a lamb, I have carried you close to my heart. <u>Isaiah 40:11</u> One day I will wipe away every tear from your eyes. <u>Revelation 21:3-4</u> And I'll take away all the pain you have suffered on this earth. <u>Revelation 21:3-4</u> I am your Father, and I love you even as I love my son, Jesus. <u>John 17:23</u> For in Jesus, my love for you is revealed. <u>John 17:26</u> He is the exact representation of my being. <u>Hebrews 1:3</u> He came to demonstrate that I am for you, not against you. <u>Romans 8:31</u> And to tell you that I am not counting your sins. <u>2 Corinthians 5:18-19</u> Jesus died so that you and I could be reconciled. <u>2 Corinthians 5:18-19</u> His death was the ultimate expression of my love for you. <u>1 John 4:10</u> I gave up everything I loved that I might gain your love. <u>Romans 8:31-32</u> If you receive the gift of my son Jesus, you receive me. <u>1 John 2:23</u> And nothing will ever separate you from my love again. <u>Romans 8:38-39</u> Come home and I'll throw the biggest party heaven has ever seen. <u>Luke 15:7</u> I have always been Father, and will always be Father. <u>Ephesians 3:14-15</u> My question is...Will you be my child? <u>John 1:12-13</u>

I am waiting for you. <u>Luke 15:11-32</u>

Love,
Your Dad
Almighty God

This beautiful letter is in video format:

"Father's Love Letter" (6:42mins):
 http://www.fathersloveletter.com/

This depiction of God expressing his thoughts in so many different ways really puts in perspective his vast love for all his children. Loved for "whose" we are rather than what we do is what we all long for, because then we know that we are loved no matter what.

"Saved by Love - Kathryn Scott (Lyrics)" (3:07 mins):
https://www.youtube.com/watch?v=78o3WjWuBZ8

God is a good, good Father. Listen to this song and take it all in!

"Chris Tomlin - Good Good Father (Audio)" (4:57mins)
https://www.youtube.com/watch?v=CqybalesbuA

What child can't help but feel empowered with a father that constantly builds them up and speaks life over them? God gave me a revelation of this as I meditated on his unconditional love:

> **God loves us exactly as we are. Then, he watches us transform into the greatest, truest version of ourselves because of his unconditional, unfailing, unwavering love. When we feel loved for who we are, without any conditions attached, we are instantly empowered.**

The comedian Michael Jr. illustrates this "Father's love" so poignantly in his own life illustration. You can watch it at:

"Short: Delivery Room | SuperSoul Sunday | Oprah Winfrey Network" (2:57mins):
https://www.youtube.com/watch?v=XeFRLdVEdCE

When we are encouraged and told how special and loved we are, especially by the "fathers" in our lives, we flourish and become confident women; sure of whom we are in Christ.

There is a very powerful sermon on being a confident woman by Christian author and speaker, Joyce Meyer.[3] She talks about 7 secrets of a confident woman. The first secret - she is loved unconditionally. When you can rest in the assurance of a love that never lets you go, a supernatural strength rises up in you that you cannot deny. The rest of the secrets of a confident woman are simply a result of being secure in his love.

A confident woman takes action or initiative in situations, she does not live in "what-ifs", or "if only", she has a positive attitude, she refuses to live in fear, she avoids comparisons, and she recovers from setbacks.

Here is a video reinforcing confidence in godly women. Be blessed by it's message!

"A Special Word For Women | The Secrets Of A Confident Woman" (5:24 mins):
https://www.youtube.com/watch?v=QEjiWlaZND0

God is calling you to be this kind of woman!

God wants you to be confident in and through him; not confident in yourself and what you can do in your own strength.

"I can do all things through Christ who strengthens me." (Philippians 4:13 NKJV)

Your confidence comes because he lives in you, therefore, draw upon his confidence; he IS your confidence!

"(We) who worship by the Spirit of God, and glory in Christ Jesus... have no confidence in the flesh." (Philippians 3:3 ASV)

In order to know this love and feeling of being confident in him, you need to get his word in your heart. If it is difficult to do on your own, do it with a group of people or a friend.

Challenge each other and pray for each other to read his word. Write the scriptures down on cue cards and put them up around your house in places you see all the time, put the scripture to a tune in your head that is easy for you to remember! There are so many ways to help you recall his word when you need it! Using a version of the bible that is easy to understand also helps to make it meaningful and helps the words to resonate with you. Whatever you have to do, start reading and memorizing his word and you will soar on wings of eagles and never look back!

Victorious Verse

"I have hidden your word in my heart that I might not sin against you. Praise be to you, O Lord; teach me your decrees." Psalm 119:11-12

Mighty Melody

"Reckless Love" by Cory Asbury, "How He Loves Us" by David Crowder Band, and "Nobody Loves Me Like You" by Chris Tomlin
Soak up the lavish love he has for you.

Armour in Action

Choose a passage about God's love that is close to your heart and make a point of memorizing it this week. Put the verse on cue cards and put one on your bathroom mirror, on your fridge, or in your room where you will see it daily. Tell someone close to you that you are memorizing that particular scripture so they can help to keep you accountable. Watch God's power work in your life as you get his word in your heart. Let the Father speak life over you through his word!

For some inspiration, watch this earthly father speak life over his daughter! How much more does our heavenly Father speak life over us?

"Dad Motivates Daughter for School" (1:23 mins):
https://www.youtube.com/watch?v=pC4WTc3CT5w

Notes:

_____
_____
_____
_____
_____
_____
_____
_____
_____
_____
_____
_____
_____
_____
_____
_____
_____
_____
_____

Introduction to Pillar **3**

RADIATE CHRIST

When you present Christ to the world, "pure" embodies who Jesus is. "You were bought with the precious blood of Christ's death. He was a pure and perfect sacrificial Lamb." (1st Peter 1:19 ERV)

Therefore, in order to be more like him, purity must be part of who you are.

In September 2012, Jessica Harris wrote a piece entitled, "5 Reasons Purity Rings and Pledges Don't Work".[1] She had some interesting thoughts after years of working with young people who were walking through the season of their life where purity was an issue. She found that participating in a "purity challenge" or just wearing a ring to symbolize your purity wasn't enough; they are good ideas, but we also need to remember the following things:

    1. Purity is a heart choice.

    With all the emphasis placed on abstinence, purity rings might well be renamed abstinence rings. Abstinence and purity are not the same. Purity actually has very little to do with sex. Sexual acting out is the ultimate manifestation of impurity. Anybody—Christian or not—can be abstinent. Purity is a heart attitude that affects how you live your life, not just how you use your body.

    2. Purity requires God's strength.

    Because abstinence involves your physical interactions with another living, breathing, human being, it can be accomplished through sheer grit, determination, logic, or fear. Because purity is more personal and less visible, it requires the working of God's Holy Spirit in your life. It requires His grace and His enabling in order for you to live a life that honours and glorifies Him.

3. Purity is not a one-time choice.

It is an important decision, yes, but it is also a daily decision. Purity is a daily, even moment-by-moment battle. Preparation for that battle does not take place in one moment. Victory is not guaranteed because of choices you made yesterday. Sign all the contracts you would like, but it is a daily battle to remain pure.

4. Purity is ultimately your decision.

We can be guilty of treating purity rings and contracts like the 21st Century chastity belt. A parent may have placed the ring on you; therefore you must be pure. No. They have given you a piece of jewellery; you have to choose to be pure.

5. Purity is a lifestyle, not simply a part of your life.

I call this Jesus-fish Syndrome. You slap a Jesus fish (Icthys) on your car and it makes no difference what you do in that car, people should be able to notice, by the Jesus fish, that you are, obviously, a Christian. I have seen the same happen with purity ring wearers. One young woman I taught was overtly sexual and immodest. When I tried to approach the subject with her, she stopped me and showed me her hand, "I have a purity ring," as if it were her license to do whatever she liked. It was her proof that she was, in her opinion, pure, but her life spoke loudly to the contrary. That ring had provided her with a false sense of purity.

That being said, purity rings can be a great reminder of a choice to remain pure, but are by no means a prerequisite for purity. Choosing to wear a purity ring or choosing to sign a pledge is not the same as choosing to be pure. Purity goes deeper than a fear of STDs or the whole 'emotional super glue' speech. It is more than waiting until your wedding night to have sex. Purity even goes deeper than promising to never look at porn again. Purity addresses how you approach and worship an Almighty and Holy God, and it is a choice you are helpless to make without Him.

In closing, many have had an abusive past that has taken away their innocence, or as you get older, you do things you regret. God can wash you "as white as snow" (Psalm 51:7). No matter what your situation, you are a "priceless" daughter of a King!

'"Priceless"- for KING & COUNTRY (Lyrics)"' (3:40mins): https://www.youtube.com/watch?v=-ZrB5dxdXsk

See God's hand in cleansing, and see how he sees you.

From Day 15 to 21 we are going to be talking about purity, guarding your heart, and accountability in all areas of your life. When it comes to relationships, purity can be a difficult thing to maintain.

Find a friend you can confide in, and vow to walk in purity together; keeping each other accountable.

To see it from God's perspective, here is a prayer for a young woman from God regarding your purity. Pray it over yourselves and your accountability partners:

Purity Prayer from God

For Daughters of the King:

Dearest Daughter, you are a precious gift and I am proud of the young woman you are becoming. I wish for you the very best this life has to offer and I encourage you to maintain a level of holy character in all your thoughts, actions, and in your attitude. Please take honour in your body and hold tight to your gift of virginity. Don't take lightly the treasure you bestow, but take joy in that which you will so intimately share with another.

Follow the ways of pure truth; take confidence in your commitment to purity, modesty, and self-control. Be patient my dear! Wait! Continually guard your heart. If you struggle and walk the line of self-destruction, take confidence in the POWER of the Holy Spirit who has equipped you with the WILL to stand strong. You are precious! Valuable to God! You ARE worth waiting for!

May you be blessed in your choice for abstinence. May you understand your worth to me! May you be surrounded by the Holy Spirit as you walk in purity.

Here is some 'wisdom' in regards to sexual purity and sexual sin:

"Should Couples Live Together before Marriage?" (4:56 mins):
https://www.youtube.com/watch?v=KnjQQVJ2Tqk

"5 Dating Tips | Pastor Steven Furtick" (6:12 mins):
https://www.youtube.com/watch?v=pjC_8inYjwQ

"Paul Washer - Are You a Virtuous Woman? (Sermon Jam)" (8:47 mins):
https://www.youtube.com/watch?v=PG6up3F7t7c

"BY HIS WOUNDS WE ARE HEALED" (ISAIAH 53:5)

Before beginning Day 15 on "consecration", I want to make sure you realize how hard the devil is fighting for you in the spiritual realm. Unfortunately, the devil will continue to fight for evil and try to use your past wounds to keep you from the plans God has for you. John and Stasi Eldridge explain this so poignantly in their book "Captivating" (2005).

> "The wounds you have received have come to you for a purpose from the one who knows all you are meant to be and fears you." (pg. 75)

The devil FEARS you! John and Stasi Eldridge remind us that we embody the beauty of God, and we can also bring life into the world, therefore "satan's bitter heart cannot bear it....he assaults her with a special hatred." (pg. 85) In essence, you are hated by satan because of your power and your beauty.

You must remember that not only are you "passionately loved by the God of the universe, but we are also hated by his enemy." (pg. 91)

In order to fight back against satan's schemes, let's take some time to focus on and deal with your past. Then our wounds can have no power against us!

Sadly, these wounds that are brought on by your actions or the actions of others can cause you to feel less than. We need to address our wounds before we can heal and consecrate ourselves for the Lord.   John and Stasi explain:

> "As a result of the wounds we receive growing up, we come to believe that some part of us, maybe every part of us, is marred. Shame enters in and makes its crippling home deep within our hearts.......shame makes us feel, no believe, that we do not measure up.....if we were not deemed worthy of love as children, it is incredibly difficult to believe we are worth loving as adults. Shame says we are unworthy, broken, and beyond repair." (pg.73)

Stasi and John go on to say in Chapter 6 (Healing the Wound, pgs. 92-110), that you need to go through a process in order to fully heal the wounds from your past so you can set your heart free. Only then can you move forward into all God has for you. I have walked through these steps, and they have begun a great healing in my heart! The steps are as follows:

1- Invite Jesus In- we must give him permission to go into the places we have shut out to anyone
2- Renounce the Agreements You've Made- with wounds, come messages to our soul- "you are worthless, you're a disappointment, etc." When we agree with these messages, we are saying they are true. We need to renounce these agreements and unlock the door to Christ's healing.

3- Find Your Tears- stop pretending to hold it all together. Let the tears come and allow yourself to feel again....let it all out.

4- Forgive- forgive those who have hurt us- this does not say what they did was ok, it just helps you to let them go. This process tells your heart that whatever happened to you "hurt" and "it mattered". We also need to forgive ourselves for any hurt we have caused ourselves because of poor choices.

Watch Stephen Furtick as he speaks on forgiveness:

"This is key to forgiveness | Pastor Steven Furtick" (18:48 mins):
https://www.youtube.com/watch?v=sHoapBtEobM

5- Ask Jesus to Heal You- give him the pieces of your broken heart and allow him to put them back together like only he can. Remember, that God CAN and WILL heal your broken heart, but you must give him ALL the pieces by fully surrendering your wounds to HIM.

6- Ask Him to Destroy Your Enemies- ask him to set you free from whatever has a stronghold on you.

7- Let Him Father You- ask him to love you with his strong and tender love. Ask him to go with you into the deep places of your wounded heart and hold you and protect you and keep you safe in his love.

8- Ask Him to Answer Your Question- ask him the questions that you may have looked elsewhere to find the answers to. "Do you see me?" "Am I Captivating?" and "Do I have a beauty all my own? Show me my beauty!"

Dealing with your wounds in a healthy way and facing them "head on", allows you to focus on the victory that God has for you in the midst of your pain....or maybe even because of your pain.

See the victory because the battle belongs to the Lord, he is fighting on your behalf! This song is a sweet reminder of this very concept! Listen to it and proclaim your victory in Jesus' mighty name!

"See A Victory | Live | Elevation Worship" (6:03mins):
https://www.youtube.com/watch?v=YNd-PbVhnvA

When you go through your own inner healing, you can then be "holy" and "set apart" for HIS purposes. Consecration is the obvious next step. Continue to be bold in your journey, mighty princess of the KING!

Craig Groeschel speaks of facing your wounds, healing, and moving forward in order to become a great warrior for HIS kingdom. End off by listening to this challenging sermon:

"What Every Warrior Needs to Hear – Warrior" (37:14 mins):
https://www.youtube.com/watch?v=4fJAaxspReA

Day *15* RADIATE Christ

CONSECRATION IS NECESSARY

"Consecrate yourselves and be holy, because I am the Lord your God."

Leviticus 20:7

There are times in our lives when we devote ourselves to studying for an upcoming test, preparing for a job interview, setting new goals, praying, or meditating on God's word. We set aside time for the things in our lives that are important to us; things that pull and lead us toward our purpose.

Jesus did this too. He set aside time to heal the sick, meet with his Father and his disciples, pray, talk to crowds, and feed the hungry. He was always making time for the work he came to do, and reflecting on why he was here.

Not only did he consecrate himself, there were also times when other people consecrated Christ.

There was a woman named Mary who poured expensive perfume on the feet of Jesus, then wiped them with her hair. (Luke 7:36-38)

Mary anointed Jesus and knew that her actions had a purpose- some say it was an act of worship, while others say the act was symbolically preparing Christ for his burial. There is a purpose and a time to everything!

God also has a purpose and plan for each one of us here on the earth, just as he did for his son, Jesus. You need to set yourself apart and allow God to mold and shape you. We all go through times in our lives where God works on and speaks to our hearts. This is called "consecration".

Consecration is defined as "devoting, setting apart, or dedicating to some purpose. It is making something an object of honour or having great respect for it."[1]

When you consecrate yourself, you set your body apart; dedicating it to God's purposes; making it an entity of honour for God, something to be revered or respected.

On Day 5 of this journey, I touched on this topic of respecting your body.

1st Corinthians is so very important, it is worth quoting again. "Do you not know that your body is a temple of the Holy Spirit, who is in you, whom you have received from God? You are not your own; you were bought at a price. Therefore honour God with your body." (1st Corinthians 6:19)

In addition, the book of Corinthians goes on to say, "you were bought at a price." (1st Corinthians 7:23)

Our world tells women that their body is their own and that they can do whatever they want with it. Many women do not realize the consequences of this thought. The world also can give young men the wrong idea that women are objects, or that purity for men isn't "cool".

When we don't do what is honourable with our bodies in God's eyes, we are really telling Jesus that his sacrifice wasn't good enough.

Remember, "He died for all, that those who live should no longer live for themselves but for him who died for them and was raised again." (2nd Corinthians 5:15)

In other words, live for him, because he gave his life for you. Therefore, living for him means honouring him with your earthly body and making sure, you treat it as a temple; and remembering not to make your temple an idol of any form.

As I mentioned in Day 5, not only did my physical well-being become an idol, but also I dressed in a way to attract attention from men. I wore low cut tops, and tight-fitting clothing that showed my body too well. I was sad and hurting inside from rejection I had suffered previously. I said to myself, my body is my own; I can flaunt it and do what I want with it. As a result, it got me into some unwanted relationships, and made me feel condemned and ashamed for allowing my body to be an object instead of something holy and of God. God worked on me spiritually in many ways over the years following those experiences. I remained single and allowed God to consecrate, or set me apart, and work on my heart.

It was during this time that I had the joy and privilege of working in a small Christian school as a teacher, becoming accountable to my students and colleagues. I realized once again that my body was in fact a temple, and that it should be covered appropriately and treated as sacred. I wanted to save that physical desire for the person God was preparing for me. What a gift to one day give your future spouse!

The following is an example of a letter written by a young woman, (Lee Jordan, 2016),[2] who took this covenant with a future spouse seriously and decided to write this to the spouse she knew God was preparing for her. She understood that God had set her apart, and she was consecrating herself for the man God had for her. She had written other letters in her Christian walk to her "future husband", and this is the final letter to her spouse that she would be united with in a few hours. What a beautiful gift to give her husband!

Dear Future Husband,

It's hard to believe that this is the last time I'll ever write a Dear Future Husband letter to you because in just a few short hours you will no longer be my future husband but instead will become my forever husband. It's hard to believe that the day we've dreamed of since we met is finally here. It's hard to believe that our forever starts today. It's hard to believe that I have the privilege of marrying a man like you—a man who loves like Jesus does, a man who serves with His whole heart, a man who is strong and brave, and a man who lets God lead His life no matter the cost.

But on the other hand, it's not that hard to believe because that's just the kind of the God we serve—a God who is faithful to work "all things together for the good of those who love Him" (Romans 8:28).

When I was 13, my dad gave me a purity ring. Engraved inside of the band are the words: true love waits. In that moment, I promised to wait for my future husband and even signed a purity pact without hesitation (although I had no idea just how difficult that road could be). Nonetheless, I've worn that ring since the day it was given to me and done my best to be true to the promise my little middle school heart made to my earthly father, my Heavenly Father, and you, my Future Husband.

It wasn't always easy waiting for you. It wasn't always easy when boys would lose interest when I said no. It wasn't always easy to explain to people all the reasons why I believed you were worth waiting for without even knowing your name yet. All I knew was that God's design is more beautiful than anything this world could dream up—and that was worth waiting for even when it was hard.

When I felt like giving up, I'd think of you and then I would write to you. I dreamed of one day giving all those letters to the man I married so that he would see how truly important he was long before I ever met him. Today, you are that man. And although some have since been misplaced, I pray you treasure these letters I've written to you over the years.

As I step out of my single life and into the mystery of marriage with you in Jesus name, I'm giving to you the purity ring my daddy placed on my hand when I was a young 13-year-old girl. In its place, I'll wear the wedding band that you'll place on my finger today as your bride.

Because you are and always have been the future husband that God designed for me, the one I've prayed for, hoped for and waited for all these years.

Although it's been a long road of waiting, God has walked with me through the steps of lonely seasons, heartbreaks, loss, frustration and so much more to prepare me to become a wife worthy of your love. Looking back, every single one of those steps that brought us here were so beyond worth it. And I know without a doubt that you are worth it and I'd do it all over again if I had to.

So as I walk down that aisle toward you today, I want you to know that I believe that walk is so much more than a ceremonial motion or formality. Each step represents the steps that God has walked with me through to bring me to this moment as I take this big step in becoming your wife.

Today we give Him everything. Today, we give each other everything.

I can't express to you how overwhelmed I am by the faithfulness and goodness of God in His blessing of me with you as my husband and I joyfully give you my hand, my heart and my life from now until the end of time.

Love,
Your Forever Bride

Like this young woman alluded to, love should not be awakened too soon. The scripture "Do not arouse or awaken love until it so desires," (Song of Songs 2:7b), became a verse very dear to my heart as God prepared me for my husband.

I wanted to be pure and holy for the man God was preparing me. His word promised that in spite of my past mistakes with relationships, he would "wash me....whiter than snow." (Psalm 51:7)

I was humbled that he would wash away my sins. God refined and allowed me to be a role model for my students, especially the young women, in this area of my life. God can wash away your sin and consecrate you too. Consecration is such a beautiful transformation when God is doing the work!

Then, God rocked my vanity even more. Consecration went to a completely new level.

A couple of my students, (Ashley and Trevor), had a mother who was very sick with cancer. I had the privilege of meeting their mom, Denise, while she was sick in the hospital. What a mighty woman of God! Even though she knew she had very little time left on earth, she praised God and stayed true to her faith. She is still an inspiration and role model for me today on how she lived her life, taught her children, and stood strong in her faith during the midst of her circumstances. She ended up succumbing to her illness just a few short weeks after I met her, which was right before a new school year.

The school was small and everyone was like family. We all rallied around Ashley and Trevor and decided to turn this horribly sad situation into something good.

Where I resided, there was an event called "Hair Massacure". The event was about people supporting their loved ones who were fighting cancer, or ones they'd lost, by attaining donations to shave their head.

[The bible tells us to "speak up for those who cannot speak for themselves." (Proverbs 31:8a)

This was our way of supporting so many adults and children in cancer wards, as well as honouring the people we had loved and lost. The event itself funds the "Make a Wish" foundation that grants wishes to terminally ill children. What an amazing cause to be a part of! The event still continues to this day!]

Our school's response was amazing, with the majority of the students participating. Some were shaving their heads in honour of Denise, and some were cutting off their hair to donate for wigs for cancer patients. It was truly amazing! God was using this tragedy to bring us together!

I had mentioned to Ashley, that we should shave our heads together, but I didn't prepare myself for what that really meant.

When the day finally came, we sat nervously in our chairs. The clippers started to make that familiar buzzing noise. We held hands and felt the first row of our shoulder-length hair fall to the floor. The cool air against our scalp was such a strange feeling, and I began to cry. I focused on myself as I lost sight of why we were there and for whom we were doing this. I remember Denise's mom, Linda, bending over to encourage me. She had just lost her daughter, and she was encouraging ME! My tears flowed throughout the entire head shave while I realized that I was losing a part of my identity as a woman.

When the final row of hair was gone, we felt our fuzzy heads. I stood up, wiped my eyes, and decided that there would be no more tears. Here I was a healthy, strong person who had chosen to shave my head for people I loved. I thought about the women who had died from this disease like Denise, my grandmother, and my mother-in-law, and those who were sick and never had the choice; they lost their hair because of being gravely ill.

Then I decided, "No more feeling sorry for myself!"

All the kids were extremely supportive of me, Ashley, Trevor and others who had shaved their heads. Being surrounded by a community of people who loved you, no matter what, sure helped in the next few months and years of my journey.

In the weeks and months following the event, God began to speak to me about my identity and about consecration. I had put so much of my identity in my outer appearance, that when my hair was taken away, it was like my security blanket had been lifted from me. I felt like a protective barrier had been shattered, making me truly vulnerable in so many ways. God started defining my new identity and I began to read the book of Leviticus about being set apart and "holy". No longer was it about me.... it was about who I was in Christ. What a revelation!

Now, when I am getting ready in the morning, I'm not doing it to impress others, I'm doing it to look good for God and give him my best, so he gets the glory. I want to put my best foot forward for God who loves me unconditionally.

Our identity should be in Christ. He says, we are "fearfully and wonderfully made." (Psalm 139:14) How can we NOT identify with a God who created us with such a passion? Consecrating us and "setting us apart" to be used for his purposes and plans for our lives really does make us realize that he deserves ALL the praise, ALL the glory, and ALL the honour that we can give him!

Victorious Verse

"For it is written: 'Be holy, because I am holy.'" 1st Peter 1:16

Mighty Melody

"Identity" by <u>Lecrae</u> and "Refiner's Fire" by <u>Brian Doerksen</u>

Armour in Action

Are there some ways you could be less worldly, and more set apart? Think of at least two ways you could challenge yourself to bring honour and glory to God. Maybe it is dressing more appropriately; maybe it is keeping your thoughts pure; maybe it is not putting your identity in your appearance. Write a prayer asking God to consecrate you, and allow you to become more holy, therefore becoming more like Christ.

Take some time right now; write a Dear "Future Husband" letter. Share your heart with him about your struggles or ideas of staying pure. Put it in a safe place. Maybe you will give it to him in the future. Write a letter anytime you have some thoughts that you want to share with him. Keep all the letters in a box! What a beautiful gift to give your husband one day.....sharing your heart!

Notes:

Day *16* RADIATE Christ

YOU ARE BEYOND PRECIOUS

"A wife of noble character who can find? She is worth far more than rubies."

Proverbs 31:10

When you are going through the process of consecration, or being set apart like Christ, you begin to realize how precious you are in God's sight.

It is unfortunate that society sees certain people, or even the unborn, as disposable. Their lives are thought to be somehow less meaningful. There is a young man with Down syndrome by the name of Frank Stephens. He courageously made a speech before Congress in the United States reminding the world of the importance of life, no matter what! We are all, indeed, a masterpiece that he has intricately formed for his purposes and plans!

"Frank Stephens' POWERFUL Speech On Down Syndrome" (7:14 mins): https://www.youtube.com/watch?v=vtS91Jd5mac

Just as God was pleased with his son Frank, as he delivered his speech and stood up for "life with Down syndrome", God was also pleased with his own son, Jesus. "This is my Son, whom I love; with him I am well pleased." (Matthew 3:17)

Which means he is pleased with us, because we are formed in his image, "So God created man in his own image, in the image of God, he created him." (Genesis 1:27)

It is so humbling to know that God deemed us so important, that he wanted to make us like his own son.

Important or as precious as God sees us, many times we don't see ourselves as he does. We act or speak in ways that show our lack of respect for ourselves.

Mentioned in Day 15, I used to dress very immodestly because I felt sad inside and longed for love from men instead of looking for love from my heavenly Father. I was enjoying the attention I was getting; not understanding it would lead me down roads to heartbreak. In the end, I needed to really seek the face of God to heal my heart and become whole again.

Many women dress in a way to bring attention to themselves. They don't realize that modesty is revealing your dignity and feelings of self-worth; it's not about hiding your body in a burlap sack. We hold a lot of power with our bodies, because men are hard-wired to be visual beings.

Here is a quote from professional boxer and social activist, Muhammad Ali (2000)[1], talking to his two daughters, as they arrived at his house wearing clothes that were far from modest:

> "'Ana, everything that God made valuable in the world is covered and hard to get to. Where do you find diamonds? Deep in the ground, covered and protected. Where do you find pearls? Deep down at the bottom of the ocean, covered up and protected in a beautiful shell. Where do you find gold? Way down in the mine, covered over with layers and layers of rock. You have to work hard to get them.' He looked at me again with serious eyes and said, 'Your body is sacred. You're far more precious than diamonds and pearls, and you should be covered too.'"

This quote is a valuable reminder of how sacred our bodies really are. God values what the world does not. His kingdom is in direct opposition to the world and everything in it.

We see evidence of this when we look at the well-known 31st Proverb. In verses 10-31, it focuses on what a wife of noble character is. In other words, she is a deep, classy, spiritual woman who is confident in her role as a strong wife and mother. A mentor to me, Betty Fraser, pointed out in one of her teachings that this passage of scripture mentions the woman's arms and hands five times.

God must deem these parts of our body as important if they are mentioned multiple times. She is constantly using her hands, arms, and fingers to help the poor, provide for her family, and be a good example to her children and community.

This Proverb is very important to me and God put it on my heart to memorize Proverbs 31:10-31 for my wedding day. I recited it for my husband that afternoon in front of family and friends. They witnessed me promising to be the wife God was calling me to be; a wife focused on godly traits, not traits the world deemed as important.

For example, outward appearance is not where the kingdom of God has its focus. Outward beauty comes and goes, it is "fleeting". Therefore we need to place our trust and hope in our God and what he sees as valuable.

Proverbs 31 speaks so much truth about our outward appearance:

"Charm is deceptive, and beauty is fleeting; but a woman who fears the Lord is to be praised." (Proverbs 31:30)

Watch these clips on a Proverbs 31 woman! A great reminder of what God sees as important!

"Proverbs 31 | A Woman Who Fears The Lord Is To Be Praised" (11:11 mins):
https://www.youtube.com/watch?v=UNHM5Jg6x74

"Proverbs 31 Woman" (13:48 mins):
https://www.youtube.com/watch?v=Dk1JcnwERj8

When you have a "fear" of God, you have an awe and respect for him that goes beyond comprehension. Moreover, the respect you have for your heavenly Father causes others to look at your life and see his light shining through you, because your life reflects his character. When your heart lines up with God's heart, this is true beauty indeed!

As the saying goes, "beauty is only skin deep". Outer beauty is something that the world deems as important, but it is our inner beauty and reverence for God that will last.

Here is a video that really puts "beauty" in perspective.

"Real Simple" (51 secs):
https://www.facebook.com/realsimple/videos/10154500870388163/

Also, this story from a sermon I once heard by Pastor Greg Fraser, retold in my own words, really speaks to our concept of beauty:

> The children gathered around the stage and waited in anxious anticipation for the beautiful princess to appear. The children whispered with excitement and eagerly held their breath as the lights dimmed and the music began to play. The spotlight seemed to dance as it searched the stage for the young lady making her appearance. Finally, to the children's delight, she began to float across the stage. A hush fell over the children as they were in awe of her beauty. She danced gracefully and sang a beautiful song as her glittery gown swayed magically about. As she sang, she studied the faces of the little boys and girls that were mesmerized by her performance. There were blonde, red, chestnut, and strawberry heads with twinkling eyes and she was touched by their innocence. As she glided across the stage, she caught a glimpse of a young boy out of the corner of her eye. He was shrinking back in the shadows, almost as if he didn't want to be seen. As she finished her performance and the boys and girls "ooohed and ahhhed", she made her way off the stage, down the stairs, and into the sea of children. They all stared up at her as though she was an angel and she stroked heads and faces as she whisked by. She made her way to the little boy in the shadows, knelt down, and held his face in her hands. As she

tilted his head up, she saw he was disfigured and was ashamed of his scars. She kissed his forehead and lovingly wiped his face of the tears that had escaped his deep, sad, brown eyes. She whispered in his ear that he was special and loved, as all the other boys and girls longed for that moment with the breathtaking princess. That day, many children learned what true beauty really was.

This story is a great picture of what our Saviour can do for you.

We are in awe of him and his beauty. He lives in our hearts, and knows when you are broken, alone, and feel far from perfect, and he kisses our face as we hide in the shadows, and tells us how much we are loved and adored. John and Stasi Eldridge (2005, pg. 112), drive this point home when they write, "A woman becomes beautiful when she knows she's loved."

First and foremost, this love comes from our Father in heaven, as we are his beloved children. If only we could see ourselves through his eyes!

Listen to the song "Through Your Eyes" by Britt Nicole and be reminded of his love!

"Britt Nicole - Through Your Eyes (Acoustic)" (3:48mins): https://www.youtube.com/watch?v=KwXakPxsg9g

When you see yourself through the eyes of Christ, you can focus on how brilliantly and meticulously he created you. Your outer appearance and imperfections should not be where you put your attention!

Instead, see your spirit, which is the true beauty to God. Focus on your inner qualities; don't put your identity in your appearance.

1st Peter describes this so well, "Your beauty should not come from outward adornment, such as braided hair and the wearing of gold jewellery and fine clothes. Instead, it should be that of your inner self, the unfading beauty of a gentle and quiet spirit, which is of great worth in God's sight." (1st Peter 3:3-4)

The cycle of our beauty being so outwardly based must be broken! We are beautiful vessels with so much to share. We have treasure inside of us that no one else has; we have a song to sing that no one else can share with this world. My prayer for each one of you is that you will continue to allow God to use you as a vessel of beauty in an ugly world. In a world that tries to tear you down, and tell you that you're not enough, know that God made you more than enough, and he longs for you to share your treasure deep inside you.

> "You are beautiful. Your beauty, just like your capacity for life, happiness, and success, is immeasurable. Day after day, countless people across the globe get on a scale in search of validation of beauty and social acceptance. Get off the scale! I have yet to see a scale that can tell you how enchanting your eyes are. I have yet to see a scale that can show you how wonderful your hair looks when the sun shines its

glorious rays on it. I have yet to see a scale that can thank you for your compassion, sense of humour, and contagious smile. Get off the scale because I have yet to see one that can admire you for your perseverance when challenged in life. It's true; the scale can only give you a numerical reflection of your relationship with gravity. That's it. It cannot measure beauty, talent, purpose, life force, possibility, strength, or love. Don't give the scale more power than it has earned. Take note of the number, then get off the scale and live your life. You are beautiful!"

Dr. Steve Maraboli (2009)[2]

If you see yourself through God's eyes, he can mold you and shape you more effectively. You can then focus on what the kingdom of God sees as important! When you allow your inner beauty to take precedence over your outer beauty, his kingdom purposes will reign in your life and you will make a difference in this world far beyond what you could ever hope for or imagine!

Watch as this woman puts outer and inner beauty in perspective. It really makes you think about how much this world stresses our outer appearance, as opposed to the "jewel" inside!

"The Gift-Wrap & The Jewel. By Wanda B. Goines" 1:20 mins:
https://www.youtube.com/watch?v=2YxCR2a-sxI

I want to finish today with a poem God laid on my heart about beauty. I pray it speaks to you as powerfully as it spoke to me when I wrote it!

BEAUTY

I asked God what beauty was, and I felt his Spirit whispered soft as could be.
He told me beauty wasn't a feeling, it was Jesus working in and through me.

While the world lies and tells us that beauty is in our makeup or painted nails,
God showed me beauty is so much more, as he slowly lifted the veil.

He revealed to me a dimension that I had never seen.
He showed me that beauty gives HIM the glory, and to take the focus off of me.

Beauty is not found in flawless skin, or the color of our hair.
Beauty points others to our Saviour, it's literally everywhere!

Beauty is in the strength we muster, when times in life are tough,
Beauty is when we keep going, when we feel like giving up.

Beauty is in the fuzzy head of a woman whose hair has fallen out.
While walking through cancer and chemo, she knows what suffering is all about.

Like the beautiful woman that I knew, just 35 years old,
Who herself in her last days while dying of cancer, praised God and was so strong and bold.

She is an inspiration to me, to this very day.
She showed me that beauty was in her strength, as she stayed the course, come what may.

Beauty is in the scars of a woman who's had a mastectomy.
She courageously faces death square in the eye, while still holding onto her dreams.

Beauty is in the words of a loyal friend who's lost their husband too.
Beauty is in the warmth of their embrace, when crying is all you can do.

Beauty is when we find the courage to pick up and move on.
We define a new normal for ourselves, even though they're gone.

Or some of us have to grieve the loss of someone we love who's still alive,
To dementia, divorce, illness or addiction, our grief is where beauty resides.

For it's through this journey of overwhelming loss, when we face our own doubts and our fears,
And we turn sadness and anger into gratitude, indeed, true beauty lives here.

Beauty is in the woman who has been abused, who feels so scared and alone,
But she allows God to heal and restore her heart, instead of allowing it to turn to stone.

For God will redeem this horrendous act, the shame and guilt she'll defy.
She will be hope for so many, and out of the ashes she'll rise!

Beauty is found in a woman, whose anxiety and fear can paralyze.
But she quotes 2nd Timothy 1:7 to the devil, and seeks counsel from the wise.

She remembers that God has not given her a spirit of doubt and of fear,
But of power, love and sound mind, faith and peace truly live here!

Beauty is the love of a mother when she holds her first born child,
Beauty is also in the heart of a woman who chose to be childless, and with God was reconciled.

Beauty is in the resolve of a woman who never bore a child of her own.
But she has a mother's heart that's beyond lovely- seeds in so many others she's sown.

Beauty is also found in the despair of a mother when God takes her child home,
Beauty is when she places her trust in God, when she feels so lost and alone.

Beauty is when we stop and seek God's face when we feel as though we've failed.
Because we know that in the end there's victory, His kingdom WILL prevail!

Beauty is telling our daughters that they are strong, smart, important, and kind.
Beauty is encouraging her to be who God has called her to be, and to focus on her heart and her mind.

Beauty is teaching her that "girl power" begins with God's power granted from above.
She can do ALL THINGS through Christ, because of his grace and his love.

Beauty is leading by example when we follow the passion inside our soul,
Beauty is watching our daughters fulfill their calling, like watching a butterfly's wings unfold.

Beauty is in the heart of a teenager, whose life is going so wrong,
But she has a faith that God is shaping her character, and she trusts God to help her sing a new song.

Why is God's beauty found in all these things you ask?
For we've all been taught that beauty should be hidden behind a mask.

A mask that exudes perfection, but makes us feel like we're not enough,
Real beauty is inside God's children- we are his diamonds in the rough!

Beauty is not found in our size, or the numbers on the scale,
Beauty is in Christ's hands and feet, as they hammered in the nails.

It all began on the Mount of Olives, when he said "Father, take this cup from me."
Beauty was when he surrendered to God, "Not my will, but YOUR will, let it be."

For his own will became secondary to what his Father was doing.
Beauty was when an angel came and strengthened him, because it was God's plan he was pursuing.

Beauty is the grace he had on the cross for the thieves on either side,
Beauty is when he said to one of them, "Indeed, you will be with me in paradise."

Beauty was in his final moments, as he thought of others before himself.
"Forgive them father, for they do not know what they are doing." As he literally went through hell.

And as those around him mocked and sneered, his death, he did not fear it.
He humbly hung his head as he cried out, "Father into your hands I commit my spirit."

So thank-you Jesus for showing me the real meaning of beauty.
As women of faith, we must go forth like Christ and preach the gospel-it's our duty!

Remember that beauty is about Jesus And bringing him the glory.
We need to look outside ourselves and see that everyone has a story.

Tell other women when you see their beauty that shines from the inside out.
Because being there for our sisters, is what the gospel is all about.

A helping hand, a listening ear, encouragement when another is down,
Not letting the world know it was crooked to start with, when you straighten your sister's crown.

Beauty is found in all these things, not on the magazines with which we're inundated,
But beauty was made to build us up, not tear down what God created.

So help us God, to keep our eyes on you when the world tears us down and apart,
Remind us Lord, that beauty is all about you, as it resides where you are, in our hearts.

Victorious Verse
"The Lord does not look at the things man looks at. Man looks at the outward appearance, but the Lord looks at the heart." 1st Samuel 16:7b

Mighty Melody
"Beautiful You" by Jonny Diaz, "Beautiful" by Micah Tyler and "Who You Say I Am" by Hillsong Worship

Watch this clip on beauty. It has a lot of "ugly" truth.

"DEAR GIRLS, YOU'RE UGLY" (4:23mins):
https://www.youtube.com/watch?v=v129rsjYGeI

Armour in Action
Do you see yourself as precious and more than enough?
Or do you see yourself as full of imperfections, always striving to be something more?
Ask God to show you your strengths and reveal your inner beauty to you, in other words, your gifts he has given you for this world.
Allow him to help you focus on your heart, and ask him to help you see your outward appearance as an enhancement of the beautiful treasure within.
Write a prayer to him expressing your deepest inadequacies and fears, along with your hopes and strengths. Ask God to help you give up self-defeating things such as expecting perfection, negative self-talk, being a people pleaser, having a fear of failure, and criticizing others because of our lack of confidence.
Finally, thank him for all he's doing and going to do in you and through you and watch the following message on your worth as a daughter of the King of kings! Hopefully, it will remind you of your value and worth in Jesus Christ.

"Who You Are: A Message To All Women" (3:36mins):
https://www.youtube.com/watch?v=uWi5iXnguTU

Notes:

_____
_____
_____
_____
_____
_____
_____
_____
_____
_____
_____

Day *17* RADIATE Christ

YOU ARE CHOSEN

"A voice came from the cloud, saying, 'This is my Son, whom I have chosen; listen to him.'"

Luke 9:35

Just like Jesus, you are chosen. He longs for you to know that there is a great purpose and plan for your life. You are not here by chance or coincidence. In addition, while you are here, immerse yourself in his undying love. Understand that he is your Daddy and he longs to spend time with you. Moreover, as you spend time with him, he is able to refine you so he can use you for his glory and to draw people unto him.

Listen to these songs about being "chosen". Let them minister to your spirit and remind you that God is deliberate in all he does. Things don't happen by chance or "coincidence"; think of it instead as "Christ-incidence". When you truly believe you are not here by accident, that he in fact chose you to fulfill what only YOU can do on this earth, you can then take that message of hope to others!

"Sidewalk Prophets ~ Chosen (Lyrics)" (3:09 mins):
https://www.youtube.com/watch?v=Y1ymenyfDjs

"Chosen (feat. Elle Limebear) [Lyric Video] - Kathryn Scott | Speak to Me" (4:48 mins):
https://www.youtube.com/watch?v=xc-rpHDeKA0

Drawing people to God is not about what we say, but mostly how we live. As in the words of Dr. Steve Maraboli (2013),[1] "I find the best way to love someone is not to change them, but instead, help them reveal the greatest version of themselves."

Sometimes our lives will be the only bible some people will ever read.

A quote that is commonly associated with St. Francis of Assisi, but has been disputed in recent years as a generalization of his original quote, is "Preach the gospel, and if necessary, use words."[2]

There is a sermon I remember listening to a few years ago, that was entitled "Fruitcake and Ice cream" by pastor and public speaker Louie Giglio (2012). It was such a poignant example of a young woman living out the gospel that it touched my life, and I've never forgotten it. Here is the story retold in my own words:

As the story begins, he speaks of a young woman in college (Ashley) whose parents divorced when she was young, and she ended up living with her Dad. Her Mom remarried a Christian man, and they had a son together. Well, Ashley and her Dad wanted nothing to do with God and that "Christianity" stuff. They thought it was all just a crutch and she actually thought her Mom's family was a little crazy because of their love for God.

Well, it turns out, Ashley had a boyfriend, and she shared an apartment with him. She was quite the partier and indulged in alcohol and all the activities that go along with worldly college life. One day, during class, Ashley felt sick, so she went back to the apartment in the middle of the day, and found her boyfriend cheating on her. She decided to kick him out of the apartment and put a sign up for a new roommate.

As it happened, a young lady who had a strong faith in God replied to the ad and moved in with Ashley. The new tenant lived by example and was always there to listen when Ashley struggled with her ex-boyfriend. Ashley would sleep with him from time to time, and yet she would still see him with other girls and this broke her heart.

Ashley had a diary that she wrote in almost every day. In it, she started to refer to the young lady living with her as "fruitcake" because she prayed, read her bible, and even went to bible studies.

"Fruitcake" was saving herself for marriage, and Ashley couldn't understand why she was still a virgin and why she would go to faith conferences on weekends instead of drink and party and enjoy college life. The young lady, "fruitcake", offered to pray with Ashley on occasion when she was really struggling. Ashley would laugh it off and think the girl was a little crazy just like her Mom. However, what she liked about "fruitcake" was she was not judgemental, as she felt some Christians were, and they would eat ice cream together as "fruitcake" listened to her problems. She was a great listener and never offered to fix her situation. She would just say she was sorry life was so difficult for Ashley, and offer to pray for her.

As time went on, "fruitcake" continued to pray for Ashley behind closed doors. God was working on Ashley's heart. Eventually, Ashley came to a point in her life where she was so broken and so sad inside, that she ended up wanting a relationship with Christ. "Fruitcake" led her in a prayer to accept Jesus into her heart. She began really seeking out a relationship with God, and ended up going to a bible study with "fruitcake" where she cried and realized God's love for her.

In just a few short weeks, Ashley went from being broken and alone to having a personal relationship with God and feeling a love that can only come from her heavenly Father.

Only a few short months after accepting Christ, Ashley was killed in a car accident. Now her story is told around the world and inspiring others to live for Christ as "fruitcake" did. "Fruitcake" simply loved Ashley like Jesus, which allowed her to speak into her life and eventually lead her to Christ. What an awesome testimony!

God used 'fruitcake'; she was 'chosen' and allowed God to use her as an instrument in Ashley's life. She was, in fact, a living bible to Ashley. Like Christ, she loved Ashley and gained relationship with her, and God did the rest.

Here is Pastor Louie Giglio sharing Ashley's intimate life story from her diary.

"Fruit Cake And Ice Cream" (26:57mins):
https://www.youtube.com/watch?v=wjOyuI2R9bY

Here is the song that Pastor Louie Giglio spoke of; the one that Ashley heard at bible study (at the 19 minute mark in the video). God is indeed MIGHTY to save!!!

"Mighty To Save - Hillsong [With Lyrics]"(6:55 mins):
https://www.youtube.com/watch?v=5Sqb9hvJjb8

It really is that simple to make a difference as we reflect the love of Christ.

As we live our lives, what we do speaks far louder that what we, say. We need to be Christians that long to be more and more like Christ. When we reflect him to others, it draws them to his love.

A childhood story by Robert Fulghum in *Chicken Soup for the Teenage Soul* (1997, pg. 134-135)[3] reinforces this concept.

> "'When I was a child, during the war, we were very poor and we lived in a remote village. One day, on the road, I found the broken pieces of a mirror.
>
> A German motorcycle had been wrecked in that place. I tried to find all the pieces and put them together, but it was not possible, so I kept only the largest piece. This one, and, by scratching it on a stone, I made it round.
>
> I began to play with it as a toy and became fascinated by the fact that I could reflect light into dark places where the sun would never shine- in deep holes and crevices and dark closets. It became a game for me to get light into the most inaccessible places I could find.
>
> I kept the little mirror, and, as I went about my growing up, I would take it out in idle moments and continue the challenge of the game. As I became a man, I grew to

understand that I am not the light or the source of light. But light- truth, understanding, knowledge- is there, and it will shine in many dark places only if I reflect it.

I am a fragment of a mirror whose whole design and shape I do not know. Nevertheless, with what I have I can reflect light into the dark places of the world- into the black places in the hearts of men- and change some things in some people. Perhaps others may see and do likewise.'"

As Christians reflect HIS light, we hold the answers to a world that is so desperate and hurting.

In the book of John, Jesus so eloquently put it, " 'If the world hates you, keep in mind that it hated me first. If you belonged to the world, it would love you as its own. As it is, you do not belong to the world, but I have chosen you out of the world.' " (John 15:18-19)

To close this day's journey, I've included a poem I wrote. A tragedy involving the death of 3 RCMP officers and the wounding of two others in Moncton, New Brunswick, in June of 2014 prompted me to write it. We are all "chosen" and need to radiate Christ and change the world one life at a time, just like "fruitcake".

In the wise words of Paul, "In him we were also chosen, having been predestined according to the plan of him who works out everything in conformity with the purpose of his will." (Ephesians 1:11)

BE THE CHANGE

Why is not for us to ask, we trust God through and through.
He will turn all things for good, his promises are true.

So many sad, hurting people in this chaotic place.
Sometimes I do question the whole human race.

But I know that God is on his throne.
In the midst of it all, we are not alone.

Everyday life will go on in spite of these tragic events.
Praying that people will be drawn to Christ- the beloved son God sent.

For this world is fleeting, and things change from day to day,
But God is the same forever and ever, and will be tomorrow and today.

So thankful for my Saviour, I put my hope in him,
as this world gets darker and the future seems so dim.

God's heart is broken once again for families feeling loss.
All he can do is point mankind to his son on a wooden cross.

The answer to this world is Jesus, who died so long ago.
He wants to walk beside us and wants us all to know....

Our lives are but a single breath- A moment frozen in time.
Our lives our his, they're not our own, as he whispers "You are mine."

We could throw our hands high in the air, and say "Where are you God?"
But we must remember we're his hands and feet- we're his staff and rod.

We are his valued instruments, we all have a part to play.
He is the loving potter, we are the precious clay.

We need to be the change in the places that we live.
Be Jesus Christ to all we meet, show them how to give!

Then maybe those who are hurting will see and feel God's glory,
And we will help to change their lives, and rewrite the next sad story.

Victorious Verse

"But you are a chosen people, a royal priesthood, a holy nation, a people belonging to God, that you may declare the praises of him who called you out of darkness into his wonderful light." 1st Peter 2:9

Mighty Melody

"Chosen Ones" by Blanca, "Love Them Like Jesus" by Casting Crowns, and "Radiate" by Hannah Kerr

Armour in Action

Is there someone in your life that God has put there to love like Jesus? Pray for that person. Live your life like it is the only bible they will read. God will work in their lives and lead them to salvation in his time. Just trust him. Remember that you are not their saviour, all you can do is point them to the "Saviour" by loving them like Jesus.

Notes:

_____
_____
_____
_____
_____
_____
_____
_____
_____
_____
_____
_____
_____
_____
_____
_____
_____
_____
_____
_____
_____
_____
_____
_____
_____
_____
_____

Day *18* RADIATE Christ

SEEING WITH THE EYES OF CHRIST

"I pray that the eyes of your heart may be enlightened in order that you may know the hope to which he has called you, the riches of his glorious inheritance in the saints, and his incomparably great power for us who believe."

Ephesians 1:18 -19a

Jesus never looked down on others. Everyone he met had worth and He always met them in the midst of their circumstance. He eventually challenged them to go to the next level after building a relationship. We need to learn to be more like Christ when dealing with the downtrodden of society and the less fortunate.

Jesus put this so eloquently when he said, "For I was hungry and you gave me something to eat, I was thirsty and you gave me something to drink, I was a stranger and you invited me in, I needed clothes and you clothed me, I was sick and you looked after me, I was in prison and you came to visit me.........I tell you the truth, whatever you did for one of the least of these brothers of mine, you did for me." (Matthew 25:35-36, 40)

We are to see Jesus in everyone we meet. Just because society deems one individual as more important than another, doesn't mean we should. I remember teaching in the public school system and making sure that the kids understood that the janitor of the school was just as important as any teacher, or even the principal, for that matter! They play a vital role in schools, just like anyone else. I remember students throwing garbage in front of them and telling them to pick it up because "that was their job". I couldn't believe they were so rude and cruel! From that moment on, I made a point of teaching all my students that everyone has worth.

I was inspired to write the following poem when a friend and fellow colleague, who also happened to be a janitor, had passed away.

Just a Janitor...

"They're just a janitor," they said, as they threw paper on the floor
"It's their job to clean our mess," and they laughed and walked out the school door.

I sat at my desk and listened, as a tear rolled down my face.
Don't they know how much they care? How much pride they take in this place?

The next day the students came to school to learn arithmetic,
but instead they learned about life, and I hoped that it would stick.

"Just a janitor?" I said, as I held back angry tears.
"Always treat them with respect, for they are so important here!"

They are not "just a janitor", they're important like you and me.
They're a part of the fabric of this school, a huge part of this family.

They work so hard to make this place shine for you and I.
They're a shoulder for teachers to lean on, when the day has gone awry.

Their hearts break for so many, hurting and broken kids,
they care much more than you'll ever know, and love like Jesus did.

They teach us about humility, as they mop and sweep our floors.
They do a thankless, dirty job, as they wipe down our walls and our doors.

They discipline students and put them to work, when they're going through some strife.
They get them doing various jobs, but, more importantly, teach them about life.

They truly have a heart for all the people in the school.
So don't treat them like "just a janitor", don't be a thoughtless fool!

The students realized that day how special janitors really are,
they're the glue that holds our schools together, they are our shining stars!

So if you are a janitor, please know this from the heart.
We love and appreciate all of you, as you play your vital part.

You're NEVER "just a janitor", you're always so much more.
And Paul, we hope to see you again, when we walk through heaven's door.

The idea of role modeling this worth, to students, was made evident by "walking the walk". For example, our Leadership class had the privilege every Christmas of cooking and serving turkey dinner to the homeless in the inner city. The students, sat and talked to them, fed them, blessed them, and saw that they were no different from us. It was truly life changing. I tried to teach the students that they should see people through Christ's lenses, which is a supernatural experience. Most people would simply pass these people by if they saw them on the street, but we were able to minister to them in so many different ways! What a blessing for all of us to put the love of Christ into action!

Recently, I saw some social media experiments done online where they put an "actor" on the streets in sub-zero temperatures. In fact, it was an actor posing as a homeless child. He had nothing on but a t-shirt and jeans, and had nothing but a plastic garbage bag to keep warm. As he lay on the sidewalk inside his garbage bag and shivered, for over TWO hours, no one helped him. People just stared at the young man, walked by as they held shopping bags in their hands and hurried to their destinations. After all that time, the only person who offered the boy comfort, and the coat off his OWN back, was another homeless man. He hugged the boy and began to talk to him, as Christ would have, as he shielded him from the cold. It was truly amazing to see this man, who had nothing, stop to help the boy. Our world is desensitized to other people's pain. We are so "self" focussed.

Watch this video on seeing others through the eyes of Christ.

"What If we saw others through God's eyes" (4:25mins):
https://www.youtube.com/watch?v=1AbT1lT7Bu8

We need to pray that God would continue to give us HIS eyes to see. Then compassion and kindness would be second nature to us.

Jesus showed this compassion to the woman at the well in the book of John. The woman came to draw water at the hottest part of the day, which was strange, as people would usually wait until the morning or evening to draw water when it was cooler. People shunned her because of her immoral lifestyle, but Jesus knowing her history, accepted her and ministered to her.

As she drew water, Jesus asked her for a drink. In this exchange, Jesus broke three Jewish customs.

First, he talked to a woman.

Second, she was a Samaritan woman, a group that the Jews despised, "'You are a Jew, and I am a Samaritan woman. How can you ask me for a drink?'" (John 4:9)

Lastly, drinking from her cup or jar would have made him unclean. Needless to say, the woman was a little shocked when Jesus asked for a drink. Eventually, Jesus started talking to her and although they had never met before, he knew her history and offered her 'living water'.

"'If you knew the gift of God and who it is that asks you for a drink, you would have asked him and he would have given you living water.'" (John 4:10)

She had to look past her hurt and relationships and see the gift of eternal life Jesus was offering.

Jesus always had such a sweet way with words! He said to her, "'Everyone who drinks this water will be thirsty again, but whoever drinks the water I give him will never thirst. Indeed, the water I give him will become in him a spring of water welling up to eternal life.'" (John 4:13)

Jesus was able to offer this woman the gift of eternal life, as well as receiving an invitation to stay in her village and speak to the people about the kingdom of God! He was granted favour because of his humility, and the fact that he saw relationships with people as more important than "spiritual" rules, customs, or laws of the day.

Pastor Steven Furtick has his take on this story of the woman at the well from John 4.

"The Thirst Trap | Pastor Steven Furtick" (57:45mins):
https://www.youtube.com/watch?v=4JCcFD7GkBU

With Jesus, relationships were vital. He always put relationship above everything else.

Another amazing example of Jesus seeing relationships as more vital than "law" is when he came to the aid of a woman caught in adultery in the book of John, chapter 8. The teachers of the law and the Pharisees brought her before Jesus.

"'Teacher, this woman was caught in the act of adultery. In the Law Moses commanded us to stone such women. Now what do you say?'" (John 8:4-5)

What Jesus said was simple, yet profound, "'If anyone of you is without sin, let him be the first to throw a stone at her.'" (John 8:7b)

Jesus was saying, yes, this woman had sinned, but who is perfect? All the people holding stones to throw at her were sinners therefore, who were they to judge?

Paul said it like this: "For all have sinned and fall short of the glory of God, and are justified freely by his grace through the redemption that came by Christ Jesus." (Romans 3:23-24)

God is a God of mercy. Mercy is 'compassion or forgiveness shown toward someone whom it is within one's power to punish or harm'. That's why we call him "Kyrie Eleison", which translates from the Greek, "Lord, have mercy."

The song "Kyrie Eleison" by Mr. Mister reminds us of HIS mercy while on our journey!

"Mr Mister - Kyrie Eleison" (4:19 mins):
https://www.youtube.com/watch?v=belrNpqqA2g

It is only because of God's mercy and grace that we are free from sin! Judging other's sin is just futile, as we are all sinners. Our job is not to judge other's wrongdoings, but instead, to love them by seeing them with the eyes of Christ, establishing relationship with them and encouraging them to the next level. It is ludicrous to think we can play judge and jury when it comes to the sins of others, especially after seeing what God's word has to say about it!

Nicole Johnson's depiction of judging others is so very powerful:

"Dropping Your Rock (Preview) by Nicole Johnson" (4:17 mins):
https://www.youtube.com/watch?v=X3NALPQwc_A

In the book of Matthew, Jesus drives this point home when he says,

> "'Do not judge, or you too will be judged. For in the same way you judge others, you will be judged, and with the measure you use, it will be measured to you.....why do you look at the speck of sawdust in your brother's eye and pay no attention to the plank in your own eye? How can you say to your brother, 'Let me take the speck out of your eye, when all the time there is a plank in your own eye?'" (Matthew 7:1-4)

I remember Pastor Greg Fraser making his point in a sermon when he held a long 2X4 in front of his eye pretending the "plank" was in his eye, all the while, trying to remove the speck in his brother's eye, and almost killing him in the process! As he turned and tried to "help" his brother, the piece of wood swung wildly about, his brother ducking and literally missed being hit by this plank by just inches every time this person tried to help!

It was quite amusing, but in the same way, it got the point across of how ridiculous we are when we are judging others.

It was his very blunt way of saying what Mother Teresa so beautifully put in these same words, "If we judge people, we have no time to love them."[1]

How true! The plank gets in the way when we are trying to love others! Give us your eyes Lord, free of judgement and of "planks"!

When we are distracted with judgement, forgiveness takes a backseat. When we've been hurt, we want to point fingers and judge, instead of forgiving, letting it go, and letting God do the rest. Max Lucado, pastor and author, sums up this idea of forgiveness so eloquently[2]:

> "The key to forgiving others is to stop focusing on what they did TO you, and start focusing on what God did FOR you."

Jesus, help us to keep our eyes on you and not on ourselves and our situation. I hear you calling us deeper; to less judgement, and more of your love, which leads to forgiveness. Thank you for who you are. With your strength, grace, and mercy, forgiveness can be an integral part of our relationships.

Forgiveness- Jesus is Calling

Forgiveness was bought with your precious blood.
So why is your sacrifice just not enough?

When I'm bitter and hurt and screaming inside,
Or when I'm upset and I'm sad, and can't lay down my pride.

When someone else's choices inflict so much pain,
When I feel like I'm getting walked on again and again.

"Forgive them once more? It's not fair! It's a chore!"
But I forget on that cross it was my sin that you bore.

You draw me towards you, saying, "My daughter, keep your eyes on the prize.
Come and sit solemnly at the foot of the cross, and look into my weary eyes."

In your eyes I see the betrayal and hurt that you endured for me,
You were scourged, rejected and tortured, as you hung upon a tree.

You were beaten and whipped beyond recognition, and thorns had pierced your brow.
You were spat on, disgraced, and hated, for my freedom here and now.

So when I feel self-righteous and justified to stay in my filth and my sin,
Lord Jesus help me willingly to be honest and look deep within.

God you search me and you know me, indeed you have set me apart.
Your eyes don't see my evil flesh, instead, they see into my heart.

When my ego wants to rise up and I am at a loss,
Help me to remember the holes in your flesh, as you died on that cursed cross.

Help me see the face of your mother, trembling as she watched your cruel fate.
Her heart shattered into a million pieces, as she tried to shield you from their scorn and their hate.

And in the midst of your crucifixion, with pain gripping you like a vice,
You took your eyes off yourself and comforted a criminal saying: "Today, you'll be with me in paradise."

May I remember all you went through, as you journeyed on that path.
Knowing you would die so we could live, taking on the world's sin and their wrath.

To forgive is to honour your sacrifice, and say thank-you for shedding your blood.
For when we let our flesh selfishly rise up, we're saying "Your sacrifice wasn't enough."

So help me Lord Jesus daily, to be a reflection of you.
Help me to be "different", and shine for your kingdom, in all I say and do.

Watch this clip on forgiveness. Truly heart-wrenching when someone has unimaginably hurt you, but with Christ, forgiveness IS possible!

"Corrie Ten Boom: a message on forgivness" (4:21 mins):
https://www.youtube.com/watch?v=hH9nwFb87u4

Finally, listen to this song about brokenness and the scars of our past. It will get your eyes off of your pain and onto God, right where they should be!

"I Am They - Scars (Lyrics) ♪" (3:51 mins):
https://www.youtube.com/watch?v=It1XzDf-pFo

Victorious Verse

"Love your neighbour as yourself." Mark 12:31a

Mighty Melody

"Give Me Your Eyes" by <u>Brandon Heath</u> and "What Mercy Did For Me" by <u>Crystal Yates, Micah Tyler, and Joshua Sherman</u>

Armour in Action

It is human to want to judge others. We've all done it.

Ask God to forgive your judgemental attitude at times, and to give you the eyes of Christ so that you can see others as Christ sees them.

The next time you feel like you are quick to judge, remind yourself to remove the plank from your own eye first.

Remember that we have all sinned and fall short of God's glory.

Lastly, remember the wise words from Mother Teresa, "If you judge people, you have no time to love them."

Notes:

_____
_____
_____
_____
_____
_____
_____
_____
_____
_____
_____
_____
_____
_____
_____
_____
_____
_____
_____
_____
_____
_____
_____
_____
_____

Day *19* RADIATE Christ

TRUST YOUR FATHER WITH ALL THINGS

"Trust in the Lord with all your heart and lean not on your own understanding."

Proverbs 3:5

Notice the above Proverb says to trust God with ALL your heart - not some or part of it, but all! God knows that if he has all of your heart, he can use you more effectively for your calling.

Proverbs 4 also talks about how precious our heart is. "'Lay hold of my words with ALL your heart; keep my commands and you will live....hold onto instruction, do not let it go; guard it well, for it is your life." (Proverbs 4:4,13)

God is driving home the fact that his commands and instruction will lead us to life- abundant life! When we start to try to do things on our own and "follow" our heart instead of "guarding" it and trusting what he has for us, we become disconnected from him.

We touched on Proverbs 4 on Day 4 when I referred to this concept of guarding your heart. Your heart is part of your flesh, which is easily swayed; therefore it can lead you astray. If you ask God to guard it and protect it, he is faithful to help you. When I was single and praying for the man God had for me, I had a saying on my bathroom mirror by Max Lucado, Christian author, which I read many times in a day.

"A woman's heart should be so hidden in God that a man needs to seek Him just to find her!"[1]

These were powerful words for me. God was asking me to trust him, and he would provide all my needs, especially when it came to my desire for a husband.

Jesus reminds us in the following verse that it is not our job to worry and fret about the future. All we have to do is keep our eyes fixed on him, his kingdom, what he called us to do, and our needs will be met according to his purposes for our lives.

"'Therefore I tell you, do not worry about your life, what you will eat or drink; or about your body, what you will wear. Is not life more than food, and the body more than clothes? Look at the birds of the air; they do not sow or reap or store away in barns, and yet your heavenly Father feeds them. Are you not much more valuable than they? Who of you by worrying can add a single hour to his life?

And why do you worry about clothes? See how the lilies of the field grow. They do not labour or spin. Yet I tell you that not even Solomon in all his splendour was dressed like one of these. If that is how God clothes the grass of the field, which is here today and tomorrow is thrown into the fire, will he not much more clothe you, O you of little faith? So do not worry, saying, 'What shall we eat?' or 'What shall we drink?' or 'What shall we wear?' For the pagans run after all these things, and your heavenly Father knows that you need them. But seek first his kingdom and his righteousness, and all these things will be given to you as well. Therefore, do not worry about tomorrow, for tomorrow will worry about itself. Each day has enough trouble of its own." (Matthew 6:25-34)

This is much easier said, than done. Just giving all your hopes, fears, desires, and worries over to God- it sounds easy but giving up control of your life is a very uncertain thing. It is a human desire to want to control your situation and everything in it. Surrender your will, have faith and trust in God that his plan is much better than what you could ever have planned for yourself!

You become more like Christ when you surrender your will and give your life over to him. Jesus was constantly surrendering his will to his Father in heaven; including his fate on the cross.

He prayed on the Mount of Olives as he contemplated his death, "'Father, if you are willing, take this cup from me; yet not my will, but yours be done.'" (Luke 22:42)

Then, while being arrested, Simon Peter struck the high priest's servant cutting off his right ear.

Jesus was surrendering once again to his Father as he commanded Peter, "'Put your sword away! Shall I not drink the cup the Father has given me?'" (John 18:11)

Finally, when his work on earth was done, as he hung on the wooden cross, he said, "'It is finished.' With that he bowed his head and gave up his spirit." (John 19:30)

He allowed his Father's will to be done over everything else. What a supreme example of laying down one's life and will for the greater good. It is because of his genuine love for us that we can fully trust him. Unfortunately just because we CAN trust him, doesn't mean we always DO.

You may find walking with Christ and trusting him difficult at times. You might find yourself consistently pushing him off the throne of your life. You take control of the "small stuff", instead of trusting that God sees the big picture, and knows what is best for you.

For example, in my journey to find my husband, I was blessed to see God's hand at work in my life as I continually surrendered. He not only was preparing my husband, but he was preparing my heart as well!

Instead of simply focussing on the worldly, superficial aspects of love and marriage, I was more concerned with the preparation of my inner being and letting the Holy Spirit guide me in my decisions. I began to understand that it was a lot easier on my heart to let God guide my steps than to be caught up in the "fairy tale" world of my prince charming sweeping me off my feet and living a perfect life.

As little girls, we long to be the princess in a story where our knight in shining armour comes in to rescue, love and protect us, as we live "happily ever after." That's why little girls play dress up and love weddings and romance. It is hard-wired into us. However as we mature, God begins to show us that in order to make wise decisions, we must allow his love to nurture our hearts so that his will can be done in our lives.

Here is a quote by an unknown author[2] that really speaks to this concept of making wise decisions regarding a potential mate:

> "Teach your daughter's the difference between:
> A man who flatters her, and a man who compliments her
> A man who spends money on her, and a man who invests in her.
> A man who views her as property, and a man who views her properly.
> A man who lusts after her, and a man who loves her.
> A man who believes he's a gift to women, and a man who believes she's a gift to him.
> Then, teach your sons to BE that man!"

What a revelation! So much wisdom here regarding the man God is preparing for us!

Again, when praying about our potential mates, just as we put our own names in 1st Corinthians 13 in Day 12, if you are contemplating dating a person, place his name in where the word "love" appears.

For example, let's use the name 'Michael'.

"Michael is patient, Michael is kind. Michael does not envy, Michael does not boast. Michael is not proud. Michael is not rude, Michael is not self-seeking, Michael is not easily angered, and Michael keeps no record of wrongs. Michael does not delight in evil, but rejoices with the truth. Michael always protects, always trusts, always perseveres. Michael never fails."

When you do this exercise, remember no person is going to be perfect, just like you aren't perfect. Just ask God to guard your heart, and allow him to give you peace regarding the relationship. If God guards your heart, no person with ill-will towards you can get close enough to cause damage because his spirit will help you to discern their intentions.

One of the ways God showed me to guard my heart was to dress in a way that glorified him. For me, modesty had always been taught growing up, but for a few years, after feeling rejected and unloved, I began to gain attention from men in the wrong ways. Being modest was always important, but I lost sight of it for a while because of my hurting heart.

Recently, I watched a group of young men do a song on YouTube titled "Virtue Makes You Beautiful". It really hit home the idea of what a man of integrity wants in a woman. Watch the video and see what you think.

"Virtue Makes You Beautiful" (3:22mins):
https://www.youtube.com/watch?v=oartlE7rKuM

This song is full of truth. It tells women that their beauty is found in their integrity, their speech, their respect for themselves, and in their virtue. Virtue is defined as "showing high moral standards" and some of the synonyms that pertain to virtue are purity, dignity, worthiness, respectability, goodness, righteousness, integrity, morality, decency, nobility, and honour.

I would most certainly want to be known as a woman of virtue! However, for that process to take place, God had to lead me through a lengthy process of changing my heart and learning to guard it along the way.

He really put Proverbs 31 verses 10-31 on my heart and as stated earlier, I decided to memorize the passage to prepare my heart for my husband to be. Trusting God with this aspect of my life gave me freedom from worry and doubt. I was even able to quote these verses by memory to my husband on our wedding day in front of our family and friends. What a testimony to God's faithfulness! Here I was saying my vows to my husband to love and honour him all the days of my life, and I was able to share scripture that involved the foundation God laid in me as he was preparing my heart for marriage. Not only was it humbling, but a great honour and privilege to see the fruit of God's work in me as it culminated with our wedding day!

Be known as a woman of virtue! God will do his work in you too, if you allow him. However, you must continually trust and surrender your will to him. As I said, it won't always be easy...in fact, it will probably be downright difficult to trust him fully at times, but the rewards in your life will surpass anything you could ever hope for or imagine!

1st Corinthians says it brilliantly when Paul writes, "...stand firm...let nothing move you. Always give yourselves fully to the work of the Lord, because you know that your labour in the Lord is not in vain." (1st Corinthians 15:58b)

In other words, when you stand firm and submit to his plans instead of your own, you will get eternal, not temporal, results. Then your success in God's kingdom will far outweigh anything you could have done on your own strength.

Victorious Verse

"He who trusts in the Lord will prosper." Proverbs 28:25b

"A wife of noble character who can find? She is worth far more than rubies." Proverbs 31:10

Mighty Melody

"Trust and Obey" by Big Daddy Weave, "Just to Be With You" by Third Day, and "While I'm Waiting" by John Waller

Armour in Action

Read Proverbs 31:10-31. Memorize a portion of this scripture or all of it, depending on what God puts on your heart. Make it a song to your heavenly Father about trusting him with all things, including your future husband. Ask him to help you submit to his plan for your life, just as Christ did. In the process, he will teach you to guard your heart.

Listen to the "remix" Proverbs 31 woman and pray that he will continue to mold you and shape you into the woman he created you to be, while guarding your heart in the process:

"Proverbs 31 Virtuous Woman (Remix) Ft. Mike B - Christian Music Videos" (5:25 mins): https://www.godtube.com/watch/?v=09MEFMNU

Notes:

_____

_____

_____

_____

_____

_____

_____

_____

_____

_____

_____

_____

_____

_____

_____

_____

_____

_____

_____

_____

_____

_____

_____

_____

Day *20* RADIATE Christ

WAY BEYOND ME

"Greater is he who is in you than he who is in the world."

1st John 4:4 (NASB)

As discussed in Day 19, submitting to God's plan is more rewarding than trying to follow your own agenda. We know that if we claim not to need God in our everyday life, we aren't aspiring to his call for us. We need him and his strength daily to carry out the calling he has on our life.

You may be caught up in the world around you or in your own "pity party" to see what is right in front of you. You are so enamoured with your short-sighted problems or hurts that you fail to see God's big picture. We don't see how God can use our hurts for his glory. Michael Jr. has his take on this.

"Michael Jr - How God Uses Our Hurts and Failures" (30:22mins):
https://www.youtube.com/watch?v=wqbLOIzEZs4

When you are so focussed on the hurt and the bad, you can't see the healing and the good. It`s like having a black sheet of paper in front of our eyes trying to look through a pinhole, rather than putting the sheet down and looking through the picture window God has placed before us. It makes more sense to try and see things through God`s eyes!

One example of a person focused on a dark pinhole is when they are caught up in depression. They lose sight of what is important, and they begin to become discouraged and lose hope. They take their eyes off God and put them onto their situation and themselves and feel lost and alone.

As mentioned before, but bears repeating - I found myself in this situation a few years ago and I felt as though darkness and confusion was all around me. I remember sitting on my bed and crying out to God as I contemplated my life and why I had to walk through such a difficult time. I was so scared and unsure of what the future would bring. God met me right there in that room and spoke to me from a devotional book I had. I actually heard an audible voice tell me to open the book that lay beside me, so I did and read the day`s devotion.

It started off with a verse that brought comfort to my heart, "Cast all your cares on him, because he cares for you." (1st Peter 5:7)

Feeling as though my whole world was falling apart, and seeing death as my only way out, the following devotion caused me to see that God did care and I needed to trust him with the gift of my life. It went something like this[1]:

> My daughter went through a period last fall when she was fearful about dying. I remember having similar fears when I was her age and I didn't know how to handle them. 'The only thing I can tell you,' I said, 'is to pray. Tell God about your fears.'
>
> One of the hardest lessons to learn as we grow up is that we are ultimately not in control. We may do many things to think we are in control; we may even manipulate our lives so that we are as much in control as possible. Nevertheless, we really don't have a whole lot of power.
>
> Therefore, we must learn to turn our worries, fears, and all that we try to control over to God. Moreover, we must learn to trust God's providence.

I felt warmth all over my body that I couldn't explain. All I could do was cry uncontrollably, as I realized that this physical warmth that had wrapped around me, and had comforted me in one of my darkest hours, was the Holy Spirit. God's mercy and love had come into my bedroom that night and saved me from myself. He held and rocked me gently as I cried tears of deep sorrow and grief.

There I was; a sad, depressed young woman, who could not see my own hand in front of me because of the darkness that surrounded me. But my mighty, powerful God shone his light into my room that night and showed me I was his beloved daughter and that he wasn't finished with me yet! His plans for me were far greater than I could ever hope for or imagine. I was going to make a difference in the world, I just needed to take his hand and trust him!

These two songs by Zach Williams really have spoken to me as I look back on my story. God never gave up on me. Thank you Jesus!

"Zach Williams - Rescue Story - Red Rocks Amphitheatre Official Video" (4:07 mins): https://www.youtube.com/watch?v=Q3aP5iuJITg

"Zach Williams - Survivor (Live from Harding Prison) (Live)" (4:11 mins): https://www.youtube.com/watch?v=GtX2dat1UVQ

Like me, there was another young woman who walked this same journey of depression. She, too, realized God's hand was on her life. Florence Nightingale was a blessing to so many injured and wounded soldiers during the Crimean War (October 1853- February 1856). Even though she helped so many, it is interesting to know that she, herself, struggled.

It was written about Florence by <u>Spartacus Educational</u>[2] that she was, "unhappy; suffered from bouts of depression and feelings of unworthiness. She wondered what her purpose was. Unlike her mother and sister, who were content to do good works on the estates in the upper class, she pondered on the need for charity and the causes of poverty and unemployment."

Going deeper into Florence's thoughts, her diary revealed a woman who had very real struggles.

"In May 1850, Florence, having read some of the very sombre poems by William Cowper, wrote in her diary that she could identify with his 'deep despondency'. And on Christmas Eve, she wrote, 'In my thirty first year, I can see nothing desirable but death...I cannot understand it. I am ashamed to understand it.'

She also wrote, 'my present life is suicide' and 'oh weary days- oh evenings that seem never to end- for how many years I have watched that drawing room clock...it is not the misery, the unhappiness that I feel is so insupportable, but I feel this habit, this disease gaining ground upon me and no hope, no help. This is the sting of death. Why do I wish to leave this world? God knows I do not suspect a heaven beyond, but that He will set me down in St. Giles, at a Kaiserswerth, there to find my work.'

Like Florence, if your depression is so bad that your life seems totally meaningless, try to make your life meaningful to a few other people. By doing this, you will make it more meaningful to yourself again, too. This is what Florence Nightingale did (on a much larger scale), and for her, it worked.

In other words, to find your way out of depression and darkness, look for a way to serve others! This woman, who was known for having founded modern nursing and improving care to wounded soldiers during the Crimean War, turned her deep-rooted feelings of depression into a positive self-sacrificing life. She was known as the 'lady with the lamp' for tending the sick throughout the night in the military hospitals.

In a keynote address by Lynn McDonald, (2005),[3] she outlined Florence's deep desire to make a difference in the world around her. Lynn stated,

> "Florence believed that God wants us to act, to reflect God's glory to the world by making it better, with practical achievements. Healing the sick was doing this, showing God's goodness by doing His work in the world.....throughout her life Nightingale liked people who did things, who saw a need, heard a call, and went out and acted. She greatly appreciated missionaries—David Livingstone was her hero. Her fondness for John Wesley similarly was for his willingness to go and do."

Lynn McDonald went on to say that,

> "Nightingale wrote a letter to her father that summarized the Prophet Samuel's call to dedicate his life to God and serve only him. Very much like Samuel, is how Nightingale saw her own calling:
>
> 'It strikes me that all truth lies between these two: man saying to God, as Samuel did, Lord, here am I, and God saying to man as Christ did, in the storm, Lo it is I, be not afraid. And neither is complete, without the other. God says to man in suffering, in misery, in degradation, in anxiety, in imbecility, in loss of the bitterest kind, most of all in sin, Lo, it is I, be not afraid. This is the eternal passion of God. And man must say to him, Lord here am I to work at all these things.'
>
> Nightingale in fact had kept saying, 'Here am I, send me,' to God for years after her 'call to service.'"

I heard a wise person once say, "Timing is up to God, obedience is up to you."

If you are willing to be used as an instrument, as Florence Nightingale was, God can do things in your life that go way beyond what you could ever dream.

Paul wrote in Ephesians, "Now to him who is able to do immeasurably more than all we ask or imagine, according to HIS power that is at work within us, to him be glory.....throughout all generations, forever and ever! Amen!" (Ephesians 3:20-21)

Therefore, not only is his power working in us to fulfill our calling, but also he gets all the glory for our actions. What an awesome God we serve! His own son Jesus had the greatest calling on his life and his father was working through him in order for it to come to fruition. Just like Christ, God is working in and through us, and he is MORE than faithful to complete the work he has started!

Lastly, watch this clip to remind you of God's power in and through you. Keep going, warrior princess....keep walking in and towards your purpose!

"WOMAN OF GOD! - Listen To This Everyday To Change Your Life" (12:48 mins): https://www.youtube.com/watch?v=tVWim82tVT0

Victorious Verse
"He who began a good work in you will carry it on to completion until the day of Christ Jesus."
Philippians 1:6

Mighty Melody
"Beyond Me" by Toby Mac and "Made to Live" by Hawk Nelson

Armour in Action
Do you have a calling on your life that seems much bigger than you could do by yourself? Do you have a dream? Write it down and keep praying about it. If God keeps putting it on your heart to do it, know that he will give you the tools to accomplish it, no matter how big or crazy it may seem! Trust him; he knows what he is doing!

Notes:

Day *21* RADIATE Christ

THE CHARACTER OF CHRIST

"Let us run with perseverance the race marked out for us."

Hebrews 12:1b

John Stephen Akhwari from Tanzania, injured and struggling to cross the finish line, was coming into the stadium over an hour after the first runner had finished the race. It was the 1968 Summer Olympics marathon, and he was slowly but steadily making his way along the track. With the finish line now in his sights, he limped onward. After he had officially crossed the finish line, he told reporters that his country sent him 5000 miles to finish the race, not to simply start it, so he never gave up.....he didn't quit! What a supernatural illustration of strength and dignity! Here is the video link:

"Olympics Inspiration: Finish the Race, Not Just Start It!" (2:41mins):
https://www.youtube.com/watch?v=k6oW9uYtJnA

Another athlete who had an amazing story of overcoming is Louie Zamperini who was a USA Olympian. He not only survived in a raft in the middle of the ocean for 47 days after his bomber crashed into the water in World War II, but he survived living in a series of Japanese prisoner of war camps. While there, he was beaten and abused beyond what most prisoners could handle, yet his spirit remained strong.

After being liberated when the war was over, he went on to marry and have children, and eventually met with some of his wartime captors and forgave them for the horrific abuse he endured. There was a movie made about him in 2014 titled "Unbroken" and it's a heart-wrenching story of a man who just wouldn't give up in the face of adversity.

This story epitomises many character traits of Christ: strength, courage, integrity, commitment, determination, diligence, perseverance.....what a powerful story of the resilience of the human spirit! Truly unbelievable!

A more recent story of an athlete representing strength in adversity is a young woman who had an inoperable brain tumour. She played basketball for Mount St Joseph University in Cincinnati. She was instrumental in raising funds for cancer research and was known for her courageous outlook on life with her "never give up" attitude. Because of her diagnosis, she had very little time left on this earth. Nevertheless, known for making the most of every day, she encouraged others to do the same. She passed away April 10, 2015, at the tender age of 19, but her impact will leave a ripple effect for years to come.

Here are a couple of clips of this young woman, honoring her courage.

"Lauren Hill: 'I didn't know what God had sent me for' " (4:00 mins):
https://www.youtube.com/watch?v=f1muhCO2XEI

"Lauren Hill One More Game ESPN Video ESPN" (7:09 mins):
https://www.youtube.com/watch?v=etGiC7GQJRc

I'm sure we can all think of touching stories of people overcoming odds that are stacked against them, or having admirable strength when facing hardships, but none of them will ever come close to Jesus' story of overcoming death and satan after being tortured and crucified. He is the one person that we are created in the image of.

In the book of Corinthians, Paul says, "Now the Lord is the Spirit, and where the Spirit of the Lord is, there is freedom. And we, who with unveiled faces all reflect the Lord's glory, are being transformed into his likeness with ever-increasing glory, which comes from the Lord, who is the Spirit." (2nd Corinthians 3:17-18)

In order to go through this "transformation" and become more like him, you must spend time with him and develop a relationship. Who you hang out with, you will become.

Pastor Greg Fraser used to say, "Show me your friends, and I'll show you your future." How true! Your friends are a reflection of you! Therefore, if Jesus is your friend, you will reflect his traits and attributes.

When I was teaching in the private Christian school, our focus was on teaching the students about the character traits of Christ. More than anything else when raising a child, the most important thing to see is that their character is developing and they are transforming into the likeness of Christ. We used a curriculum by Accelerated Christian Education that listed the character traits of Christ. The list was a good reminder of all that he was and all that we can hope to be.

If you look at the character traits below and see ones that you struggle with, it will allow you to grow in those areas and become more like him. The ones that you do well can be used to reflect Christ to those around you.[1]

Appreciative, Attentive, Available, Committed, Compassionate, Concerned, Confident, Considerate, Consistent, Content, Cooperative, Courageous, Creative, Decisive, Deferent, Dependable, Determined, Diligent, Discerning, Discreet, Efficient, Equitable, Fair, Faithful, Fearless, Flexible, Forgiving, Friendly, Generous, Gentle, Honest, Humble, Joyful, Kind, Loyal, Meek, Merciful, Observant, Optimistic, Patient, Peaceful, Perseverant, Persuasive, Prudent, Punctual, Purposeful, Resourceful, Respectful, Responsible, Secure, Self-controlled, Sincere, Submissive, Tactful, Temperate, Thankful, Thorough, Thrifty, Tolerant, Truthful, Virtuous, Wise, and Zealous

Many times the Olympics illustrate inspiring human qualities. Here are a few examples of them:

"5 MOST INSPIRING OLYMPIC MOMENTS" (8:09mins):
https://www.youtube.com/watch?v=6AkjRbSj6W4

Many of us already embody many of these character traits, even though we find it difficult to display. We are meant to be a mirror to the world but we are a work in progress daily, aiming to become more and more like Christ. Having a solid character, as Jesus did, is something we all want to be remembered for.

While character can be comprised of both mental and moral qualities that make up a person, I found a definition that summarizes what I believe a Christian's character should be.

Character is "the stable and distinctive qualities built into an individual's life which determine his or her response regardless of circumstances."[2]

The 16th president of the United States, Abraham Lincoln, said,

> "Character is like a tree and reputation like its shadow. The shadow is what we think of it; the tree is the real thing. Our character is much more than just what we try to display for others to see, it is who we are even when no one is watching. Good character is doing the right thing because it is right to do what is right."[3]

Build your character on experiences, as you go through trials and pain in your life. Don't let a victim mentality cause you to waste your trials. During fiery trials, many times you may only see the ashes, but God helps us to see the beauty. Isaiah 61:3 states that he will "bestow on them a crown of beauty for ashes."

Remember, that out of your pain, your passion and purpose will be birthed! Therefore, there is hope in the midst of your trials!

TD Jakes reminds of this passion and pain correlation:

"Bishop T.D. Jakes on How to Give Birth to Your Dreams | SuperSoul Sunday | Oprah Winfrey Network" (4:54 mins):
https://www.youtube.com/watch?v=_uq0ybgoc0g

Paul reminds us of this, "....but we also rejoice in our sufferings, because we know that suffering produces perseverance; perseverance, character; and character, hope." (Romans 5:3-4)

You can look at your trials as producing growth and good things in you, or you could withdraw from God and immerse yourself in the things of the world to numb your pain. Falling in love with the things of the world and putting them above God is a dangerous situation to put yourself in. You need to remember that you may be in the world, but you don't have to love the things in it more than you love God.

John tells us, "Do not love the world or anything in the world ...the world and its desires will pass away, but the man who does the will of God lives forever." (1st John 2:15a, 17)

So what is this "will of God" that Paul speaks of? In part, it is to see you becoming more like his son Jesus. Do this by nurturing the "tree of character" that Abraham Lincoln spoke of.

The book of Isaiah speaks of this tree, but puts it in God's perspective. "They will be called oaks of righteousness, a planting of the Lord for the display of his splendour." (Isaiah 61:3)

In order for an acorn to grow into a mighty oak, it must get the nourishment, sunshine, and the proper amount of water. Once it begins to grow, it must rely on its roots. Without strong roots, the tree will not flourish. This is analogous to your life as a Christian.

In order for your "tree of character" to grow strong and healthy, you must have deep roots in Christ. Spend time with him and read his word. This is where you get nourishment. This is where you "connect" with your Saviour and begin to become more and more like him, causing you to bear fruit in your life. Without your connection to him, you will fail to make the impact on the world that he created you for.

Jesus put it very eloquently in the book of John when he said, "I am the vine, you are the branches. If a man remains in me and I in him, he will bear much fruit; apart from me you can do nothing." (John 15:5)

We are blessed to have the honour of becoming more like our role model, Jesus Christ! Thank-you God for sending your son to shape our lives around! When we go through the pressures and challenges of life, we become more and more like our Saviour- like a precious diamond being formed under the earth. What a tremendous privilege to walk through fire with him by our side.

As we are walking, we are being refined, and we become free from bondage! As the apostle John so eloquently said, "If the Son sets you free, you will be free indeed." (John 8:36)

Thank you Jesus for the blood that you shed for us, which in turn, has given us the ultimate gift of freedom; we will forever be thankful and humbled by your sacrifice.

Be encouraged as you listen to Zach William's story as he found freedom through Jesus Christ. Nothing is impossible with our mighty God!

"On the Road to Recovery with Zach Williams" (11:34 mins):
https://www.youtube.com/watch?v=-nTD5h-tFuI

His song "Chain Breaker" is one of the songs chosen for today's devotion. This specific version is so very powerful!

"Zach Williams - Chain Breaker (Live from Harding Prison)" (4:09 mins):
https://www.youtube.com/watch?v=6WtV1XtqsW0

Victorious Verse

"Where the spirit of the Lord is there is freedom. And we, who with unveiled faces all reflect the Lord's glory, are being transformed into his likeness with ever-increasing glory, which comes from the Lord, who is the Spirit." 2nd Corinthians 3:17-18

Mighty Melody

"Different" by Micah Tyler and "Chain Breaker" by Zach Williams

Armour in Action

Go back and look at the list of the character traits of Jesus. Write down 2 traits that you struggle with. Ask God to give you opportunities to practice these traits in the week ahead. Pray that he would guide you to take the steps you need to take to become like him in all ways. Ask for his wisdom in growing to be the woman he is calling you to be.

Notes:

_____
_____
_____
_____
_____
_____
_____
_____
_____
_____
_____
_____
_____
_____
_____
_____
_____
_____
_____
_____
_____
_____
_____
_____
_____

Introduction to Pillar 4

REFLECT INTENTIONALLY

When you reflect, you are thinking very deeply, giving careful consideration, or reviewing in your mind so that you can learn from your experiences and attain heights that you did not know were possible. Reflection allows you to look back in hindsight, and set new goals based on your experiences. This is essential if you want to grow physically, emotionally, and spiritually.

Growth comes with looking inside and allowing that introspective approach to lead you in a healthy relationship with God, yourself, and others. In order to understand *what* reflection truly is, we need to look at another definition of "reflect".

Another important definition of reflection is to cast back light off of a surface, and not absorb it. An object that reflects light on many different levels is a diamond. Christians are like diamonds in many different ways.

First, when diamonds are in their original form, they have very little value. Only after a skilled diamond cutter makes very precise cuts and it is polished to a brilliant lustre that it becomes beautiful and valued. Just like the diamond, a Christian is transformed by the power of God and you radiate his beauty!

Secondly, diamonds have to be subjected to tremendous pressures deep beneath the earth in order to become created. As a Christian, you will come up against trials and pressure which will help to produce character, and will allow you to become all God has created you to be!

Thirdly, a diamond doesn't possess its sparkle and shine until part of it is cut away. Isn't it interesting that value is added to a diamond when something is taken away? Likewise, as a Christian you have the blood of Christ that removes, or takes away, your sin. Then, you become righteous and you are strengthened because of his sacrifice. What an awesome gift he gave you by dying on the cross!

Finally, in order for a diamond to emit its brilliance, it must REFLECT the light glittering upon its surface. Just like the diamond, you can't reflect God's glory in the darkness. Instead, walk in his light and therefore shine for all to see!

As you submit yourself and your life daily over to God and allow him to keep chipping away all the unwanted things in your life, you become more of who he created you to be. You will begin see yourself becoming more brilliant and valuable just like a precious diamond!

You can only become a brilliant diamond when you take the time to pause and reflect on what God is doing in and through you. Reflection inwardly results in reflecting HIS glory outwardly to the world. Shine from the inside out for all to see!

Listen to the song "Diamonds" by Hawk Nelson (3:02mins) and be encouraged! If you are willing, God will refine you and cause you to reflect Christ to the world!
https://www.youtube.com/watch?v=Yf1ARbpBOgA

Day 22 REFLECT Intentionally

GET OUT OF YOUR TENT SO YOU CAN SEE THE STARS

"Then I heard the voice of the Lord saying, 'Whom shall I send? And who will go for us?' And I said, 'Here am I. Send me!'"

Isaiah 6:8

Sometimes we are so caught up in our lives and situations that we forget to look up and see all that God has done, and is going to do, for us.

God reminded Abraham of all his promises when he took him out of his "tent" and said, "'Look up at the heavens and count the stars- if indeed you can count them....so shall your offspring be.'" (Genesis 15:5)

Abraham focused on the fact that he and Sarah were childless; he couldn't see the power and faithfulness of a mighty God. God knew what he had promised Abraham; he just wanted him to fully trust him and have faith. Just like Abraham, you may not see the magnificent things that God is doing in your life because you tend to focus on the little things.

I remember once contemplating life while rollerblading. I was watching the sidewalk for cracks and potholes so I wouldn't trip and fall. A still small voice inside prompted me to look up. It was in that very moment a blue heron on the lake beside me spread his wings and took off. He had about a 6-foot wingspan, and it was a sight of beauty as it gracefully glided silently through the night air. I would have missed it if I had been looking down. It was in that moment God said to me, "Look up, focus on me, and I will richly reward you with blessings beyond what you could hope for or imagine!"

It was during this time in my life, that I was having trouble trusting God. Would he give me my dreams and desires? I wanted a family, but I was a single career woman. In addition, I had to trust God to set a very special person in my life free from addiction.

Along with my longings and desires for a husband and family, I longed for women who were Christians, to "speak life" into me. There is something about women building each other up. When we are encouraging each other, it helps us to sense our worth and know we are loved and accepted on our journey towards Christ.

God knew the desires of my heart. He just wanted me to seek him first before he would begin to bless me with the longings of my heart. His word confirmed this when I read, "Delight yourself in the Lord and he will give you the desires of your heart." (Psalm 37:4)

In the years that followed, I dedicated my life back to God. I was baptized, sold my house, quit my job, and moved in with my parents and went to Discipleship school.

As a culmination to our year in Discipleship school, we went on a mission trip to Mexico that changed my life forever. I was seeking God on a new level in my life. He became someone I spent time with not because I HAD to, but because I WANTED to. I began to memorize scripture and get it in my heart. God softened my spirit and he allowed my desires and longings to happen. He provided good Christian women in my life, and we encouraged each other. He began to set my friend free from addiction as he began to seek Christ. He granted me an amazing husband, and now I am blessed with a beautiful daughter and son. I could see his hand in so many aspects of my life; I couldn't deny his power and saw firsthand that he is a God that keeps his promises.

During this time, I also attended a retreat where many fellow Christians loved me unconditionally. It was then that I began to take my eyes off myself and put them on the big picture that God was painting right before my very eyes. I found myself able to reflect on my situation instead of distracting myself with work.

When we all allow ourselves to take the time to stop and reflect we can renew our spirit and begin to have a different, more positive perspective on what is happening in our lives.

At this retreat, a chapel segment was part of our day. While there, having one-on-one time with God, worship songs were playing softly in the background. "Here I am Lord" began to play and tears began to trickle down my face.

Basically, the song was telling God that I was there to do his will. He was asking who to send, and it was clear that it was me.

Listen to the song and hear how God loves when we are willing and open to hear his voice.

"Here I am Lord" (4:10mins):
https://www.youtube.com/watch?v=otaSC_NHICw&list=PLpCgdd_367jok8YecTcy8U4JUmXuELwUz

As these words washed over me, I walked to the altar and knelt there before the Lord. I lifted my hands and asked him to send me where he wanted me to go. I realized in that moment my life was not my own, and that ultimately God was in control. I had purpose IN and THROUGH him!

Remind yourself of God's purposes and plans for your life.

"What is Your Purpose? Christian Motivational Video" (7:35mins):
https://www.youtube.com/watch?v=ce4I5h0grXI

This is a revelation to realize that "your" purpose isn't about "you"! When you surrender and give God access to all areas of your life, you can truly live for HIM!

For over 30 years of my life, I had tried to do things my way and just fit God into the empty spaces, but now, he was beginning to become the hub of the wheel, and everything in my life began to flow from him. This is the way it should be; God is the center and because of his hand in all things, my life speaks of his mercy and grace instead of my life speaking of all my successes and accomplishments. At the end of our lives, none of the awards and recognition will matter. What will live on are the eternal bonds we have made while on the earth....the people we have touched...our relationship with our Saviour...these are the things that will last beyond the grave!

Moreover, to think I would not have stumbled upon this revelation if had I not stopped to reflect and take time to make God's priorities my own!

Therefore, reflection and prayer are key components for your spiritual growth. If you allow yourself to be constantly inundated with what is happening around you, you fail to have those moments of true connection with your creator, thus constantly repeating the same things and expecting different results.

When you know better, you do better, which is what you will find out when you pause and reflect on who you are and how you got there.

The bible tells us many times to "be still", or "wait patiently on God".

Psalm 46:10a "Be still and know that I am God."

Psalm 37:7a "Be still before the Lord and wait patiently for him."

Psalm 27:14 "Wait for the Lord; be strong and take heart and wait for the Lord."

The prophet Zechariah (2:13a) also confirms this when he says, "Be still before the Lord, all mankind."

The act of "being still" is overlooked in today's culture. Everything is moving so fast. Ask God to help you pause, reflect and be still. He loves to see his children rest and be restored, as this is when we can hear his voice very clearly and concisely. And when we are listening to his voice, there is no limit to what he will do in and through us!

Listening to God and hearing his voice will lead to breakthrough and action. How is God preparing YOU today for a breakthrough?

"3 Signs God Is Preparing You for a Major Breakthrough" (6:58 mins):
https://www.youtube.com/watch?v=TXa9LWqAAoM

Victorious Verse

'Again Jesus said, "Peace be with you! As the Father has sent me, I am sending you."' John 20:21

Mighty Melody

"Here I Am" by <u>Downhere</u> and "I Surrender" by <u>Hillsong Live</u>

Armour in Action

Pray to God and tell him you are available and ready to be used as his instrument. Tell him you are willing to be sent wherever he needs you. As long as we are willing, he will use us. Thank him for the opportunities he has given you in the past, and for the ones still to come. Write down a time recently when you felt as though God used you for his purposes. Be encouraged by his plans for your life!

Notes:

_____
_____
_____
_____
_____
_____
_____
_____
_____
_____
_____
_____
_____
_____
_____
_____
_____
_____
_____
_____
_____
_____
_____
_____
_____
_____
_____
_____

Day *23* REFLECT Intentionally

COME AS YOU ARE-
THANKFULNESS IS THE KEY

"Come to me all you who are weary and burdened, and I will give you rest."
Matthew 11:28

We all can think of ways in which we are imperfect and list our shortcomings very easily, whereas it may take some time to think about our strengths and the gifts God has placed in each one of us.

Our world has convinced us that we will never be enough. We always need to strive to be someone or something we are not, because being ourselves is just mediocre or average, which will not suffice.

Please stop that mentality right now - end it. God tells you to come to him just as you are and he will not only accept you, but he will celebrate all that he has created you to be! Isn't that amazing? It almost sounds too easy!

There is a young man by the name of Jonathan Pitre that is a beautiful example of living his life just as he is. He has a disease called Epidermolysis Bullosa (EB). This disease requires constant dressing changes, and wrapping like a mummy, so his skin lesions are not exposed to friction and create blisters. Eating is difficult, as food going down his throat causes blisters as well. Children who have this disease are called "butterfly children" because their skin is as fragile as a butterfly's wings.

He presented the realities of his daily life to the world so he could help, fundraise, and encourage others. He truly lives with a burden that never goes away. It is constant and painful, and he faces it head on.

Jonathan sees himself as a warrior and an ambassador for others with the disease and his goal is to raise funds to help fight the disease. In order to do that, he did a documentary to show the world how he fights pain and suffering daily and to raise awareness. Watch his story and be humbled.

"TSN Original: The Butterfly Child" (12:43mins):
https://www.youtube.com/watch?v=iuYxGtuBSgk

What a perfect example to "come as we are" and be ambassadors. Just as Jonathan was an ambassador for his disease, we too, can be ambassadors for Christ. Paul confirms this in 2ⁿᵈ Corinthians 5:20a "We are therefore Christ's ambassadors." Our stories and testimonies can allow others to step forward and be light as well.

Here is a moving clip on being ambassadors for Christ. Just like Jonathan, he has work for you to do!

"God is Preparing You to Work for Him! // Ambassadors of Christ" (29:49 mins):
https://www.youtube.com/watch?v=nOaS_JFCqAE

Another example of a person presenting herself just as she is; Shawn Johnson was an Olympic gold medalist at the age of 16. Listen to her story:

"Shawn Johnson - Second Edition" (4:46mins):
https://www.youtube.com/watch?v=7lyr5PYt2II

When she was real about her predicament and what they had gone through, she was able to reach many people. Here is a news story that came about that touched thousands of hearts.

"Olympic gold medalist Shawn Johnson opens up about her miscarriage" (5:56mins):
https://www.youtube.com/watch?v=NxdMU7HlnP4

Like Shawn, I believe we all come to different sets of crossroads in our lives and we literally have to choose which way we will go. Will you follow God's path, or will you continue on the road of "self".

The road of "self" is what many of us choose because at the time it may seem easier or more fun. In reality, it is not, because we are constantly at war in our spirit. We have no peace.

More often than not, following Christ will be difficult and you will have to go against the ways of the world. Although it may not be easy, you have the peace of Christ which will pull you through. Nothing can be a substitute for having that peace. When you have it, you can move mountains. With God's peace, you can do anything; Luke 1:37 reinforces this concept: "For nothing is impossible with God."

The bible tells us, "Do not worry or be anxious about anything, but in everything, by prayer and petition, with thanksgiving, present your requests to God. And the PEACE OF GOD which transcends all understanding will guard your hearts and minds in Christ Jesus." (Philippians 4:6-7)

What a promise! In other words, when you worry about something or are anxious, focusing on your blessings, and being thankful is the key to entering into God's peace! Moreover, that peace is beyond what you could ever comprehend. It will actually blow your mind to realize the depths of his peace! What a huge revelation! However, in order to acquire this peace, you need to stop, reflect on your situation, surrender your worries and anxieties, turn them into thankful petitions to Christ, and in exchange, he grants you his unimaginable peace. Therefore, instead of being a WORRIER, be a WARRIOR, so the fruit of peace will be evident in your daily life! Again, either WORSHIP or WORRY can come out of your mouth....which one will it be? Your choice!

In Colossians, Paul reinforces this concept, "Let the peace of Christ rule in your hearts, since as members of one body you were called to peace. And be thankful." (Colossians 3:15)

Again, the concept of peace and thankfulness being linked is supported. In order to be thankful, you need to take the time to think about God's blessings in your life. In order to do this, pause and remove yourself from the distractions of the world. Only then can the static of the world grow silent, and you can "tune in" to God. He will remind you of the many things to be thankful for; just be willing to take the time with him.

I find that my most memorable experiences with God the father are when I've totally made him my focus. It's like bathing in his presence, and his glory and grace envelope me like warm water surrounding my body.

In the book of Isaiah, he says, "You will keep in perfect peace all who trust in you, all whose thoughts are fixed on you!" (Isaiah 26:3 NLT)

So again, the prophet Isaiah notes the idea of God's peace being with you; when you fix your gaze on the Father, the world simply fades into the background and you can fully submit to his plan! Then, his peace will guard your heart and mind and you will be free from worry and stress because you know he is in control and he is guiding you daily!

It is much easier said than done. If you fix your eyes on Jesus, his peace will automatically be with you. Sure, that sounds all well and good in theory, but there will be times in your life when things may seem overwhelming. When simply trusting in God takes all that you can muster, and peace seems like a faraway concept in the midst of your storm.

During these times, remember to get prayer and support from those around you that are journeying with you. Encouragement from others will help you to keep your focus where it needs to be, and peace will be yours when there is chaos around you.

Like the "butterfly child", Jonathan, did with his disease, and Shawn did with her miscarriage, they connected to people who were in the same circumstances and showed others that that they were not alone.

When people realize they are not alone, they become empowered; their fears, worries, and anxieties seem to be less daunting. There is power in the support of others as they cheer you on.

Along with the power you find in people that will support and pray for you, there is unbelievable power in the word of God. This power can be used to propel you towards your purpose as you intentionally reflect and give thanks along the way. Only then you will be able to stand back and give him all the glory, while you walk in purpose and bask in his perfect peace.

As an addendum to our previous story about Jonathan and the light he was to the world, here is a recent video about his passing:

"Jonathan Pitre's mother, Tina Boileau, talks about her son: 'I don't know how to live without him'" (4:08mins):
https://www.youtube.com/watch?v=1gf5BmJZyyI

When you have lived a life that God calls you to live and you live it well, the length of your life is not the focus, it is the DEPTH, or HOW you lived that length that speaks volumes! Thank-you Jonathan for your courage and strength in adversity. You are a true hero!

Victorious Verse
"Whatever you have learned or received or heard from me, or seen in me--put it into practice. And the God of peace will be with you." Philippians 4:9

Mighty Melody
"Grateful" by Elevation Worship, "Come As You Are" by David Crowder Band, and "Satisfied" by Chris Tomlin

Armour in Action
Watch these clips and help them to motivate you to start your day with God and to be thankful.

"Start Your Day With God - Morning Inspiration to Motivate Your Day" (5:13 mins): https://www.youtube.com/watch?v=-JB8so2U44Q

"Start Each Day With God - Morning Inspiration to Motivate Your Day" (4:55 mins): https://www.youtube.com/watch?v=PgR6cJbXqqw

Write a list of 10 things you are thankful for in your life. If you have more, write them down! Practice looking at God's hand in your life instead of your situation. As I like to put it, start your day with a cup of "T" (or thankfulness).

Watch this clip on being grateful.

"How To Thank God 'Even Though' | Pastor Steven Furtick" (10:09 mins): https://www.youtube.com/watch?v=5GsINTk6tdo

A song that echoes this pastor's message is:

"MercyMe - Even If (Official Lyric Video)" (4:16 mins): https://www.youtube.com/watch?v=B6fA35Ved-Y

Practice thankfulness on a daily basis. If you have trouble doing this, focus on being thankful for one thing a day for an entire week or even month. See his power and peace come into your life and take away your stress and anxiety.

It is a great way to show others how God is working in your life. They will see a difference in you and you can tell them you have a thankful heart for all God's blessings!

Notes:
_____
_____
_____
_____

Day *24* REFLECT Intentionally

REPLENISH SO YOU CAN POUR OUT

"Peace I leave with you; my peace I give you. I do not give to you as the world gives. Do not let your hearts be troubled and do not be afraid."

John 14:27

God's peace is something we all long for. I have found that it is not a place we "arrive"; we need to choose his peace in the midst of the joys and sorrows in our lives.

As Jesus states above in the book of John, he freely gives us his peace, therefore we have access to it at all times.

In the words of Big Daddy Weave in their song "Hold Me Jesus", they write about having a knowledge that God will never leave us in times when mountains look big compared to our faith. He is mighty and powerful, but he is also our humble king who brings us peace.

"Hold me JESUS by: Big Daddy Weave w/lyrics*" (3:51mins):
https://www.youtube.com/watch?v=xdYKjnjpm6I

In a world that surrounds us with fear and anxiety, you can find yourself in a constant state of being on edge. This may cause you to see the difficulties in your life as a barrier. During these times, not only does God want to be the powerful, majestic lion, or King of glory in your life; but he also wants to be the gentle, quiet lamb or Prince of peace. You just need to let him.

There are so many voices telling you how to be, who to be, what to be...it can be overwhelming. You will only have peace when you listen to HIS voice in your situations and fears.

Jesus said, "My sheep listen to my voice; I know them, and they follow me." (John 10:27)

In the same chapter, Jesus continues to say that not only do his sheep know his voice and follow him, but "he goes on ahead of them." (John 10:4)

This is so very important and is the key to your walk with your Saviour. You need to know that he always goes ahead of you. He is the leader, the shepherd, your example. Because he is your example, you need to see how he handled situations in his life and therefore, learn from him.

There is a story in the book of Luke that illustrates how Jesus constantly poured out to others; he taught and preached to crowds, performed miracles, healed the sick and gave people advice. He knew his life and ministry would be short on earth, so he understood "what" he had to do and he knew "why" he had to do it. He understood that in order for him to carry out his "what" and his "why", he needed to spend time with his father and replenish himself. His father gave him the strength to focus on his purpose here on earth.

As I listed previously, part of that purpose was healing people. So many blind, mute, leprous, demon-possessed, diseased people needed Jesus' help. One person in particular was a woman who had an issue with bleeding for over twelve years and no one could heal her.

The story goes on to say,

> "She came up behind him and touched the edge of his cloak, and immediately her bleeding stopped. 'Who touched me?' Jesus asked.
>
> When they all denied it, Peter said, 'Master, the people are crowding and pressing against you.'
>
> But Jesus said, 'Someone touched me; I know that power has gone out from me.'
>
> Then the woman, seeing that she could not go unnoticed, came trembling and fell at his feet. In the presence of all the people, she told why she had touched him and how she had been instantly healed.'
>
> Then he said to her, 'Daughter, your FAITH has healed you. Go in peace.'"
>
> (Luke 8:44-47)

This woman had "radical faith". Listen to this minister preach about exercising your faith, just like this woman did.

"Woman with the Issue of Blood - Min. Sean Edwards" (6:57mins): https://www.youtube.com/watch?v=z_qGe2H-BPk

Wow! This woman went from a "nobody", to a "somebody", to a "daughter". She realized her position in the kingdom that very day! What a moment of true revelation! She was changed forever!

Not only was this woman changed, but Jesus was also changed.

Jesus knew when he healed someone, power would leave him. He was wise enough to know that whatever he put out, he had to put back in.

He would spend alone time with his Father to replenish his spirit and gain back what he had given to others.

 Here are some of his times of being replenished:

"Very early in the morning, while it was still dark, Jesus got up, left the house and went off to a solitary place, where he prayed." (Mark 1:35)

"Immediately Jesus made the disciples get into the boat and go on ahead of him to the other side, while he dismissed the crowd. After he had dismissed them, he went up on a mountainside by himself to pray. When evening came, he was there alone." (Matthew 14:22-23)

"One of those days Jesus went out to a mountainside to pray, and spent the night praying to God." (Luke 6:12)

"But Jesus often withdrew to lonely places and prayed." (Luke 5:16)

You can see how important it was for Jesus to replenish his spirit and spend time with God. He made it a priority in his life and I encourage you to do the same.

This story by Wayne Rice titled "Table for Two" from *Still More Hot Illustrations For Youth Talks* (1999)[1] really makes you look at how you are spending your time:

> "He sits by himself at a table for two. The uniformed waiter returns to his side and asks, 'Would you like to go ahead and order, sir?' The man has, after all, been waiting since seven o'clock- almost half an hour. 'No thank-you,' the man smiles. 'I'll wait for her a while longer. How about some more coffee?'
>
> 'Certainly, sir.'
>
> The man sits, his clear blue eyes gazing straight through the flowered centerpiece. He fingers his napkin, allowing the sounds of light chatter, tinkling silverware, and mellow music to fill his mind. He is dressed in sport coat and tie. His dark brown hair is neatly combed, but one stray lock insists on dropping on his forehead. The scent of his cologne adds to his clean-cut image. He is dressed up enough to make

a companion feel important, respected, and loved. Yet he is not so formal as to make one uncomfortable. It seems that he has taken every precaution to make others feel at ease with him. Still, he sits alone.

The waiter returns to fill the man's coffee cup. 'Is there anything else I can get for you, sir?'

'No thank-you.'

The waiter remains standing at the table. Something tugs at his curiosity. 'I don't mean to pry, but.....' His voice trails off. This line of conversation could jeopardize his tip.

'Go ahead,' the man encourages. His voice is strong, yet sensitive, inviting conversation.

'Why do you bother waiting for her?' the waiter finally blurts out. This man has been at the restaurant other evenings, always patiently alone. Says the man quietly, 'Because she needs me.'

'Are you sure?'

'Yes.'

'Well, sir, no offense, but assuming that she needs you, she sure isn't acting much like it. She's stood you up three times just this week.'

The man winces, and looks down at the table. 'Yes, I know.'

'Then why do you still come here and wait?'

'Cassie said that she would be here.'

'She's said that before,' the waiter protests. 'I wouldn't put up with it. Why do you?'

Now the man looks up, smiles at the waiter and says simply, 'Because I love her.'

The waiter walks away, wondering how one could love a girl who stands him up three times a week. The man must be crazy, he decides. Across the room, he turns to look at the man again. The man slowly pours cream into his coffee. He twirls his spoon between his fingers a few times before stirring sweetener into his cup. After staring for a moment into the liquid, the man brings the cup to his mouth and sips, silently watching those around him. He doesn't look crazy, the waiter admits. Maybe the girl has qualities that I don't know about. Or maybe the man's love is stronger than most. The waiter shakes himself out of his musings to take an order from a party of five.

The man watches the waiter, wonders if he's ever been stood up. The man has, many times. But he still can't get used to it. Each time, it hurts. He's looked forward to this evening all day. He has many things, exciting things, to tell Cassie. But, more importantly, he wants to hear Cassie's voice. He wants her to tell him all about her day, her triumphs, her defeats....anything, really. He has tried so many times to show Cassie how much he loves her. He'd just like to know that she cares for him, too. He sips sporadically at the coffee, and loses himself in thought, knowing that Cassie is late, but still hoping that she will arrive.

The clock says nine-thirty when the waiter returns to the man's table. 'Is there anything I can get for you?'

The still empty chair stabs at the man. 'No, I think that will be all for tonight. May I have the check please?'

'Yes, sir.'

When the waiter leaves, the man picks up the check. He pulls out his wallet and sighs. He has enough money to have given Cassie a feast. But he takes out only enough to pay for his five cups of coffee and the tip. *Why do you do this, Cassie,* his mind cries as he gets up from the table.

'Good-bye,' the waiter says, as the man walks towards the door.

'Good night. Thank you for your service.'

'You're welcome, sir', says the waiter softly, for he sees the hurt in the man's eyes that his smile doesn't hide.

The man passes a laughing young couple on his way out, and eyes glisten as he thinks of the good time he and Cassie could have had. He stops at the front and makes reservations for tomorrow. Maybe Cassie will be able to make it, he thinks.

'Seven o'clock tomorrow for party of two?' the hostess confirms.

'That's right,' the man replies.

'Do you think she'll come?' asks the hostess. She doesn't mean to be rude, but she has watched the man many times alone at his table for two.

'Someday, yes. And I will be waiting for her.' The man buttons his overcoat and walks out of the restaurant, alone. His shoulders are hunched, but through the windows the hostess can only guess whether they are hunched against the wind or against the man's hurt.

As the man turns toward home, Cassie turns into bed. She is tired after an evening out with friends. As she reaches toward her nightstand to set the alarm, she sees the note that she scribbled to herself. *7:00*, it says. *Spend some time in prayer.* Darn, she thinks. She forgot again. She feels a twinge of guilt, but quickly pushes it aside. She needed that time with her friends. And now she needs her sleep. She can pray tomorrow night. Jesus will forgive her.

And she's sure he doesn't mind."

This story truly is heartbreaking, as many of us have probably put Jesus in the same predicament; we have good intentions to spend time with him, but we end up choosing other things instead. Jesus created women to be very relational in nature, so he understands this and longs to spend time with us daily.

God also created women to be nurturers, so being replenished is necessary as we pour out to others, and we can only "pour out" when our cup is filled by Jesus himself.

Being there to soothe and encourage others in their time of need just comes naturally to us. Sometimes, to our detriment, we focus so much on others that we have no time or energy left to focus on ourselves.

A great way to think about self-care is to remember what they tell you to do during an emergency on an airplane. After going through seatbelt and lifejacket demonstrations, they show you how to use an oxygen mask. They tell you that if you are with a child, to put on your mask first before putting it on the child. The key here is that you are of no use to others if you do not help yourself first. It's a simple concept that is very difficult for many women, but it is crucial if you want to live a peaceful and purposeful life in the midst of many distractions.

Jesus grants this peace to the woman we talked about earlier with the issue of blood. She was burdened with this bleeding for so long that it became a distraction in her life, and as a result, she probably lost her peace along the way.

Jesus ends the conversation with the woman with these words, "Daughter, your faith has healed you, GO IN PEACE." (Luke 8:48)

What a great reminder to you, as a young woman, to choose peace in the midst of your demanding lives and circumstances!

One final example of a woman pouring her love on others and receiving peace from the Saviour is the parable of the woman who poured perfume on the feet of Christ.

The story is one of a "sinful" woman who had learned that Jesus was eating at the house of a Pharisee (who was a very religious person of the day).

This is her story, "She brought an alabaster jar of perfume, and as she stood behind him at his feet weeping, she began to wet his feet with her tears. Then she wiped them with her hair, kissed them and poured perfume on them." (Luke 7:37b-38)

The Pharisee who had invited Jesus to his home was disgusted, because he knew this woman was "sinful" and shouldn't be touching Jesus.

Jesus knew what the man was thinking and he answered his concerns with these words,

> "'Do you see this woman? I came into your house. You did not give me any water for my feet, but she wet my feet with her tears and wiped them with her hair. You did not give me a kiss, but this woman, from the time I entered, has not stopped kissing my feet. You did not put oil on my head, but she has poured perfume on my feet. Therefore, I tell you, her many sins have been forgiven, for she loved much. But he who has been forgiven little loves little.'" (Luke 7:44-47)

Then, as he said to the woman with the issue of blood, he conveys his peace to her, "'Your faith has saved you; GO IN PEACE.'" (Luke 7:50)

"A woman washes Jesus' feet with her hair and tears (Luke 7:36-50)." (4:35 mins): https://www.youtube.com/watch?v=ii5wfxCgeK4

Once again, Jesus illustrates that he can restore you and bring you the peace that you long for. You simply have to choose the peace that only he can give.

By choosing peace in the midst of whatever your circumstance may be in, you are allowing yourself to be shaped and formed into HIS image. He IS the Prince of Peace, so you must embody peace too if you long to be more like him.

Victorious Verse
"A heart at peace gives life to the body." Proverbs 14:30a

Mighty Melody
"Pour My Love on You" by <u>Phillips, Craig, and Dean</u> and "Holy Spirit" by <u>Jesus Culture</u>

Armour in Action
In your times of reflection, prayer and being quiet with God, ask him to help you to choose peace and continue to do so despite what is going on around you.
Thank him for his peace that surpasses understanding.
Thank him for your giving heart, and make sure that you are putting aside time for yourself so you can continue to pour out to others.
Make time this week for something you really enjoy doing. Put it on your schedule so you make sure you do it!

Notes:

_____
_____
_____
_____
_____
_____
_____
_____
_____
_____
_____
_____
_____
_____
_____
_____
_____
_____
_____
_____
_____
_____
_____

Day *25* REFLECT Intentionally

REFLECTION LEADS TO REVELATION

"Where there is no revelation, the people cast off restraint; but blessed is he who keeps the law."

Proverbs 29:18a

If I put the above verse in my own words, it would read, "where I don't have discipline and vision in my life, I tend to have chaos and a lack of restraint, but if I have order, self-control and abide by God's laws, I will be blessed!"

This verse makes so much sense. Discipline equals blessing. When you are disciplined, you can train your mind to smash the limits you have place on yourself so that your perceptions can't hold you back. You are capable of far more than you think you are. The minute you allow chaos to reign in your life, your self-discipline goes down the drain. Where there is no self-discipline, there is no order.

The kingdom of God is all about order. There is a season and a purpose for everything. Nothing happens by accident, or out of disorder. God has a plan and it is deliberate and full of life. You will be blessed in so many ways if you truly seek his will.

Nevertheless, at times, bad things happen to good people and you may be angry with God or may have fallen away from your faith because of a deep wound. In the midst of your pain, trust God.

"TRUST GOD FIRST | YOUR WHOLE LIFE WILL CHANGE" (12:31 mins): https://www.youtube.com/watch?v=iYAxKTApgQA

In the midst of the hurt or chaos, order takes a back seat, and you may not see the grand plan of what God has for you because of your sadness and sorrow.

On Day 18, you watched a clip about Corrie Ten Boom. She was the Holocaust survivor who preached about the power of forgiveness through Jesus Christ. She would often quote this embellished version of "The Weaver" or "Tapestry Poem" by American minister and composer Grant Colfax Tullar[1]:

My life is but a weaving
Between the Lord and me;
I may not choose the colors—
He knows what they should be.

For He can view the pattern
Upon the upper side
While I can see it only
On this, the underside.

Sometimes He weaves in sorrow,
Which seems so strange to me;
But I will trust His judgment
And work on faithfully.

'Tis He who fills the shuttle,
And He knows what is best;
So I shall weave in earnest,
And leave to Him the rest.

Not 'til the loom is silent
And the shuttles cease to fly
Shall God unroll the canvas
And explain the reason why.

The dark threads are as needed
In the Weaver's skilful hand
As the threads of gold and silver
In the pattern He has planned.

What a beautiful depiction of the sad and dark times in our lives. When we really reflect and look back on them, we can see how God can use our sorrow to help us build who we are today.

Pastor Steven Furtick talks of this pain In our lives being used for God's purposes.

"The Point Of Pain | Pastor Steven Furtick" (8:17mins):
https://www.youtube.com/watch?v=7rKBbOrZKXw

Hard times cause us to build strong character, which gives God glory and honour, because we will walk in purpose and maturity in our faith.

The book of James says it like this, "Consider it pure joy, my brothers, whenever you face trials of many kinds, because you know that the testing of your faith develops perseverance. Perseverance must finish its work so that you may be mature and complete, not lacking anything." (James 1:2-4)

Paul in the book of Romans echoes James when he writes, "Not only so, but we also rejoice in our sufferings, because we know that suffering produces perseverance; perseverance, character; and character, hope." (Romans 5:3-4)

Finally, Peter says,

> "In this you greatly rejoice, though now for a little while you may have had to suffer grief in all kinds of trials. These have come so that your faith, of greater worth than gold, which perishes even though refined by fire, may be proved genuine and may result in praise, glory and honour when Jesus Christ is revealed." (1st Peter 1:6-7)

Not only do your trials build character and make you stronger, but also they allow you to help and minister to others.

People that have gone through hard times can walk with others through their valleys and show them that they are not alone. They have been in their "shoes" and can empathize with their situation. They have received comfort from God primarily when they walked through it, and in turn, can pass that comfort onto others.

Paul writes to the Corinthians and says,

> "Praise be to the God and Father of our Lord Jesus Christ, the Father of compassion and the God of all comfort, who comforts us in all our troubles, so that we can comfort those in any trouble with the comfort we ourselves have received from God. For just as the sufferings of Christ flow over into our lives, so also through Christ our comfort overflows." (2nd Corinthians 1:3-5)

Here is a prime example of this Christ-like comfort —my friend, Diane, went through the painful loss of her grown child, her husband, and her beloved pet all within a few years. I saw her strength daily as she helped and listened to others. She comforted friends as they told her about their hurts and struggles.

One time in particular, a mother came to her about her son that had been diagnosed with a serious illness. The mother was devastated. My friend was able to listen, minister to the woman, and comfort her because of the valley she herself had walked through. I truly admired her strong spirit and her ability to love others as Jesus did, even though she had many hurts of her own.

She passed away in June, 2020, and I miss her influence in my life tremendously. She made a difference in the lives of so many; she listened to me, gave me advice without judgment, and she inspired me to keep going in spite of setbacks or pain.

There is always a silver lining when it comes to our burdens and troubles. In the words of Paul, "And we know that in all things God works for the good of those who love him, who have been called according to his purpose." (Romans 8:28)

I'm sincerely thankful that God is so gracious and merciful. He gives you beauty for ashes (Isaiah 61:3) and is always working for your good. When I stop to reflect, I see God's hand in all things around me; through my family, my friends, my husband, my children, his word...he is working everywhere.

He is omniscient, meaning he knows everything about me, and he is omnipotent, meaning he has unlimited power and is able to do anything. Moreover, because I have him on my side, I also have power and I'm able to do anything! He gives me everything I need.

Psalm 28:7 says, "The Lord is my strength and my shield; my heart trusts in him and I am helped."

When you take the time to reflect on God's power in your life, he reveals to you who he is calling you to be. You are a warrior in his kingdom called to battle.

"YOU ARE MORE THAN A CONQUEROR ▶ CHILD OF GOD HD (MOTIVATIONAL)" (4:04 mins): https://www.youtube.com/watch?v=AB98vIGrlGI

Because we have the power of God working in us, when we boldly walk in his purposes for our lives, we can then engage in battle for others and allow God to work in their lives through us.

The bible says we are to "Speak up for those who cannot speak for themselves, for the rights of all who are destitute. Speak up and judge fairly; defend the rights of the poor and needy." (Proverbs 31:8-9)

You do this by engaging in the spiritual battle going on around you, praying for those in need and taking action when called to do so. God will give you direction through his word and will reveal the places where he wants you to be. Just be obedient, listen to his promptings from the Holy Spirit and never let fear get a foothold.

You are a fearless daughter of the King of Kings! Walk that out as you remember the wise words of Paul, "For you did not receive a spirit that makes you a slave again to fear, but you received the Spirit of son ship. And by him we cry, 'Abba, Father.'" (Romans 8:15)

Watch these two videos on overcoming fear and begin to realize that your destiny is on the other side of fear! Rise up mighty warrior princess and fight your fears with the King of Kings in your corner!

"NOTHING CAN STOP YOU CHILD OF GOD! HD" (15:50 mins): https://www.youtube.com/watch?v=Yf6okxpJGmw

"Keys That Will BOOST Your Faith And Belief Today!" (13:36 mins): https://www.youtube.com/watch?v=ja8dRnPZLCY

And as you fearlessly advance, let him lead you by his word and example and Jesus will radiate God's glory to you! "The Son is the radiance of God's glory and the exact representation of his being, sustaining all things by his powerful word." (Hebrews 1:3a)

Be reminded of his great power and might. End with watching this clip on who God really is!

"Who is God? - Very Powerful Video" (8:13 mins):
https://www.youtube.com/watch?v=X2dZbRwS7qo

Victorious Verse
"For you did not receive a spirit that makes you a slave again to fear, but you received the Spirit of son ship. And by him we cry, 'Abba, Father.'" Romans 8:15

Mighty Melody
"No Longer Slaves" by Jonathan David & Melissa Helser and "You Are Life" by Hillsong Worship

Armour in Action
Speak God's promises over your life and the lives of others! His word has the power over fears and trials!

Write a prayer that includes the following:
>   -ask him to give you victory over your fears
>   -ask him to allow his word to wash over you, cleanse your heart, and help you comfort others
>   -as you reflect on his word, ask him to speak to you, guide your steps and grant you
>   the privilege of doing his will

If you have a chance, look at the website below. The author of the blog has a wonderful depiction of a weaving- front and back. "Traci" will bless you with her thoughts.
https://www.beneathmyheart.net/2016/01/life-is-a-tapestry/

Notes:
_____
_____
_____
_____
_____
_____
_____
_____
_____
_____
_____
_____
_____
_____
_____
_____
_____
_____
_____
_____
_____
_____

Day *26* REFLECT Intentionally

STORMS BRING RAIN NECESSARY FOR GROWTH

"So neither he who plants nor he who waters is anything, but only God, who makes things grow. The man who plants and the man who waters have one purpose, and each will be rewarded according to his own labour."

1st Corinthians 3:7

When you see others going through strife, you think if you just try harder, or pray more fervently for them, the situation will change in your time. You forget that you only see a small piece of the pie. Like the apostle Paul states in the opening verse for today, we simply plant seeds in those around us, but God is the one who makes these seeds germinate and grow into something beautiful; in HIS time!

You get discouraged because things aren't happening in your time and God doesn't seem to be working fast enough. You throw up your hands and give up on people. Write them off. God never writes people off. He is always working; sometimes you are just too impatient.

When we lived on Vancouver Island, we saw rain, rain, and more rain. The overcast sky can get old, and many people suffer through deep valleys of depression, as the wind, rain, and cooler weather hammer on their bodies and souls.

We don't look out our front window and wait for our lawn to grow. We inherently know that spring is coming with warmer temperatures, and the grass will flourish in time.

We forget that all the greenery we see around us is a direct result of the rain and the rain is essential for growth! Too much rain can get you down, and you can start focusing on your dislike of the rain instead of what the rain will eventually bring.

Just as we needed the physical rain on the island, we need spiritual rain in our lives as well.

You need to continue to ask God for HIS eyes to see what is going on around you. He is the one that causes the spiritual growth and resulting fruit in your life and in those around you. You simply have to listen to his still, small voice and your role becomes more and more clear.

Listen to this "interview" with God. It reminds us that his still, small voice is always with us, no matter what! Praise you Jesus that YOUR faithfulness reminds US to stay faithful, in each and every situation!

"Interview with God" (3:32 mins):
https://www.youtube.com/watch?v=oXdkappiOWc

Your job is to continue to be faithful and plant seed. You may never see the fruit of your labour, but that is not the point. One day you may get to heaven and see all the people you prayed for were touched by your acts of kindness; that they always remembered a certain conversation you had with them or a heartfelt prayer you prayed with them.

What you say and do DOES make a difference. Just be obedient and continue to sow seed where God prompts you. He sees everything you do, that's all that matters!

In Hebrews, Paul confirms this when he says, "God is not unjust; he will not forget your work and the love you have shown him as you have helped his people and continue to help them." (Hebrews 6:10)

You may not see your rewards now, but in heaven when you lay your crowns at the feet of your Saviour, you will be richly rewarded as you spend eternity with your king.

Once again, I remember Pastor Greg Fraser making up a story to help drive this point home. He said, "Think of your life being on a big screen when you get to heaven, for all to see!" Isn't that a cool way to think about it? I could sit down with my tub of popcorn and see all the people whose lives I touched and all the people who are in the kingdom because of my actions.

If this was the case, I would want my life to be a blockbuster hit up in heaven, with real substance. I wouldn't want it to be a one, two, or even three star movie- 5 stars would be ideal!

There are so many people whose movies would be beautiful to watch – authors, mothers, missionaries, nurses, evangelists, martyrs, warriors....the list goes on and on. Each of us has something special and divine to offer this world. No one has more value than another.

Unfortunately, there are cases where the world puts labels on people and deems them as less important, or even disposable. For example, people with a disability may be looked upon as having a lesser value than your "average" person has.

There is a story of a father named Heath White who struggled with the news that his second daughter was going to be born with Down syndrome. He desperately wanted his wife to abort the baby. To make a long story short, his wife refused and he went through a period of acceptance after his daughter Paisley was born. God really worked on his heart and showed him how his love for his daughter could overcome any disability. He began to run marathons with her and even went so far as to tattoo the words "Down Syndrome" across his chest. There is no doubt he inspired many to rethink the idea of aborting a child with a disability, as they can be one of the greatest gifts to this world and can teach us a lot about ourselves. Watch his story at:

"The Reason - Heath & Paisley White" (3:59 mins):
https://www.youtube.com/watch?v=NncLUa8YSts

This circumstance definitely speaks to us of hope coming from something that can seem so devastating.

Many times, when you are in the middle of a dark time in your life, you can't see how the circumstances will ever be beneficial, but you have a God that is bigger than your circumstances and will turn ALL situations for good so that you will accomplish what he has put you on this earth to do!

"God intended it for good to accomplish what is now being done." (Genesis 50:20)

In the midst of another's struggle, someone else may find hope.

Watch these two clips- one of a little girl walking for the first time, and the other of a woman taking her first breaths unassisted. These videos illustrate so candidly how hope can come from adversity; truly the message of the gospel!

"4-Year-Old With Cerebral Palsy Takes First Steps on Her Own" (1:02 mins):
https://www.youtube.com/watch?v=gMltrWMfYTg

"First Breath After Lung Transplant" (2:25mins):
https://www.youtube.com/watch?v=cq6wjjN73Q0

After watching the last clip, this song reminds us that he gives us the breath in our lungs; something that many of us take for granted everyday! And as we walk through challenges, we can keep our eyes on HIS greatness!

"Casting Crowns - Great Are You Lord (Live)" (6:34 mins):
https://www.youtube.com/watch?v=FaP8fKAR2Og

I know there have been many times in my life where the storms seem so unnecessary, and I wondered why I had to walk through those times. Somehow, God always reminded me that in order for growth to happen, the storms have to be endured. And not only do we endure the storms, sometimes, we can even dance in the rain!

Here are a couple of songs that speak to this idea of living life fully while IN the storm.

"Casting Crowns - Praise You In This Storm (Official Lyric Video)" (5:03 mins):
https://www.youtube.com/watch?v=0YUGwUgBvTU

"Eye Of The Storm - [Lyric Video] Ryan Stevenson" (5:31 mins):
https://www.youtube.com/watch?v=X2FqFLKisys

Here is a poem I wrote while staying in a desolate campground so full of sad and lonely people. God showed me his faithfulness even when the situation seemed dark and hopeless. Again, he always turns all things for good if we keep our eyes on him! And when we keep our eyes on him, our thoughts will automatically focus on what is true, noble, right, pure, lovely, admirable, excellent, or praiseworthy. (Philippians 4:8)

GOD'S FAITHFULNESS

Campers, gravel, dusty roads, muck and mud after the rain,
God whispers through this campground to so many who are lonely and in pain.

I can look and see with my earthly eyes,
And see a place some would despise...

But you teach me to look with the eyes of Jesus,
Even in this barren, desolate place, you never, ever leave us.

You're in the joyful face of our bright-eyed baby's smile,
You are the peaceful, angelic look on the face of this sleeping child.

You're even in the determined face of my husband at the end of his day,
His utter exhaustion turns to joy, as he sits with our daughter and plays.

You are the scent of the wild roses all around me in full bloom,
You're even in the swaying dandelions in their sea of yellow hues.

You're in the playful chipmunk holding his treasure so tight,
You're in the beautiful sunrise, and the sunset late at night.

You're in the songs of the bustling birds I hear as I walk by,
You're also in the great expanse of the perfectly painted sky.

We've seen your hand at work here, ever since we first arrived,
We've watched a brown, dead landscape turn into something so green and alive!

You've shown me when I take my eyes off myself and my situation,
I can do small acts of kindness that can start to change a nation!

Because whenever we look around, we can choose to see,
All the misery, pain, and sorrow, and we miss opportunities.

A chance to be light to someone, a chance to encourage another,
The chance to lift someone's spirits, to be "Jesus" to our sisters and brothers.

To pray for lost souls on a worksite, living in a sea of pain,
Or to bring fresh bread to a stranger in the middle of the pouring rain....

You've shown us how blessed we really are, you've shown us many answers to prayer,
Wherever we roam through this vast country, your love is displayed everywhere.

On the drive home from Alberta your love and faithfulness was plain to see,
When the brightest rainbow was shown to us as a reminder that you are all we need.

So thank-you God for all you've shown me on this beautiful life adventure,
And I'm thankful for the ones I love most, and I'm so thankful we're here together.

Sometimes, it comes down to the things in our life that could "break" our spirit, but they end up making us stronger. I remember a young lady I grew up with that was involved in a gymnastics accident at her school. She ended up being in hospital with a broken neck and needed years of rehabilitation. During the gruelling weeks and months in the hospital after her accident, she began to feel sorry for herself and started to become angry. She had a nurse that basically put it into a nutshell for her. She said, "Margaret, you can be bitter, or you can be better. You decide which one." She said from that day on, she chose to be better.

Like Margaret, we can allow difficult times to make us better or bitter. The choice is up to you. And if you choose better, God can work through you and display his glory! What a way to really live!

"For our present troubles are small and won't last very long. Yet they produce for us a glory that vastly outweighs them and will last forever! So we don't look at the troubles we can see now; rather we fix our gaze on things that cannot be seen. For the things we see now will soon be gone, but the things we cannot see will last forever." (2nd Corinthians 4:17-18 NLT)

End today's devotion with this video of brokenness. It is only through being broken that God can truly use us for his purposes. What a privilege it is that God can use our lives to display HIS glory!

"This Video will Change the Way We Look at BROKENNESS - Voddie Baucham" (32:37 mins)
https://www.youtube.com/watch?v=M_Q6ZSzV8iQ

Lift HIM high when you are broken, and deep down in the valley! Enjoy!

"Vertical Worship - Yes I Will (Official Lyric Video)" (3:53 mins):
https://www.youtube.com/watch?v=NrTv39-IG4M

Victorious Verse

"In him we were also chosen, having been predestined according to the plan of him who works out everything in conformity with the purpose of his will." Ephesians 1:11

Mighty Melody

"Sweetly Broken" by David Crowder Band, "New Wine" by Hillsong Worship and "Broken Vessels (Amazing Grace)" by Hillsong Worship

Armour in Action

Write down something in your life that has made you a stronger person or allowed you to grow. Write a prayer of praise to God thanking him for turning all things for his good and purposes. Thank him for the rainbow at the end of the storm that shows his faithfulness!

Notes:

_____
_____
_____
_____
_____
_____
_____
_____
_____
_____
_____
_____
_____
_____
_____
_____
_____
_____
_____
_____
_____
_____
_____
_____

Day *27* REFLECT Intentionally

DRINK FROM HIS CUP

"'Abba, Father,' he said, 'everything is possible for you. Take this cup from me. Yet not what I will, but what you will.'"

Mark 14:36

I can only imagine the agony Jesus was going through in his final hours; the gruesome beatings, being spat on, having a crown of thorns driven into his head, death by crucifixion...something I can't even begin to comprehend. Try to imagine how God must have felt. He watched his son beg to take this cup from him. Worse than that, his Father indeed had the power to make it all stop, or even send a legion of angels down to rescue Jesus, but he knew he couldn't. He knew his son had to go through these horrible events in order to save you and me. He died knowing you might never love him in return....wow, that is true love with no conditions, no strings attached.

Not only did Jesus show us this love through his actions, but also the bible says, "God IS love. Whoever lives in love lives in God, and God in him." (1ˢᵗ John 4:16)

Therefore, if God loved his son Jesus that much, he also has that same love for each one of us.

A touching story from a young boy who heard from God when he was doing chores on his ranch shows this special bond in such an innocent way.

After the young boy had to put a beloved pet down because of a birthing situation gone wrong, he cried out to God and asked him why things had to be that way. The little boy told God that the cow was special to him, and God spoke to him saying his son was special to him too, but he had to experience the same thing when he lost his son.

Therefore, God knows exactly what you are going through and he understands. You just need to trust him.

To watch Logan's story, you can find it at:

"Logan, the Sky Angel Cowboy" (2:23mins):
https://www.youtube.com/watch?v=zCdZwitrNoY

This boy experienced first-hand the love from our Saviour. Amazing, when you really think about it- God truly understands any loss you experience in your life, and loves you unconditionally through the pain. Love can help you overcome all things.

A group of professional people posed this question to a group of 4 to 8 year-olds, "What does love mean?" The answers they got were broader and deeper than anyone could have imagined:

"When my grandmother got arthritis, she couldn't bend over and paint her toenails anymore. So my grandfather does it for her all the time, even when his hands got arthritis too. That's love." Rebecca - age 8.

"When someone loves you, the way they say your name is different. You know that your name is safe in their mouth." Billy - age 4

"Love is when a girl puts on perfume and a boy puts on shaving cologne and they go out and smell each other." Karl - age 5

"Love is when you go out to eat and give somebody most of your French fries without making them give you any of theirs." Chrissy - age 6

"Love is what makes you smile when you're tired." Terri - age 4

"Love is what's in the room with you at Christmas if you stop opening presents and listen," Bobby - age 7

"If you want to learn to love better, you should start with a friend who you hate," Nikka - age 6

"There are two kinds of love, our love and God's love. But God makes both kinds of them." Jenny - age 8

"Love is when you tell a guy you like his shirt, and then he wears it every day." Noelle - age 7

"Love is like a little old woman and a little old man who are still friends even after they know each other so well." Tommy - age 6

"Love is when your puppy licks your face even after you left him alone all day."
Mary Ann - age 4

"When you love somebody, your eyelashes go up and down and little stars come out of you." Karen - age 7

"Love is when Mommy sees Daddy on the toilet and she doesn't think it's gross."
Mark - age 6

Although these children had some sweet definitions, Jesus' love for you surpasses them all. He is the only person that will never let you down.

The world carelessly throws the word love around so much that we use it in the silliest of situations. We say we love peanut butter or cookies, yet we profess to love our parents in the same breath! Love used to be such a sacred word, but it seems to have little meaning anymore.

Unlike the love of the world, the love you experience from God is true and eternal. His love for you will never fail.

Psalm 136:1 is a wonderful reminder that his love is always there, "Give thanks to the Lord, for he is good. His love endures forever."

This phrase 'his love endures forever' continues throughout the whole psalm- in all 26 verses! What a testimony to his love and faithfulness in your life! He will always be there loving us; it is us who fail to fulfill our relationship with loving him as we should. We get distracted; we find other things to place on the throne of our lives to take his place. Instead of letting him be Lord in our life, it is a constant battle to see what will fill our day. God is always patiently waiting to love us... it is our job to let him.

Knowing that love and trust go hand in hand with our Father, listen to this convocation speech given on trusting God.

"TRUST GOD FIRST - One of The Most Inspiring Videos Ever (very powerful!)" (14:20mins):
https://www.youtube.com/watch?v=FrNamnkxzkA

God longs for us to fall deeper in love with him and trust him wholeheartedly. The only way we can do this is through spending time with him. Just like any other relationship in our lives, love and trust are built on quality time spent and getting to know their character. God is waiting for us to spend time with him.

I remember a powerful letter that a teacher gave our whole class in grade 5. I still keep it in my bible and it reminds me of his everlasting love and his longing to be in relationship with us.

My Daughter,

I just had to send a note to tell you how much I love and care about you. I saw you yesterday as you walked with your friends, and I waited all day hoping you would want to talk with me also. At evening, I gave you a golden sunset and a cool breeze, and I waited....but you never came. It hurt me, but I still love you because I am your friend.

I saw you fall asleep last night and I longed to touch your brow, so I spilled moonlight upon your pillow. Again, I waited, wanting to rush down so we could talk. I have so many gifts for you. But you awoke late, today, and rushed out. My tears were in the rain.

You've looked so sad and alone today. My heart aches for you because I understand...in the blue sky, and in the quiet green grass. I breathe it in the colors of the flowers. I shout it in the mountain streams and give the birds love songs to sing. I clothe you with warm sunshine and perfume the air with nature's scents. My love for you is deeper than the oceans and bigger than the biggest want or need in your heart.

If you only knew how much I want to help you! I want you to meet with my Father, too. He wants to remind you how much he cares about you. My Father is that way, you know. I have so much to share with you......just call me, ask me, and talk with me. I'll wait for you to come, but I'll never hassle you, because I love you.

Your friend,
Jesus

The God who created you desires to spend more time with you and loves you. Seek his face.

"But if from there you seek the Lord your God, you will find him if you seek him with all your heart and with all your soul." (Deuteronomy 4:29)

Allow his peace and love to minister to your spirit as you sit at the foot of the cross and look up into the eyes of the man who died for you. Whether you return his love or not he will always love you. What an unimaginable sacrifice to drink from a cup that Jesus knew would lead to his death!

I'm so thankful that he not only drank from that solemn cup, but Psalm 23 tells us that with him as lord of our lives, our cup will "overflow". (Psalm 23:5)

Let's drink from this overflowing cup he gives us for the rest of our lives, because we know he has living water that will fill our souls and we will never have to be spiritually thirsty again.

He promises this in the book of John, "Whoever drinks the water I give them will never thirst. Indeed, the water I give them will become in them a spring of water welling up to eternal life." (John 4:14)

Victorious Verse

"For God so loved the world that he gave his one and only Son, that whoever believes in him shall not perish but have eternal life." John 3:16

Mighty Melody

"The More I Seek You" by Kari Jobe and "Beloved" by Jordan Feliz

Armour in Action

Insert your name into the letter from Jesus and read it aloud. Feel the pain in his voice as he longs to meet with you repeatedly.

Write a letter back to Jesus expressing your feelings and desires to meet with him too and read it aloud to him. Or write a letter asking for forgiveness for not making time for him. Ask him to help you make time with him a priority.

Come up with a set time daily to meet with him and seek him with a deeper understanding of his love for you.

Notes:

_____

_____

_____

_____

_____

_____

_____

_____

_____

_____

_____

_____

_____

_____

_____

_____

_____

_____

_____

_____

_____

_____

Day *28* REFLECT Intentionally

DON'T WAIT FOR TOMORROW- LIVE FOR TODAY

"I have seen all the things that are done under the sun; all of them are meaningless, a chasing after the wind."

Ecclesiastes 1:14

In a nutshell, this is King Solomon's basic message in the book of Ecclesiastes: everything is meaningless in our lives...as pointless as chasing after the wind, unless we are centered on God and his purposes for our life.

When you are just going through the motions and you don't really have any purpose, time just seems to fade into oblivion and you get lost in the so-called "doldrums". Definition from the WFMZ-TV weather website (2011)[1]:

> "The doldrums are regions of the Atlantic and Pacific oceans that have little if any wind. This was a particular problem for sailors in the past, when they depended on the winds to propel their ships, a problem that could be potentially deadly. The doldrums are caused by solar radiation from the sun, as sunlight beams down directly on the area around the equator. This heating causes the air to warm and rise straight up rather than blow horizontally. The result is little or no wind, sometimes for weeks on end....the rising moist air in the doldrums can spawn tropical storms and hurricanes. Nearly every Atlantic hurricane arises in or near the doldrums. The unpredictability of the weather, either no winds or potential hurricanes, made the doldrums one of the least favourite sailing lanes when all that the ships had to power them across the ocean was their sails."

Therefore, like the doldrums of the sea, being in the doldrums of life, you are stagnant; stuck in a no-man's land where time seems to stand still. Life seems to have no meaning. You can drift into unchartered territory where you don't want to be…somewhere so far from the dreams and passions God has placed in your heart that you can't seem to find your way back. This is what happens when our time is not devoted to God and his plans.

Here is a reminder from Steve Harvey speaking on the dreams God has placed deep down in your heart. They are not there by accident! No matter how far you have drifted from your dreams, they will always be there to come back to, as God has only planted them in YOU! No one else on this earth can complete the work he has given you to do, daughter of the King!

"Imagination Is Everything | Motivated + | Steve Harvey" (8:14 mins):
https://www.youtube.com/watch?v=TbEMlw3ecGI

When you have time to reflect on how close you are coming to achieving your dreams, or how far you have drifted away from them, you can be excited or depressed. It is only through true reflection and goal setting that you will see your dreams happen. Without time set aside to evaluate where you have been, where you are, and where you are going, you will find yourself sadly disappointed.

When you constantly put things off until tomorrow, you aren't accomplishing all that you could. Procrastination is also a form of the proverbial "doldrums" of life. You don't seem to get anywhere. Life can seem depressing and gloomy, where there is no point to anything because every day seems to just meaninglessly fade into the next. God wants you to remember that your time here on earth is valuable. You are given a certain amount of it, and not one of us knows when our time is up.

We all live as if we are guaranteed tomorrow, yet our tomorrows are so fleeting, and are not promised to anyone. We take for granted the fact that God has given us this precious gift called life, and we squander it daily as we put things off repeatedly.

So what is the solution? What do we need to do as Christians to really live for the moment and "carpe diem" or "seize the day" as the poet Horace (23 BC) put it?

We need to look to his word. A study by Stephen May[2] on the quote "seize the day" lead him to Philippians chapter 3. He found that Paul outlined three basic steps for getting the most out of every day, and therefore living a more focused and fulfilling life.

First, find your purpose, which is to know Christ and become more like him.

"I consider everything a loss compared to the surpassing greatness of knowing Christ Jesus my Lord…I want to know Christ and the power of his resurrection and the fellowship of sharing in his sufferings, becoming like him in his death." (Philippians 3:8, 10)

Second, forget the past.

"Not that I have already obtained all this, or have already been made perfect, but I press on to take hold of that for which Christ Jesus took hold of me. Brothers, I do not consider myself yet to have taken hold of it. But one thing I do: Forgetting what is behind..." (Philippians 3:12-13a)

It's the reason the windshield in a car is much larger than the rear view mirror...because what lies ahead is vastly more important than what is behind us!

Third, we need to face the present.

"....straining toward what is ahead, I press on toward the goal to win the prize for which God has called me heavenward in Christ Jesus." (Philippians 3:13b-14)

Along with the three steps that Stephen May outlined, I would add three more steps from the next chapter of Philippians to enable you to get the most out of each day.

Fourth, always be thankful and rejoice in what God is doing, even in the valleys of your life.

Philippians chapter four, tells us to "Rejoice in the Lord always.....and with thanksgiving, present your requests to God." (Philippians 4:4a, 6b)

That way, no matter what the day brings, you will rejoice in the blessings of our Lord.

Fifth, get your mind right everyday by meditating on the things of God instead of the things of the world.

"Whatever is true, whatever is noble, whatever is right, whatever is pure, whatever is lovely, whatever is admirable- if anything is excellent or praiseworthy-think about such things." (Philippians 4:8)

Sixth, be content with your situations, no matter what, and rely on God- he will always give you the strength to keep going. This will definitely help you to "seize the day", as you focus on the positive and trust that God will always be there to provide the strength you need.

Paul says, "I have learned to be content whatever the circumstances. I know what it is to be in need, and I know what it is to have plenty. I have learned the secret of being content in any and every situation, whether well fed or hungry, whether living in plenty or in want. I can do everything through him who gives me strength." (Philippians 4:11b-13)

It is encouraging to know that you can live for "to-day" instead of your "to-do" list. Looking further into his word, you see that your time is not only valuable, but it does not belong to you.

"For Christ's love compels us, because we are convinced that one died for all, and therefore all died. And he died for all, that those who live should no longer live for themselves but for him who died for them and was raised again." (2nd Corinthians 5:14-15)

This verse reminds us that our lives are not our own, therefore our time is not our own. Christ died for every second we get on this earth. He died for us, so we should live for him! Simple concept when you think about it- live every day for a man whose death showed us his commitment and faithfulness, and whose love goes beyond anything we can comprehend.

And as we discussed how love and trust are intertwined in Day 27, watch this segment on how we need to keep our eyes on Jesus as we live for him. He is the only one we can fully trust in the chaos of our daily life.

"Trusting God in the Storm of Chaos - Motivational & Inspirational Video" (6:38mins): https://www.youtube.com/watch?v=43_wu5hDBiI

Thank you Jesus that we get to live for you, that each day truly is a gift called the "present". In the words of famous scientist, Albert Einstein, "Learn from yesterday, live for today, hope for tomorrow."[3]

If you start worrying about tomorrow, you lose your peace that you should have for today, which takes your focus off Christ, and what really matters. Distraction creeps in, and you may drift off course and into the ambiguous doldrums. Reflect on the gifts you have today and do all you are called to do instead of waiting for tomorrow, which is never a guarantee.

Finally, there here is an example of a young girl making a small difference and taking action, and in turn, saving lives. It's amazing what a ripple effect one small gesture can make!

"Teen Stops Suicide By Covering Bridge With Messages Of Hope" (3:22 mins): https://www.youtube.com/watch?v=F5HbiiKshJI

Victorious Verse

"Be very careful, then, how you live; not as unwise but as wise, making the most of every opportunity."
Ephesians 5:15-16a

Mighty Melody

"Do Something" by Matthew West and "Move" by Mercy Me

Armour in Action

Think of at least two things you've been putting off doing. Do something about them TODAY. If they are more long-term projects, you've been neglecting, start the wheel in motion to accomplishing them. Set some goals and a due date as to when they will be done. Especially if they are part of your dreams or passions, you need to achieve the baby steps to get there in order to feel truly fulfilled!

Notes:

_____
_____
_____
_____
_____
_____
_____
_____
_____
_____
_____
_____
_____
_____
_____
_____
_____
_____
_____
_____
_____
_____
_____
_____
_____
_____
_____
_____
_____
_____
_____

Introduction to Pillar **5**

RAISE OTHERS UP

Our life should be about leaving a legacy and allowing others to live their best life. Too many seniors, when asked, if they could live their life over again, wished that they would have done more that would live on after they were gone.

In order to leave a lasting legacy, we must answer the question "why" we are doing what we are doing. As the Christian comedian, Michael Jr. put it in one of his sermons (*Know Your Why*, 2017), "When you know your 'why', your 'what' has more impact because you are walking in or towards your purpose."

In order to walk in purpose, you need to outline your strengths. When you can pinpoint and capitalize on your strengths, they can be applied to the vision God has given you for your life, which will allow you to set realistic and attainable goals. Look back on your notes from Day 1 when you took the "StrengthsFinder" test.

Remind yourself about where your strengths lie! Knowing your strengths will help you set goals that will propel you towards your purpose, which will cause you to step up, make a difference, and create a ripple effect beyond your wildest imagination!

This ripple effect is the impact you will have on this dark and hopeless world. It involves your why because it is the reason you are here.

For example, my "why" is inspiring young people to walk in purpose. My "what" is teaching, writing and playing the drums, or in other words, how I will make my "why" happen. My "what" involves the gifts and talents God has placed in me in order to carry out my "why" and fulfill my legacy here on earth.

Watch this clip on your purpose and leaving a legacy. It will light a fire under you!

"CHASING YOUR PURPOSE - 2017 Motivation" (7:03 mins):
https://www.youtube.com/watch?v=ekkOFqFe5LE

Ask yourself what kind of a legacy you will leave for future generations? Will you have any regrets when you leave this earth to go home? If so, re-establish your "what" and your "why" and start walking in or towards your purpose right now! Don't waste the precious time God has entrusted to you. When you are using your time wisely, you will maximize the impact you can have on the people around you.

Jesus had a minimal amount of time on earth, so he maximized his impact by constantly revisiting the reason he was here. His "why" was the redemption of mankind, so therefore, his "what" was teaching, preaching and healing. He could only achieve his why by knowing what gifts his father had placed in him and by forming relationships with people that would support and carry on his ministry.

Like Jesus, when you find a core group of people that draw you closer to your "why", you will automatically lift others up because it will come as a natural progression of the healthy relationships you have built over time.

Therefore, by knowing and walking in your "why" and your "what", and by forming relationships with those walking with you towards your purpose, you will indeed live a life that is impactful. Live for Christ and you will have no regrets!

Living for Christ should help you to walk more fervently towards your purpose! Watch this inspiring video from Pastor Steven Furtick about handling life with Christ inside you. There is nothing that can stop you with the mighty King of Kings working in your life. You may even want to watch it every morning to pump you up!

"I Can Handle It | Motivational Track from Steven Furtick" (3:32mins):
https://www.youtube.com/watch?v=P8kgbpR1fSc

Day **29** RAISE Others Up

THE PRODIGAL

"…this brother of yours was dead and is alive again; he was lost and is found."

Luke 15:32b

This story in the bible in the 15th chapter of Luke is a well-known one. 'The prodigal' son means "wayward" - spending money, or resources, in a recklessly extravagant way.

The parable tells the story of a young son who asked his father for his inheritance early and squandered the money on "wild living". After he had spent all he had, there was a severe famine in the land and he resorted to a job feeding pigs. Life got so bad that he ate with those same pigs because he was so hungry. After a while, he got the courage up to go back home and ask his father for forgiveness.

He wasn't sure how his father would react, but Luke tells us that as he approached his father, this is what unfolded:

> "But while he was still a long way off, his father saw him and was filled with compassion for him; he ran to his son, threw his arms around him and kissed him. The son said to him, 'Father, I have sinned against heaven and against you. I am no longer worthy to be called your son.' But the father said to his servants, 'Quick! Bring the best robe and put it on him. Put a ring on his finger and sandals on his feet. Bring the fattened calf and kill it. Let's have a feast and celebrate. For this son of mine was dead and is alive again; he was lost and is found. So they began to celebrate." (Luke 15:20-24)

What joy filled the father's heart when he saw his son walking towards him! His son, thought lost! What a miracle! Our father in heaven feels the same way when a wayward child of his comes home; overcome with great joy and throws his arms around us, and kisses us just like the father in the story.

This song sums up this story perfectly!

"Phillips, Craig & Dean - When God Ran" (5:15 mins):
https://www.youtube.com/watch?v=ml1UU23yh4g

There are many prodigal sons and daughters walking around in this world and it is our job as Christians to maintain relationships, love them, and speak encouragement into their life! They don't want to hear judgemental Christians pointing out all that they are doing wrong in their lives...they simply want to be loved just like you or me. Our lives should be a reflection of how blessed they could be and all the good things that they are missing so that they will have the courage to ask for forgiveness and come home!

Is your life full of mistakes and regrets, just like the prodigal son?

Remember that you are human and "all have sinned and fallen short of the glory of God." (Romans 3:23)

You can dwell on your sin and allow it to swallow you up, or you can encourage others like Marc and use your life to spread God's message of love and forgiveness. Marc is an example of a prodigal with true humility as he shares his powerful testimony.

"The Story That Moved This Entire Middle School to Tears" (5:50 mins):
https://www.youtube.com/watch?v=Li7vpzLA9uw

Another example of encouraging others is when famous people take opportunities to speak to young people about God. Chris Pratt did this in an acceptance speech on the "2018 MTV Movie and TV awards":

"Chris Pratt's 9 Rules Acceptance Speech | 2018 MTV Movie & TV Awards" (4:15 mins):
https://www.youtube.com/watch?v=EihqXHqxri0

There are many people like Marc and Chris using their mistakes and/or opportunities to encourage others and bring them closer to God and to their purpose!

Part of encouraging others starts with humbling yourself and asking God for forgiveness. Then, you must also ask the people in your life if you have caused hurt or pain, and ask them for forgiveness as well.

I remember how humbling it was to go into my boss's office and tell him that I had been talking badly about him. I told him that as a Christian, what I did was wrong and I apologized. I think that spoke volumes to him, as he was a non-Christian.

When you lay down your pride and humble yourself, it shows people who do not have a relationship with Christ that Christians are human too; we are far from perfect. Moreover, if God is who he says he is, then his love covers all our imperfections! Remember this the next time you feel like saying something that isn't complimentary.

In fact, there is an acronym "THINK" that is easy to remember when you have the urge to say something negative about someone. Before you say it, is it True, Helpful, Inspiring, Necessary, or Kind? If it is not, you probably shouldn't be saying it!

Would you talk like that about a person, if that person were standing right there in the room? Think about all the people that you have relationships with; is their name safe in your mouth? If not, you may need to humble yourself and go to that person and ask for forgiveness. After having to do that a few times, you may just think twice before you let derogatory words come out of your mouth about God's children.

Here is a great example of a college professor that taught this lesson to his first year students. He asked them to draw a person that they really didn't like or had talked badly about recently on a sheet of paper. He then asked them to staple these pictures to a bulletin board and handed out darts. He told them to throw the darts at the pictures so they could get their frustrations out towards that person. He told them to get into the activity and the students began to laugh and joke as they threw the darts. After they had done this for a few minutes, the professor asked them to take their seats. When all the students were paying attention, he quietly began to peel the paper off the bulletin board to reveal what was behind the pictures they had drawn. It was a picture of Christ with holes in his face- a picture tattered and torn by the darts. The students then realized that their words were like weapons that not only hurt God's beloved children, but Christ himself. It caused many students to become emotional, because they never looked at their actions as hurting Jesus as well. I believe that activity changed many hearts that day.

It is not our job to judge another's heart. It is simply our job to love them. Hearts can become hardened towards others as we begin to compare ourselves, when hurt by something they said or did, or when they hurt the people that we love.

The older son in the "prodigal" story felt like this. He saw the pain that the younger brother had caused his father and it grieved him. He had stayed and been faithful to his father and worked hard for him. His hurt turned to anger and his heart was hardened towards his younger brother.

We see that as the party was going on, "the older brother became angry and refused to go in. So his father went out and pleaded with him. But he answered his father, 'Look! All these years I've been slaving for you and never disobeyed your orders. Yet you never gave me even a young goat so I could celebrate with my friends. But when this son of yours who has squandered your property with prostitutes comes home, you kill the fattened calf for him!' " (Luke 15:28-30)

There are many prodigals out there who are longing to come home. Your job is to pray for them and lift them up. Speak words of life, not death. Your prayers will be one of the tools God uses to help them build their palace of purpose.

Are you guilty of being like this older brother? Has your heart become hardened towards others, instead of having a heart of compassion towards them as our father in heaven does?

As the father in this story reacts to the older son, this is how our heavenly father sees his wayward children.

"'My son, you are always with me, and everything I have is yours. But we had to celebrate and be glad, because this brother of yours was dead and is alive again; he was lost and is found.' " (Luke 15:31-32)

Watch the "Skit Guys" perform a powerful drama on the prodigal son.

"The Prodigal" (7:26 mins):
https://www.youtube.com/watch?v=HyVlF24u5dY

Thank God, our father never gives up on us even when others do! He will always be there for us when we decide to return to him.

The following is a poem from one of my former students Kyra Laboucan (2010), that summarizes the heart that God has for all his lost children:

A Cry from the Heart of God

I miss you, I long for you my love. How long will you stand far off?
How long will you continue in your ways?
You try in vain to make things right, hoping to do it all with your own might.
Walking lifeless, looking for more, feeling empty straight through your core.
Not knowing what to do, life seems meaningless to you.
I have all you are looking for, I have all you need, look to me my love, unto my words do heed.
Please stop this lifeless living; it will soon be the end, for back into this world My Son do I send.
When He was with you, He told you of what was to come, obey every command,
to evil do not succumb.
A life of freedom to you do I wish to give, forget this lifeless living and truly live!
Be happy, be free, My life, My love, I give you My all. Until you return, forever I will call.

Thank-you Jesus for your compassion and love that sometimes seems beyond our capabilities.

Help us to remember that, "there will be more rejoicing in heaven over one sinner who repents than over ninety-nine righteous persons who do not need to repent." (Luke 15:7)

Make us more like you so we can see others through your eyes. Only then can we truly celebrate with you and welcome them home with open arms!

Or, as human rights activist and Nobel Peace prize winner, Desmond Tutu put it, "There comes a point where we need to stop just pulling people out of the river. We need to go upstream and find out why they're falling in."[1]

With God's leading and his Holy Spirit prompting us, may we be open to "going upstream", loving others, and doing God's work before someone needs to be pulled out of the river itself!

I pray a blessing on all those who are working "upstream". God give them your wisdom, your strength and perseverance, and your grace. May their labor for the kingdom not be in vain! Amen!

Victorious Verse

"But while he was still a long way off, his father saw him and was filled with compassion for him; he ran to his son, threw his arms around him and kissed him." Luke 15:20

Mighty Melody

"Welcome Home" by Brian Littrell, "The Father's House" by Cory Asbury, and "There Was Jesus" by Dolly Parton and Zach Williams

Armour in Action

Recall the quote by Mother Teresa, "When you judge people, you have no time to love them." Think of someone in your life where your heart has become hardened. Pray that God can help you to have compassion for that person and let go of the things that are holding you captive. Be free in Christ by not only asking God for forgiveness, but have the boldness and courage to go to the person and ask for forgiveness as well. You never know if your actions may lead someone to salvation and you will have a part in one of the biggest parties thrown in heaven!

Notes:

Day *30* RAISE Others Up

NO ONE IS TOO FAR GONE

"Therefore if anyone is in Christ, he is a new creation; the old has gone, the new has come."

2nd Corinthians 5:17

Do you feel guilt and shame for some of the things you may have done in your life? The good news is that Christ gives you a clean slate every day and God sees you "whiter than snow" (Psalm 51:7b) and without blemish.

In Colossians, Paul confirms this, "Once you were alienated from God and were enemies in your minds because of your evil behaviour. But now he has reconciled you by Christ's physical body through death to present you holy in his sight, without blemish and free from accusation." (Colossians 1:21-22)

Despite your sin, God seeks to have relationship with you and make you a new creation with no record of your wrongs! As long as you repent and turn to him, he can work with you. He molds and changes you into the image of his son; he sees your possibilities, not your liabilities.

You need to see potential in yourself, and in others. Try not to write anyone off as a "lost cause", "too far gone", "broken" or "too scarred" for God to create change in or to use. Jesus came to earth and died the death he did for ALL who sin. He never writes one of his children off. He always sees the potential locked away inside us all.

Watch how this teacher saw the potential in her students and, in turn, literally changed the course of their lives.

"She Never Gave Up on Her Students | Erin Gruwell | Goalcast" (10:58 mins):
https://www.youtube.com/watch?v=9VJ6Lsx5aTI

It is our job as Christians, never to lose hope or faith in another human being. You may need to set proper boundaries with some people, but you can remain praying and know that your God is willing and able to help them make their way to him. Never stop fighting any battle for the person that God puts on your heart. You can never lose faith that they will repent and begin to make their way back to God and leave that "old" self behind!

We could define true repentance as a sincere turning away, from self to God, in both the mind and heart.

As a person begins to live solely for God, it becomes less about them and more about God. Here are some thoughts on repentance by Katash Diakonia (2014)[1]:

> "In a biblical context, repentance is recognizing that our sin is offensive to God. Repentance can be shallow, such as the remorse we feel because of fear of punishment, like Cain, or it can be deep; such as realizing how much our sins cost Jesus and how his saving grace washes us clean, like the conversion of Paul".

Paul's deep conversion is a miracle! He went from murdering Christians, being a man full of hatred and anger, to a man who wrote a good portion of the New Testament, preaching God's grace and forgiveness to all who listened.

A modern day "Saul to Paul" conversion is the story of Cody Bates. Read about his unbelievable transformation in "Former drug dealer Cody Bates helps those battling addictions": http://calgaryherald.com/news/local-news/a-year-in-the-death-and-life-of-cody-bates

Here also is Cody's testimony in a powerful segment that shows the power of God. You will be in awe of the goodness of God!

"Cody Bates Testimony" (19:31 mins): https://www.youtube.com/watch?v=4HDfEsJe-qA

Stories of people such as Cody and Saul give us hope that God can, in fact, turn any situation around!

In Acts chapter nine, it outlines how God began to convert Saul into the man of God named Paul who was one of the most powerful apostles in history.

First, it states that as Saul was on his way to a place called Damascus, still uttering murderous threats against God's people, "Suddenly a light from heaven flashed around him. He fell to the ground and heard a voice say to him, 'Saul, Saul, why do you persecute me?' 'Who are you Lord?' Saul asked. 'I am Jesus, whom you are persecuting....Now get up and go into the city, and you will be told what you must do.' " (Acts 9:3b-6)

From the light flashing around him, Saul was blind for three days, and in that time he fasted as well, because God was preparing him for the work he had for him.

Acts 9:19b-20 goes on to say, "Saul spent several days with the disciples in Damascus. At once he began to preach in the synagogues that Jesus is the Son of God."

What an awesome transformation! Again, only God is able to work in such a powerful way in a person's life! Then he brings people alongside Saul (Paul) as he begins preaching the gospel.

> "When he (Saul) came to Jerusalem, he tried to join the disciples, but they were all afraid of him, not believing that he really was a disciple. But Barnabas took him and brought him to the apostles. He told them how Saul on his journey had seen the Lord and that the Lord had spoken to him, and how in Damascus he had preached fearlessly in the name of Jesus. So Saul stayed with them and moved about freely in Jerusalem, speaking boldly in the name of the Lord." (Acts 9:26-28)

First, Barnabas, "the son of encouragement" (Acts 4:36) came to support Saul, then the disciples, after hearing of his preaching in Damascus.

In the same way he used Barnabas, God will bring people beside you to support you, or he will bring you into the lives of others that need encouragement, to walk beside them and support them.

Many times, a there are people in our lives that cheer us on and help us to become all we are. It may be a coach, pastor, parent or mentor. The following clip is an excellent example of how God can place others in our lives to encourage us.

"The Death Crawl scene from Facing the Giants" (5:36 mins):
https://www.youtube.com/watch?v=-sUKoKQlEC4

Along with teachers and coaches, parents are the primary source of encouragement to a young person. A mother's love and support can bring out our very best.

Two sweet depictions of the support and encouragement of a mother can be found at:

"Thank You Mom - P&G Commercial (Sochi 2014 Olympic Winter Games)" (2:00 mins):
https://www.youtube.com/watch?v=1SwFso7NeuA

And here is a Mom speaking life over her daughter....so powerful, the words we speak over our children!

"CBN News" (3:21 mins)
https://www.facebook.com/cbnnews/videos/10157675190525393/

Dads have such an important role in their daughter's lives too! When a little girl knows she is loved unconditionally by both her heavenly and earthly father, there is no limit on what she can accomplish for the kingdom of God!

"Dads and Daughters Read Powerful Affirmations | Iris" (2:25 mins):
https://www.youtube.com/watch?v=Hkqi3D-oN8Y

"What About Me Makes You Proud? - Emotional Father's Day Video Will Make You Cry" (3:55 mins): https://www.youtube.com/watch?v=AguclSviIJI

Many people may not have caring, loving parents, so it is our job as Christians to show them what a supportive and loving person looks like. There are so many broken and defeated people in today's world, wandering aimlessly around with no purpose or meaning to their lives.

They don't know that God's plan for us is life, not death, deliverance, not destruction. We will reap consequences to our actions, but God can still work wonders in our broken lives and help to "repay us for the years the locusts have eaten." (Joel 2:25)

Yes, unfortunately, there are always consequences to poor choices, but God is about restoration.

After listening to a sermon by Blake Jennings (February 2011) on "The God of Lost Causes", I came out of it with more knowledge and understanding about this subject of restoration.

Evidence of God being willing to restore people is found in the book of Isaiah chapter 40, "Comfort, comfort my people, says your God. Speak tenderly to Jerusalem, and proclaim to her that her hard service has been completed, that her sin has been paid for." (Isaiah 40:1-2a)

When he heals us and restores us, he does it in person through his son Jesus and through his Holy Spirit who dwells in us.

Verse 8 goes onto say, "The grass withers and the flowers fall, but the word of our God stands forever." (Isaiah 40:8)

In other words, the things in this world are changing and unstable. The only thing that will last is God's word and his promises. No matter WHAT someone has done, God's promises are YES and AMEN in Christ; they can literally do ANYTHING!

Not only will he redirect you, but also he will use your story to inspire and bring hope and healing to others.

"You who bring good tidings to Zion, go up on a high mountain. You, who bring good tidings to Jerusalem, lift up your voice with a shout, lift it up, do not be afraid; say to the towns of Judah, 'Here is your God!' " (Isaiah 40:9)

When God does restore us, we can then proclaim what he has done in our lives, and our testimony becomes a testament to his goodness and love. You can use your story to preach the gospel to others who are lost.

We are all sheep in his flock; some of us have stayed close to our master and under his protection, but others have strayed. No matter where we are, he embraces us gently and lovingly.

"He tends his flock like a shepherd: He gathers the lambs in his arms and carries them close to his heart; he gently leads those that have young." (Isaiah 40:11)

God cares for you, tends to your heart, and heals you so you can bring healing to others. God's healing and restoration is not about you, it is about him. Your testimony will bring him glory, honour, and praise! Your life will be a witness and a light to lead people out of the dark. God is willing to bring healing and hope to the lost, and you are his instrument to help those who are struggling!

Not only is he willing to bring restoration and hope to the lost, but also he is able.

Isaiah tells us of the immensity of God:

> "Who has measured the waters in the hollow of his hand, or with the breadth of his hand marked off the heavens? Who has held the dust of the earth in a basket, or weighed the mountains on the scales and the hills in a balance? Surely the nations are like a drop in a bucket; they are regarded as dust on the scales; he weighs the islands as though they were fine dust." (Isaiah 40:12, 15)

Because of how vast our God is, nothing is too big for him. He holds the world and universe in the palm of his hand; therefore, no life is ever too far gone for our powerful, mighty God! If he can hold each star in his hand and call them each by name, (Psalm 147:4), he can take care of your sins and mine. He is more than capable!

Lastly, we know he is able to help the lost because, "Do you not know? Have you not heard? The Lord is the everlasting God, the Creator of the ends of the earth. He will not grow tired or weary, and his understanding no one can fathom. He gives strength to the weary and increases the power of the weak." (Isaiah 40:28-29)

When you are at your weakest moments or in your darkest hour, God comes along and gives you HIS strength and power. He is willing and able to help you in your time of need. You must be sensitive to this and again be used as God's tool to come alongside the broken and lend your strength that you've received from God as well. Join in with what God is doing and help people find hope amidst their desperate situation.

"...but those who hope in the Lord will renew their strength. They will soar on wings like eagles; they will run and not grow weary, they will walk and not be faint." (Isaiah 40:31)

Eagles are birds that we can learn much from. There is an interesting segment on eagles that I thought I would share.

"7 Leadership Principles To Learn From An Eagle" (1:38 mins):
https://www.facebook.com/CurejoyVideos/videos/654310691428875/

An eagle is a representation of freedom, strength and power. You can help others to fly like eagles by showing them they can trust God in their times of weakness.

It just makes sense to trust him and make him the center of your life, because of the strength he provides! Moreover, as you trust him, allow him to mold you and create a clean spirit in you and become a new creation in him.

Eventually, you will realize that only in him can you find true fulfillment and peace. You will see that God longs to show his love, grace and mercy to every person in darkness that will turn to him. And his grace is something you can't earn; he offers it freely to all.

Accept his gift of grace with joy, for you are his beloved daughter, and nothing can change that!

Being the daughter of a king, your beauty and worth come from him, so thank him for his gifts that he bestows on you.

Rest in his arms and know he loves you unconditionally for who you are, not for what you have or haven't done. Thank him today for his gift of love that knows no bounds!

And as you thank him for his love, remember that in order to raise others up, we must reflect HIS love to those around us who need it most. End with this song as you finish today's devotion....thank him that he is ALWAYS working in our lives, even when it doesn't seem like anything is happening from the outside, trust him above all else!

"Leeland - Way Maker (Official Live Video)" (8:23 mins): https://www.youtube.com/watch?v=iJCV_2H9xD0

This song is very special to our family. Justice, we love you and are thankful for the miracle that you are in our lives!

Victorious Verse

"The Lord is my light and my salvation; whom shall I fear? The Lord is the stronghold of my life, of whom should I be afraid?" Psalm 27:1

Mighty Melody

"Undo" by Rush of Fools and "The Only Thing That's Beautiful in Me" by Rush of Fools

Armour in Action

Think of a person that you've written off as a lost cause. Make an effort to pray for them this week and allow God's power to work in their life through you. Let the Holy Spirit guide you as to what you should be doing for this person. Maybe it goes farther than praying for them- maybe it is an encouraging phone call or meeting them for breakfast to bless them and pray for them in person. Be sensitive to what God is doing in their life!

Notes:

_____
_____
_____
_____
_____
_____
_____
_____
_____
_____
_____
_____
_____
_____
_____
_____
_____
_____
_____
_____
_____
_____
_____
_____
_____
_____
_____

Day *31* RAISE Others Up

REMEMBER WHEN YOU WERE ON FIRE?

"Therefore, since we are receiving a kingdom that cannot be shaken, let us be thankful, and so worship God, acceptably with reverence and awe, for our 'God is a consuming fire.' "

Hebrews 12:28-29

Like a fire that consumes and fully engulfs whatever material it is burning, God wants to consume the hearts of his daughters. He wants to set your heart ablaze so, in turn, you can pass the torch to others so their fire may burn brightly for others too. The only way to get on fire for God is to receive his power through his word, allow yourself to be encouraged by other believers, and spend one on one time with him really hearing and listening to his voice.

You must be aware that you are in a vicious battle for souls and satan wants nothing more than to "steal and kill and destroy", (John 10:10a), anything or anyone that gets in his way. So be prepared for battle at all times; using God's word as your sword, and faith as a shield, having the breastplate of righteousness firmly in place, the helmet of salvation on your head, the belt of truth around your waist, and "your feet fitted with the readiness that comes from the gospel of peace." (Ephesians 6:15)

Being armoured up and ready for battle is what keeps the flame alive and full of passion.

I received an email a few years back that really spoke to me. It went something like this, "Be the kind of woman that as soon as your feet hit the floor in the morning, the devil says 'Oh crap, she's up!'"

You should be a force to be reckoned with when it comes to the kingdom of God. You truly are an ambassador for Christ, which means you represent him in this foreign world.

On Day 23, we spoke of being ambassadors for Christ, and I shared a thought-provoking video, that I believe bears repeating. God IS preparing you as we speak!

"God is Preparing You to Work for Him! // Ambassadors of Christ" (29:49 mins): https://www.youtube.com/watch?v=nOaS_JFCqAE

"We are therefore Christ's ambassadors, as though God were making his appeal through us." (2nd Corinthians 5:20a)

This world is just your temporary home, one day Jesus will reunite you with him and other loved ones. That is your hope! There is so much pain, sorrow, and despair in this world, that if you put your hope here, you will be dreadfully disappointed. There are times when I wonder what this world is coming to, but then I realize that won't help anything. We need to be telling people about the hope in Jesus, so as many can come to know him as possible!

The following poem that I wrote got out some of my frustrations and grief in regards to the hopelessness of the world, after yet another mass shooting. Through writing it though, it also made me come to realize the hope we have in Christ that is victorious in ALL situations:

I'M NOT ASHAMED OF THE GOSPEL

"God help us," is all I can utter, in this troubled time.
Why do sad events keep happening? There is no reason or rhyme.

Why does the world shun you, yet in their time of need,
They're quick to speak of prayer and peace, while resting quietly in their greed?

Why does a world so full of hate reject a Saviour who came...
only to show love, kindness, and mercy, and heal the sick and lame?

Why do our schools reject you, with so much pain behind every wall?
Why do they take prayer and crosses out of their empty halls?

Why does the world say "Rest in Peace", when they do not know,
the Prince of Peace who is Jesus, because they're too busy to do so.

Why are our churches dwindling, while casinos and bars are full?
Church is just a crutch they say...what a bunch of bull!

Organized religion is a farce, they say behind their sneer,
Yet they do not know you came to earth to have relationship with them here.

You long to sit and talk with them, to hear about their day,
Yet they go about their busy lives, they don't take time to pray.

And as this world falls and crumbles, bringing such doubt and fear,
they can't hear your loving whisper, they're life's too loud to hear.

But when their time in this world ends, and they meet God face to face,
only then will they realize that earth was just a temporary place.

Our lives on earth are fleeting, our next breath could be our last,
We live like we'll never die, yet the hourglass runs out so fast.

Please God, draw them to you, no matter what it takes,
Will it take 1000 tears to fall, or a million hearts to break?

Their hearts are broken right now, as our country mourns,
But weeks, or months, or years from now, their hearts will be far from torn.

They'll return to their ruts and distractions, and tell off all those Christians,
They'll say "We don't need your God in our world, he has no place or dominion."

So as Christians we need to rise up, stop apologizing for our faith,
Show Jesus to a dying world, Help save the human race!

Stand up for Christ, don't be ashamed, he's not ashamed of you!
Stop living for this world because it'll crucify you too!

For when we pray the Lord's prayer, and say "On earth as it is in heaven",
Do we really, truly mean it, or are we just going through the motions?

We know his kingdom will have dominion from sea to shining sea,
And every knee will bow and every tongue confess that Jesus Christ is King!

So if you're sitting on the fence, not sure if God is real,
Just look at the darkness around you, and that fear inside you feel?

That fear's as real as the light that shines through the holes in Christ's hands and feet,
As he hung on that cross bearing our sins, and CRUSHED the devil under his feet!

God has and will have his way with satan, and when all is said and done,
Don't you want to stand in victory, with Jesus, God's only son?

God wants to call you by your name one day, as you walk up to those pearly gates.
As he runs towards you and embraces you, you'll be home, sealing your fate.

But while on earth you must accept this man, Jesus, into your heart,
He longs to spend each day with you, now's a good day to start!

Just tell him that you love him, thank him for his sacrifice and grace,
Ask him to come into your life, and one day when you look upon his face-

His face will show his mercy, as his Father sits on his throne above,
He'll welcome you home with open arms, and immerse you in his love.

Many things in this world want to pull you away from God. Satan is the king of lies, and he will try to distract you.

Satan loves when people not only pull away from God, but they blatantly choose to serve other gods. There is a story of a satanist who became a Christian, which is hard to believe.

"Satanist Finds Peace After Lifetime of Fear" (5:50 mins):
https://www.youtube.com/watch?v=ZYfCgZWqQk4

God truly can work miracles in anyone's life! He has a passion for his people!

Like God's passion, people can have a "fire" or "passion" for many things in this life...just look at the person at a football game that is painted from head to toe in his team's favourite colors, dancing and cheering... passionate about the organization. He never misses a game, has season tickets, a diehard fan devoted to his team.

This same mentality can carry across to our faith. We must be on fire for our team- the kingdom of God! We must see each soul as a victory for our "team" and join with our father in heaven as he celebrates!

Finally, may we be inspired by the people this pastor is talking about! God, help us to see our faith as something so valuable and precious; we could set the world on fire for Jesus if we lived our faith like these people in China!

"Church in China source @Christian fellowship TV." (3:37 mins):
https://www.youtube.com/watch?v=3S8-rfM_fV4

Victorious Verse

"Consider what a great forest is set on fire by a small spark." James 3:5b

Mighty Melody

"On Fire" by Sanctus Real and "Sold Out" by Hawk Nelson

Armour in Action

If your fire or passion for God and his kingdom has died down to just a glowing ember, ask God to ignite you and pray that his consuming fire would come into your heart and allow you to see from his perspective.

Pray Hebrews 12:28-29 and allow God to make your fire burn brighter than ever before as you pray for the salvation of at least 3 people that God has placed in your life!

Actor Matthew McConaughey made a speech at the Oscars. Help it to light your fire!

Do you have someone (God) to look up to, something to look forward to, and a dream or a hero to chase?

"Matthew McConaughey winning Best Actor" (4:30mins):

https://www.youtube.com/watch?v=wD2cVhC-63I

Notes:

_____

_____

_____

_____

_____

_____

_____

_____

_____

_____

_____

_____

_____

_____

_____

_____

_____

_____

_____

_____

_____

_____

Day *32* RAISE Others Up

INSPIRE OTHERS TO GO DEEPER

"Deep calls to deep in the roar of your waterfalls; all your waves and breakers have swept over me."

Psalm 42:7

Psalm 42 is one that I remember very well. Sitting on the stairs in my house, I was crying out to God. I was struggling in my life; a broken relationship, a friend in addiction, longing for a husband to share my life with, and I felt spiritually dry.

The psalm starts with, "As the deer pants for streams of water, so my soul pants for you, O God. My soul thirsts for God, for the living God. When can I go and meet with God?" (Psalm 42:1-2)

Focussed on my problems, I lost sight of where I needed to put my hope. I wept as I continued to read, "My tears have been my food day and night." (Psalm 42:3a)

This psalm spoke directly to my broken heart....but as I dug deeper into his word; it began to give me the answers I needed.

"Why are you so downcast, O my soul? Why so disturbed within me? Put your hope in God, for I will yet praise him my Saviour and my God." (Psalm 42:5-6a)

Instead of hanging my head and despairing in my situation, I needed to pick myself up, put my hope back in Almighty God, and start to praise him for who he is and all that he had done in my life!

"Deep calls to deep in the roar of your waterfalls; all your waves and breakers have swept over me." (Psalm 42:7). Just as this verse reminded me, I needed a refreshing waterfall to sweep over me and feel that cold water shock my system, allowing the stagnant pools of self-pity to be washed away! Only then did I realize that I was wasting too much time looking at the past and future, and I lost sight of the present.

The following poem by Helen Mallicoat (1982)[1] really drives this idea home:

My Name is "I AM"

I was regretting the past
And fearing the future.
Suddenly my Lord was speaking:

"My name is I Am." He paused.
I waited. He continued,
When you live in the past
With its mistakes and regrets,
It is hard. I am not there,
My name is not I WAS".

When you live in the future
With its problems and fears,
It is hard. I am not there.
My name is not I WILL BE.

When you live in this moment,
It is not hard. I am here.
My name is I AM.

What a beautiful picture of who our God is; he is the God of here and now. What a wonderful reminder for us to live in the gift of the present, instead of the prison of the past, or the uncertainty or frailty of the future. So many times, we take our lives into our own hands!

The prophet Jeremiah put it like this, "My people have committed two sins: They have forsaken me, the spring of living water, and have dug their own cisterns, broken cisterns that cannot hold water." (Jeremiah 2:13)

The past and the future are like these broken cisterns Jeremiah speaks of that you pour water into. Unfortunately, you keep filling them in vain, as it constantly runs out. You worry about the future, and live in regret and longing of the past. These cisterns cannot hold any water!

The present is the only cistern that can hold the living water of Jesus Christ! When you exist in the present, you are fully alive and it gives you the courage and boldness to dive fully over your head into God's fresh-flowing living water! The song "Dive" reminds us that we need to go deeper with God in order to inspire others to do the same.

The lyrics are so powerful! He basically tells us to jump in with God not just ankle deep or knee deep, or even waist deep.....we need to go in over our head! We should be fully immersed in him!

Here is a link to the song itself entitled "Dive" by <u>Steven Curtis Chapman</u> (4:04 mins):
https://www.youtube.com/watch?v=2qTXLEpS1gg

This song inspires me to go deeper. Moreover, when I go deeper, others will follow because they will witness the joy and life God breathes into me!

Jesus was an excellent example of diving into the waters of life and encouraging others to do the same. In Luke chapter five, Simon Peter had been fishing all night and came in with nothing. Jesus saw his boat at the water's edge, and challenged Simon to put his nets down again.

He said, "'Put out into deep water, and let down the nets for a catch.'" To which Simon replied, "'Master, we've worked hard all night and haven't caught anything. But because you say so, I will let down the nets.'" (Luke 5:4b, 5)

Jesus asked Simon Peter to cast his nets out yet again; he obeyed, and blessings were beyond his imagination. I'm sure it increased his faith one hundred fold!

"When they had done so, they caught such a large number of fish that their nets began to break. So they signalled their partners in the other boat to come and help them, and they came and filled both boats so full that they began to sink." (Luke 5:6-7)

The story goes on to say how astonished Simon Peter was and he fell down at his master's feet. (Luke 5:8)

Jesus calmed him by saying these simple words, "Don't be afraid; from now on you will catch men." (Luke 5:10b)

This is a picture of your Christian life. Jesus asks you to cast your nets out into the deep water, after trying to do things on your own strength like Simon Peter, and you will begin to witness God's miracle power.

Only when you let go of your nets and give God control of them, allowing him to take you deeper, will you be able to inspire others and be the fisher of men and women God is calling you to be!

Victorious Verse

"'If anyone is thirsty, let him come to me and drink. Whoever believes in me, as the Scripture has said, streams of living water will flow from within him.'" John 7:37b-38

Mighty Melody

"Over My Head" by Brian Littrell and "Dive" by Steven Curtis Chapman

Armour in Action

Spiritually, are you wading in God's living waters only ankle deep? Is there a spiritual mentor in your life who inspires you?

Ask them to pray for you to dive in over your head and get fully immersed in his presence and love. If you have yet to find a mentor, pray for God to put one in your life so that you can be inspired, and therefore, inspire others to dive into deep waters and swim with Jesus- the best lifeguard there is!

Notes:

_____
_____
_____
_____
_____
_____
_____
_____
_____
_____
_____
_____
_____
_____
_____
_____
_____
_____
_____
_____
_____
_____
_____
_____

Day *33* Raise Others Up

WE ALL HAVE VALUE

"Give yourself fully to God. He will use you to accomplish great things on the condition that you believe much more in his love than in your own weakness."

Mother Teresa[1]

"Whatever you do, work at it with all your heart, as working for the Lord, not for men."

Colossians 3:23

The world may tell you that you are not enough; that you have no value unless you get recognition, approval, or accolades from people around you. God's kingdom is in direct opposition to this mentality. He tells you that you have value regardless of what you do. You have value not only because of who you are, but also because of WHOSE you are; his child. You don't have to earn his love; it's freely given. That is why when you give yourself fully to him, as Mother Teresa put it, 'he can use you to do great things.' When you aren't focused on all your inadequacies, fears and failures, you can keep your eyes on his love, which helps you become "great" in his eyes.

This concept of getting your eyes off yourself and placing them on "Eli" (or God) is the central theme in a book by Max Lucado called "You Are Special". You can go around worrying about what others think, and focus on the wrong things, or you can rest in his love and be content knowing that you are doing his will for your life. The back cover of Max's book sums it up like this:

> "The world tells kids, '"you are special if...If you have brains, the looks, the talent.' God tells them, 'you're special just because. No qualifications necessary.' Only one of those messages will find its place in their hearts. That's why every child you know needs to hear this one, reassuring truth: 'You are precious in his sight.'" (Lucado, 1997)[2]

The book very eloquently drives home the idea that no matter how the world sees or evaluates you, God sees and adores you just the way you are.

Although it is a children's book, it is a powerful message that many adults never learned or heard growing up, so they struggle with acceptance of themselves in the eyes of others. They constantly compare themselves to those around them and wonder why they lose their joy and their peace.

Only true joy and peace can come with knowing you have value because of God's love. You don't have to "do" anything to earn that love. It is a concept that is very difficult to grasp, even for many Christians.

Sometimes, you may feel broken, condemned, or not good enough; you feel like "how could God love a sinner like me?"

If we, as Christians, can feel this way knowing the truth, imagine how the lost feel!

The book of Jeremiah echoes the words of the Lord, "I have loved you with an everlasting love; I have drawn you with loving-kindness." (Jeremiah 31:3)

In other words, God tenderly cradles you in his arms and shows you his unending love for you even when you don't feel that you are worthy of it.

A story from Inspiration Peak from an unknown author of a twenty-dollar bill's value illustrates this concept of our value, no matter what the circumstance[3]:

"A prominent speaker started off his seminar by holding up a new $20 bill. In the room of 200 people, he asked, 'Who would like this money?'

Hands started going up. He said, 'I am going to give this $20 to one of you but first let me do this.' He proceeded to crumple it up.

He then asked, 'Who wants it now?' Still the hands were up in the air.

'Well', he replied, 'What if I do this?' In addition, he dropped it on the ground and started to grind it into the floor with his shoe. He picked it up, now all crumpled and dirty with ragged edges.

'Now who still wants it?' Still the hands went into the air.

'My friends,' said the speaker, 'you have all learned a very valuable lesson. No matter what I did to the money, you still wanted it because it did not decrease in value even though its appearance changed. It is still worth $20.'

'Many times in our lives,' he continued, 'we are dropped, crumpled, and ground into the dirt by the decisions we make and the circumstances that come our way. We feel as though we are worthless. Nevertheless, no matter what has happened or what will happen, you will never lose your value in God's eyes. Dirty or clean, crumpled or finely creased and torn, you are still priceless to Him.'"

"YOUR VALUE - Powerful Motivational Speech" (3:32 mins):
https://www.youtube.com/watch?v=yBrRpb8aLwk

Psalm 17:8 (ESV) confirms your value in Christ. It says that we are "the apple of his eye."

The disciple Luke also shows us how important we are in God's eyes. He actually leaves the 99 to come to our rescue. Here is the account in Luke 15:1-7:

> "Now the tax collectors and sinners were all gathering around to hear Jesus. But the Pharisees and the teachers of the law muttered, "This man welcomes sinners and eats with them."
>
> Then Jesus told them this parable: "Suppose one of you has a hundred sheep and loses one of them. Doesn't he leave the ninety-nine in the open country and go after the lost sheep until he finds it? And when he finds it, he joyfully puts it on his shoulders and goes home. Then he calls his friends and neighbours together and says, 'Rejoice with me; I have found my lost sheep.' I tell you that in the same way there will be more rejoicing in heaven over one sinner who repents than over ninety-nine righteous persons who do not need to repent."

Listen to this song and see how special you truly are!

"Reckless Love - [Lyric Video] Cory Asbury" (5:31 mins):
https://www.youtube.com/watch?v=7GGJ8cyYNzQ

Watch Pastor Steven Furtick drive this home that we truly are important in the kingdom of God!

"You Must Be Important | Savage Jesus | Pastor Steven Furtick" (48:11 mins):
https://www.youtube.com/watch?v=G038ky_RwKg

The devil is busy trying to distract you, and thwart God's plans because he knows your importance in the kingdom. Meanwhile, God is in you and you are stronger and more loved than you know.

This means you are beyond precious to God; he cherishes each one of us. You hold a special place in God's heart. My pastor used to say God has a wallet with your picture inside. Just like a proud parent who shows off pictures of their kids, God does the same!

Matthew reiterates this (6:26), when he says, "Look at the birds of the air; they do not sow or reap or store away in barns, and yet your heavenly Father feeds them. Are you not much more valuable than they?"

This scripture drives home the fact that because he values you, he will take care of you and all of your needs, all you have to do in return is trust him.

Again, this is the message we need to bring to the world! So many people do not understand their value. They don't understand how precious they are to God who loves them so much that he sent his only son to die for them. They feel worthless and hopeless and some even fall into deep depressions and never come out of them.

A few years ago, I substitute taught a lost, sad little boy. I remember walking into the room and seeing his "cubicle" at the back of the classroom. He had walls up all around him so he couldn't see the other students and be disruptive. He was one of those "bad" kids we all know of. When I found out his story, I realized that he not only had physical walls up around him, but he had big emotional and psychological walls up as well. He was just longing for love, affection, and attention. His parents were divorced; he rarely saw his mom, and she was into drugs and was a lost soul. His Dad was a good person, doing his best, but had to work long hours on minimum wage to raise his kids.

The little boy needed someone to show interest in him and say he was special. I remember teaching him to speak life over himself and over others. He responded so positively that every time I walked into school, his eyes would light up and he would run to me. I also remember making a point of giving him little gifts like erasers that said, "You're special" on them, and he would beam at knowing someone thought HE was precious and worth their time!

There are so many people like this little boy. Longing for someone to take the time to tell him or her, they are special and loved. I believe God places us in the lives of young and old alike to build them up.

Paul in first Corinthians relays this, "Knowledge puffs up, but love builds up." (1st Corinthians 8:1b)

It's the old adage that "they don't care how much you know until they know how much you care."

Here is a beautiful example of that very concept of unconditional love and care for another human being in Mac Anderson's "Things That Grab Your Heart and Won't Let Go" (2014)[4] :

Someone Who Cares

It was a busy morning, approximately 8:30 a.m., when an elderly gentleman in his eighties arrived to have stitches removed from his thumb. He said he was in a hurry since he had an appointment at 9:00 a.m.

I took his vital signs and had him take a seat, knowing it would be more than an hour before someone would be able to see him. I saw him looking at his watch and decided since I was not busy with another patient I would evaluate his wound.

On exam, it was well healed, so I talked to one of the doctors, got the needed supplies to remove his sutures, and redressed his wound. We began to talk and I asked him if he had a doctor's appointment since he was in such a hurry. The gentleman told me no, that he needed to go to the nursing home to eat breakfast with his wife.

I asked about her health. He told me she had been at the nursing home for a while and that she was a victim of Alzheimer's disease. As we talked and I finished dressing his wound, I asked if she would be worried if he was a bit late. He replied that she no longer knew who he was—that she had not recognized him in five years.

I was surprised and asked him, "And you still go every morning, even though she doesn't know who you are?" He smiled as he patted my hand and said, "She doesn't know me, but I still know who she is."

I had to hold back tears as he left. I had goose bumps on my arm and thought, "That is the kind of love I want in my life."

True love is neither physical nor romantic. True love is an acceptance of all that is, has been, will be, and will not be.

We all long to be unconditionally loved and cared for, to feel worthy of time and affection from someone else; to know we are valued as the treasure God created us to be. It is plain to see that we must build relationships with so many that are longing to hear this message about this unconditional love. It is the message of the gospel of Jesus Christ.

He came to have relationship with us because of his unfailing love for us. Moreover, in order to have relationship with us, he had to die a horrific death on a cross. Nevertheless, three days later, he rose again! He is alive and waiting for the lost to come and see that they have value and that their identity is in Christ. However, he must use us, as vessels to reach them...so be willing to share your hope in Jesus and inspire others to do the same!

I would like to end off this day's devotion with the story of a young woman we came across on the side of the road after church. Thank-you for the privilege, God, of being used as an instrument in your hand to show others their value!

Kristine- The ANOINTED one

She'd lost her shoes on the side of the road, after walking many miles.
Trudging along in plus 40 degree heat, her belongings at her feet, in a pile.

She was standing on the side of the highway, sweaty, and tired and scared.
She needed a miracle, so God sent her one; she couldn't believe someone cared.

My friend and I picked her up, on our way home from church that hot summer night,
She climbed in my vehicle, sat down, and cried, as she told me about her boyfriend and their fight.

How she had to scramble to pick up her belongings, strewn across a highway of four lanes.
How she'd been hurt and abused too many times, and how the men in her life wouldn't change.

She'd been treated like trash by so many; she had never known a father's love,
Her earthly father was her first taste of the fact that she'd never be good enough.

Her name was Kristine, and I told her that her name meant "anointed one",
She laughed and said, "You mean ANNOYING, not anointed"; she didn't know God, or Jesus, his son.

My friend and I joined hands with her and while we prayed we cried,
Because she didn't know that Jesus loved her so much, and for her, he gave up his life.

She told us she was waiting for her ride to find her, walking along the side of the road.
So we made sure she was safe in a hotel room, so she could lay down her heavy load.

I had the chance to pray with her once again when she settled into her room.
And I prayed that her friend would find her, and that she would get there soon.

And as I drove away that night, my heavy heart was torn.
So many lost and broken women for which, Jesus, God's son, was born.

He came to give hope to this hurting world, to pay for their sins with his blood.
But so many people choose death over life; they're stuck in the mire and the mud.

They were programmed from a young age by satan himself, who used people around them as bait.
And every time they were kicked and pushed to the ground, the devil would lay and wait.

His lies of them being worthless, that they'd never amount to anything,
Was engrained in their mind so many times, it became a sick song that they'd sing.

A song that reminded them daily of the pit that they'd never get out,
A song that told them they are trash and not wanted, that trust was not theirs, only doubt.

So they live life like there is no meaning, the chaos swallows their purpose and chance to succeed.
The devil comes to rob, kill, steal, and destroy; their lives, their hopes, and their dreams.

A text came a couple weeks later, from Kristine with a bruised, blackened eye.
She tells me of her harrowing night, how she got beaten up by a group of guys.

Lord, how do I save this woman? How can I make her realize?
That you love her so much you'd die for her, and to quit falling for satan's lies.

I can't save her, Lord, that is your job, help me to trust and obey,
Help me to love her where she's at, and help me, Lord, to learn how to pray

Help her to see herself, as the daughter of a mighty, merciful King.
Help me to call out her anointing, so she'd have a new song to sing.

A song that tells of your power, a song that speaks to your grace.
And I pray, Lord, that you'd catch every tear that falls, from both her bruised and beautiful face.

When she is downcast, lift her head and show her your light in the dark.
Bind satan and send your angels around her, hold her close to your soft, Father's heart.

Help her, Lord, to see herself through the eyes of a loving father.
That you will fight for her and protect her, and that she is your precious daughter.

May she see that her value is not reliant on other's opinions or her circumstance,
But truly see herself as the princess God is calling her to be, as he lovingly leads her in a new dance.

A dance like none she's ever known, where, of something, she feels like a valued part,
Where she knows she's loved beyond measure; with Jesus as the King of her heart.

There is a movie entitled *Priceless* (2016), that shows the very real and brutal world of human trafficking. It is a faith-based drama that drives the point home that every person has value. It is a difficult movie to watch, but it displays the heart Christ has for all the people hurt and abused by this horrendous industry.

Victorious Verse
"But we have this treasure in jars of clay to show that this all-surpassing power is from God and not from us." 2nd Corinthians 4:7

Mighty Melody
"King of My Heart" by <u>Bethel</u>, "Fierce" by <u>Jesus Culture</u>, and "You Are Loved" by <u>Stars Go Dim</u>

Armour in Action
Think of three people in your life that have instilled value or worth in you by making you feel special.
Maybe they show you by spending time with you and being an encouragement to you.
Write them a letter thanking them for making "you" a priority in their life.
Make sure to tell them that you are becoming the person God is calling you to be partly because of their influence. Tell them how much you appreciate them! Also, thank God for putting these "vessels" in your life!

Notes:

Day *34* RAISE Others Up

HE CARRIES OUR BURDENS ON HIS SHOULDERS

"For to us a child is born, to us a son is given, and the government will be on his shoulders. And he will be called Wonderful Counsellor, Mighty God, Everlasting Father, Prince of Peace."

Isaiah 9:6

This scripture from Isaiah illustrates how the "government" or "weight of the world" is on the shoulders of our Saviour. While we may have felt heaviness on us at times, we know Jesus truly did carry the weight of the world on his shoulders when he took on all our sins, and all the shame that came with that, as he died for each one of us on the cross.

Many times, we've heard the saying, "I feel as though I'm carrying the weight of the world on my shoulders."

This means a person is feeling weighed down with many burdens and is struggling to cope with their situation. However, this is usually the case when one takes on more than they can handle and then wonders why they are overwhelmed. Or, a tragedy has struck their lives and they are trying to recover from it or create a "new normal".

Christ came to help carry your burdens. "I lift up my eyes to the hills; where does my help come from? My help comes from the Lord, the Maker of heaven and earth. He will not let your foot slip, he who watches over you will not slumber; indeed, he who watches over Israel will neither slumber nor sleep." (Psalm 121:1-4)

Jesus, also in the book of Matthew 11:28, reassures us, "'Come to me, all you who are weary and burdened, and I will give you rest.'"

The Ragman story by American pastor, writer, and educator, Walter Wangerin, Jr. (2004)[1] is a beautiful depiction of our Saviour taking our burdens on his shoulders. I saw this play acted out before me when I was a young girl. It was very powerful and beautiful. It illustrates his compassion and willingness to carry our burdens:

The Rag Man's Story

I saw a strange sight. I stumbled upon a story most strange, like nothing my life, my street sense; my sly tongue had ever prepared me for. Hush, child. Hush, now, and I will tell it to you.

Even before the dawn one Friday morning I noticed a young man, handsome and strong, walking the alleys of our city. He was pulling an old cart filled with clothes both bright and new, and he was calling in a clear, tenor voice: "Rags!" Ah, the air was foul and the first light filthy to be crossed by such sweet music.

"Rags! New rags for old! I take your tired rags! Rags!"

"Now, this is a wonder," I thought to myself, for the man stood six-feet-four, and his arms were like tree limbs, hard and muscular, and his eyes flashed intelligence. Could he find no better job than this, to be a ragman in the inner city? I followed him. My curiosity drove me. And I wasn't disappointed.

Soon the Ragman saw a woman sitting on her back porch. She was sobbing into a handkerchief, sighing, and shedding a thousand tears. Her knees and elbows made a sad X. Her shoulders shook. Her heart was breaking. The Ragman stopped his cart. Quietly, he walked to the woman, stepping round tin cans, dead toys, and Pampers.

"Give me your rag," he said so gently, "and I'll give you another."

He slipped the handkerchief from her eyes. She looked up, and he laid across her palm a linen cloth so clean and new that it shined. She blinked from the gift to the giver.

Then, as he began to pull his cart again, the Ragman did a strange thing: he put her stained handkerchief to his own face; and then HE began to weep, to sob as grievously as she had done, his shoulders shaking. Yet she was left without a tear.

"This IS a wonder," I breathed to myself, and I followed the sobbing Ragman like a child who cannot turn away from mystery.

"Rags! Rags! New rags for old!"

In a little while, when the sky showed grey behind the rooftops and I could see the shredded curtains hanging out black windows, the Ragman came upon a girl whose head was wrapped in a bandage, whose eyes were empty. Blood soaked her bandage. A single line of blood ran down her cheek. Now the tall Ragman looked upon this child with pity, and he drew a lovely yellow bonnet from his cart.

"Give me your rag," he said, tracing his own line on her cheek, "and I'll give you mine."

The child could only gaze at him while he loosened the bandage, removed it, and tied it to his own head. The bonnet he set on hers. And I gasped at what I saw: for with the bandage went the wound! Against his brow it ran a darker, more substantial blood - his own!

"Rags! Rags! I take old rags!" cried the sobbing, bleeding, strong, intelligent Ragman.

The sun hurt both the sky, now, and my eyes; the Ragman seemed more and more to hurry.

"Are you going to work?" he asked a man who leaned against a telephone pole. The man shook his head.

The Ragman pressed him: "Do you have a job?"

"Are you crazy?" sneered the man. He pulled away from the pole, revealing the right sleeve of his jacket - flat, the cuff stuffed into the pocket. He had no arm.

"So," said the Ragman. "Give me your jacket, and I'll give you mine."

Such quiet authority in his voice!

The one-armed man took off his jacket. So did the Ragman - and I trembled at what I saw: for the Ragman's arm stayed in its sleeve, and when the other put it on he had two good arms, thick as tree limbs; but the Ragman had only one.

"Go to work," he said.

After that, he found a drunk, lying unconscious beneath an army blanket, an old man, hunched, wizened, and sick. He took that blanket and wrapped it round himself, but for the drunk he left new clothes.

Now I had to run to keep up with the Ragman. Though he was weeping uncontrollably, and bleeding freely at the forehead, pulling his cart with one arm, stumbling for drunkenness, falling repeatedly, exhausted, old, and sick, yet he went with terrible speed. On spider's legs, he skittered through the alleys of the city, this mile and the next, until he came to its limits, and then he rushed beyond.

I wept to see the change in this man. I hurt to see his sorrow. Yet I needed to see where he was going in such haste, perhaps to know what drove him so.

The little old Ragman - he came to a landfill. He came to the garbage pits. And then I wanted to help him in what he did, but I hung back, hiding. He climbed a hill. With tormented labour he cleared a little space on that hill. Then he sighed. He lay down. He pillowed his head on a handkerchief and a jacket. He covered his bones with an army blanket. And he died.

Oh, how I cried to witness that death! I slumped in a junked car, wailed, and mourned as one who has no hope - because I had come to love the Ragman. Every other face had faded in the wonder of this man, and I cherished him; but he died. I sobbed myself to sleep.

I did not know - how could I know? That I slept through Friday night and Saturday and its night, too.

Then, on Sunday morning, I woke by violence. Light - pure, hard, demanding light - slammed against my sour face, and I blinked, and I looked, and I saw the last and the first wonder of all.

There was the Ragman, folding the blanket most carefully, a scar on his forehead, but alive! And, besides that, healthy! There was no sign of sorrow, age, and all the rags that he had gathered shined for cleanliness.

Well, then I lowered my head and trembling for all that I had seen, I myself walked up to the Ragman. I told him my name with shame, for I was a sorry figure next to him. Then I took off all my clothes in that place, and I said to him with dear yearning in my voice: "Dress me."

He dressed me. My Lord, he put new rags on me, and I am a wonder beside him. The Ragman, the Ragman, the Christ!

What a poignant depiction of our compassionate saviour! His example is not one of judgement, but of mercy and grace and is a powerful reminder of how Christ takes your hardships upon himself. You also need to remember, though, not to take on the role as the "Ragman" and try to fix the universe yourself.

Here is the overall theme of the story acted out in a powerful drama.

"Ragman" (3:21 mins):
https://www.youtube.com/watch?v=Cx776JIO4oU

I remember a time that a friend was going through a deep addiction and I took that burden upon myself to save them from hurting themselves. I became emotionally, psychologically, and physically bankrupt. I had nothing left for myself. I truly felt that I had the weight of the world on my shoulders.

Then my pastor, Greg Fraser, had some wise words for me.

He said, "Suzanne, you can't save anyone, all you can do is point them to the Saviour and let him do the rest."

Those were wise words, as many of us get in the way of what God is trying to do in the lives of those around us. God puts us in each other's path to lighten the load, not take it on ourselves. Sometimes you may be able to pray to lighten someone's load...other times you may be able to give your time or resources to help with someone's burdens. You need to be sensitive to the Holy Spirit and listen to what he is saying about your involvement in all situations.

When all is said and done, the person that you are ministering to has to realize their need for God. Realizing that he is all they need, will bring them to the end of themselves; then he can begin to do the work in their heart that only HE can do! Here's an uplifting song that illustrates this need for God in our lives!

"TobyMac - I just need U." (3:56 mins):
https://www.youtube.com/watch?v=4wNpOeakhEM

Ultimately, God is the life "changer" and "shaper". Watch this drama by the "Skit Guys" entitled "God's Chisel" and you will have a revelation of his power when it comes to changing a life!

"Skit Guys - God's Chisel Remastered" (11:33 mins):
https://www.youtube.com/watch?v=3QCkBL2DfVg

He created each and every one of us to be his masterpiece...which means we are blessed with gifts so that you may be a blessing to others, but you can't take on the role of Christ! At times, we can be a blessing, but He is their help!

"So we say with confidence, 'The Lord is my helper; I will not be afraid. What can man do to me?'" (Hebrews 13:6)

Sometimes simply praying with a person shows God's love and that he cares. This can help to ease someone's load tremendously. Encourage them with his word; let them know that you care and their mighty God cares:

> "The Lord watches over you- the Lord is your shade at your right hand; the sun will not harm you by day, nor the moon by night. The Lord will keep you from all harm- he will watch over your life; the Lord will watch over your coming and going both now and forevermore." (Psalm 121:5-8)

Do your part, then get out of the way....he is a big God- let him do his job!

Victorious Verse

"Let the beloved of the Lord rest secure in him, for he shields him all day long, and the one the Lord loves rests between his shoulders." Deuteronomy 33:12

Mighty Melody

"Shoulders" by King and Country, "How Many Kings" by Downhere and "The Passion" by Hillsong Worship

Armour in Action

Think of a person who has a heavy load right now. Ask God to show you how you could help ease their burdens. Make a plan this week to help this person with their load. If you can, share your testimony with them as well, of how God has helped you with your burdens over your life. Maybe your testimony will cause them to ask Jesus into their heart! You never know what God will do if you are willing to step out in boldness!

Notes:

_____

_____

_____

_____

_____

_____

_____

_____

_____

_____

_____

_____

_____

_____

_____

_____

_____

_____

_____

_____

_____

_____

_____

_____

_____

_____

Day **35** RAISE Others Up

JESUS OUR HUMBLE KING

"When pride comes, then comes disgrace, but with humility comes wisdom."

Proverbs 11:2

The definition of pride is having a "high or inordinate opinion of one's own dignity, importance, merit, or superiority, whether as cherished in the mind or as displayed in bearing, conduct, etc."

Pride is all about self, and you cannot gain wisdom if the focus is on yourself all the time. You can only become wise when you become more like Christ, which means being humble and focused on God and others.

Many people view humility as seeing oneself as less than. Google defines humility as "a modest or low view of one's own importance".[1] This is partly true, but the focus is not on you at all.

I believe that humility is simply affirming the worth of those around you, while being secure of our own self-worth in Christ. Or as pastor and author Bill Johnson (2006) put it in one of his sermons:

> "The world tries to tell you that you need to focus on yourself and build your self-worth
> by getting recognition and accolades; only then will you be successful. Christ says the
> opposite. Focus on others and their worth, while resting securely in the King of Kings."

How do you find your self-worth in him, and rest knowing that he is the one who builds you up, and gives you your strength? Well, you listen to who HE says you are and you speak his promises over your life. Here is a list of identity scriptures that will remind you daily of your self-worth in him.

Place your name where the blanks are and pray these scriptures over yourself as a reminder of who you are and where you get your self-worth:

_____ is a child of God. (John 1:12)

The Holy Spirit lives in _____. (1Cor. 3:16)

_____ is tenderly loved by God. (Jeremiah 31:3)

_____ is the sweet fragrance of Christ to God. (2 Cor. 2:15)

_____ is a branch on Christ's vine and Christ's friend. (John 15:1,5)

_____ is a member of Christ's body. (1 Cor. 12:27)

_____ has Christ's righteousness. (Rom. 5:19, 2 Cor. 5:21)

_____ is a temple in which God dwells. (1 Cor. 3:16)

_____ is the salt of the earth and the light of the world. (Matthew 5:13,14)

_____ is not condemned by God, and is reconciled to God. (Romans 8:1, Romans 5:11)

_____ is Christ's ambassador. (2 Cor. 5:20)

_____ is completely forgiven. (Col. 1:14)

_____ is helped by God. (Hebrews 4:16)

_____ is united to the Lord, one spirit with him. (1 Cor. 6:17)

_____ has peace with God. (Rom. 5:1)

_____ is a joint heir with Christ, sharing his inheritance with him. (Romans 8:17)

_____ may approach God with boldness, freedom, and confidence. (Eph. 3:12)

_____ is chosen by God, holy and dearly loved. (Col. 3:12)

_____ is a member of a chosen race, a royal priesthood, a holy nation, a person for God's own possession and created to sing his praises. (1 Peter 2:9-10)

_____ is firmly rooted and built up in Christ. (Col. 2:7)

_____ is one of God's living stones, being built up in Christ as a spiritual house. (1 Peter 2:5)

_____ is born of God, and the evil one cannot touch her. (1 John 5:18)

_____ has been given a spirit of power, love, and a sound mind. (2 Timothy 1:7)

_____ cannot be separated from the love of God. (Romans 8:35)

_____ should have confidence that the good work that God began in her will be completed. (Philippians 1:6)

_____ is God's workmanship. (Eph. 2:10)

_____ can do all things through Christ who strengthens her. (Philippians 4:13)

These promises illustrate that you are loved and accepted and can rest knowing your worth is in your humble Saviour who gave his life for you.

He, in fact, is the very definition of "humble", as he willingly died for you, placing your sin upon himself:

"Your attitude should be the same as that of Christ Jesus: Who, being in very nature God, did not consider equality with God something to be grasped, but made himself nothing, taking the very nature of a servant, being made in human likeness. And being found in appearance as a man, he humbled himself and became obedient to death- even death on a cross!" (Philippians 2:5-8)

I love that these verses not only remind us of his humility, but it tells us that he "took on the nature" of a servant. Here is the king of kings showing us what it is like to serve others! Wow, this is truly and utterly humbling. He even served his own disciples when he got down on his hands and knees and washed their feet.

Again, here was the master showing his followers true humility and love. ".....so he got up from the meal, took off his outer clothing, and wrapped a towel around his waist. After that, he poured water into a basin and began to wash his disciples' feet, drying them with the towel that was wrapped around him." (John 13:4-5)

His disciples were learning an important lesson that day, as Jesus said to them:

> "'Now that I, your Lord and Teacher, have washed your feet, you also should wash one another's feet. I have set you an example that you should do as I have done for you. I tell you the truth, no servant is greater than his master, nor is a messenger greater than the one who sent him.' " (John 13:14-16)

He was saying, go and be an example and light to the world, serve, and humble yourself around others. Your life is an open book for the whole world to read...make sure the story is compelling and reflecting the one who gives you your worth!

Once you begin to grasp this concept of your self-worth in him, and start living humbly, as he did, you can celebrate this with others and inspire them to find this same Christ-like humility. In turn, they will see that humility is all about lifting others up, and as they continue to do this, they'll see that Christ will lift them up as well.

Their self-worth will be defined by Christ, and will come from being transformed from the inside out. True identity should reflect what God has invested in you, and flow out as the confidence in Christ. They will have confidence in themselves because of his love and mercy, not because of what they have done or accomplished.

Sometimes though, a person you meet may not have confidence because of all the mistakes they have made. They put their eyes on themselves and tell themselves they are no good, and are worthless.

Many of Jesus' very own disciples probably felt this way. For example, Matthew, a tax collector, hung out with prostitutes and other tax collectors! Jesus saw promise and potential in him and called him to be a disciple of his. Jesus showed him his worth and then he lived up to what Jesus called him to do!

Matthew was a part of Jesus' inner circle and got to sit and glean wisdom at the feet of Christ, while becoming more and more like him every day! What a beautiful picture of what he does for us! While we live in our sin, he picks us to be more than we ever thought possible, and he continues to teach and guide us as we transform into his likeness! What an awesome God we serve!

Continue to be like our example Jesus, figuratively "washing the feet" of those around you and inspiring them to do the same. Your humility in your actions will speak much louder than any words you could ever say.

Ask God to give you wisdom regarding whom you need to serve and be an example to. Sometimes it may surprise you who God will put in your path to serve! It may take multiple times of laying down your pride and humbling yourself in order to serve another, but practice will not make you perfect. Instead, it will make you more and more into the image of Christ!

Victorious Verse

"Humble yourselves, therefore, under God's mighty hand, that he may lift you up in due time." 1st Peter 5:6

Mighty Melody

"Humble King" by Brenton Brown and "Amazing Love, You are my King" by Newsboys

Armour in Action

If you were reading the pages of your life, what would it say about humility? Would God see that you are truly humble in your life, or is it something you need to work on?

Ask him to make you humble so you can truly serve others out of a heart of gratitude for what he has done for you. Also, read the scriptures listed previously that show you where your identity lies. Ask him to show you your worth in him, as it will help you see that humility is a joy and a privilege! Is there someone God has put in your path to serve today? Be sensitive to his leading and ask the Holy Spirit for guidance in "washing the feet" of someone in your life.

Notes:

ERECTING THE 5 PILLARS AND PUTTING THE PALACE TOGETHER

" 'For I know the plans I have for you,' declares the Lord, 'plans to prosper you and not to harm you, plans to give you hope and a future. Then you will call upon me and come and pray to me, and I will listen to you. You will seek me and find me when you seek me will all your heart.' "

Jeremiah 29:11-13

In the words of famous motivational speaker Tony Robbins,

"....Life is constantly testing us for our level of commitment and life's greatest rewards are reserved for those who demonstrate a never-ending commitment to ACT until they achieve. This level of resolve can move mountains, but it must be constant and consistent. As simplistic as this may sound, taking action is still the common denominator separating those who live their dreams from those who live in regret."[1]

Being a true warrior involves ACTION. If you aren't diligent in your faith and in your walk, you will not advance against the enemy in the battle of life. The helmet of salvation, breastplate of righteousness, and belt of truth are stationary pieces of armour; but your shield of faith, sword of the spirit, and your feet fitted with the gospel of peace are the pieces that need to be active in battle.

Therefore, faith, God's word, and spreading God's hope and peace to a lost world are dynamic and alive! Use these assets to your advantage as you ACT and walk in and towards your purpose!

Look back at Day One in the "Armour in Action" section, and rewrite your strengths here. Remember the gifts God placed in you and walk boldly with God in your calling!

My strengths:

_____

_____

_____

_____

_____

God will help you to use your strengths wisely, as you answer HIS call on your life! In the words of American writer, preacher, and theologian Frederick Buechner, (1993),[2] "The place where God calls you to is the place where your deep gladness (desire), and the world's deep hunger meet."

Here are a couple of sermons by Craig Groeschel that will rev up your spirit to start taking action as a warrior for the kingdom!

"When It's Time to Throw a Punch – Warrior" (37:53 mins):
https://www.youtube.com/watch?v=NIFDmLC3NUo

"Killing Your Inner Coward – Warrior" (38:06 mins):
https://www.youtube.com/watch?v=9FpZTMf-3c4

Finally, warrior princess, reach for your purpose by conquering your fears! For when fear is overcome, your true beauty will be unveiled, causing you to unite with others that are on the same mission! With God, you are unstoppable!!

Uniting IN Purpose

I had a dream, then a vision from the Lord, of women gathering together for Christ.
Beauty was all around me, as we spoke of his light and his life.

There was such beauty on stage as we all worshipped our God and mighty King,
The performers shone like precious jewels, with every song that they would sing.

The women sung and played with authority, yet also with humility and with grace.
Their outer beauty was simply stunning, as they were clothed in fine linen and lace.

The beauty that was before me caused my human mind to wander.
My focus came off of Christ, and my insecurities I began to ponder.

But the Holy Spirt spoke to me, as myself to others, I dared to compare.
"While man looks at the outward appearance, God sees the heart", both precious and rare.

Hearts that are fully devoted to him, showing love to our sisters and brothers.
Hearts full of compassion for both friends and enemies; while loving and supporting one another.

While the world believes the lies that say-Marilyn Munroe is beauty with her "mole" strategically placed,
Beauty is hair styled and colored perfectly, or the makeup we apply to our face.

While we need to look and feel our best to be solid ambassadors for Christ,
This is not where we should place our identity, for these outward things will soon fade in this life.

Proverbs 31 says that beauty in and of itself is fleeting on its own accord,
But a woman who stands in awe of Jesus will be praised, because she is reverent and fears the Lord!

It's ok to wear your favorite perfume, just don't identify in the "brand name"
Your identity should be in that you are the daughter of a King, who has the NAME above ALL NAMES!

'Cause your "earthly" perfume may smell sweet for an hour or so, before you need to reapply,
But your "spiritual" perfume allows you to be HIS aroma to this hurting world, while being the apple of his eye.

So as we follow the desires God has placed in us, may his love draw us ever so near,
Because God IS love, and his love is perfect, and it's strong enough to cast out ALL fear!

Jesus conquered fear and death when, for our sins, he paid the ultimate cost.
So devil go back where you came from, because your lies are no match for the cross!

So when all you see are your scars and flaws, and you're feeling worthless and "less than",
Remember how Christ sees you as his precious daughter, and put your trust in the great "I AM"!

Stomp out those feelings of unworthiness; that spirit of fear can be bound.
For you have the power and love of God inside you, and the mind of Christ that is sound.

So go out and continue to make a difference, on your own devices, you need not rely.
Just allow God to give you HIS strength, for all your needs, he will surely supply.

For we are his masterpiece, made in his image, the crown of all creation!
We all have a message given to us by Christ, the HOPE of ALL the nations!

The message you have for this world will be broadcast through your purpose, the passion God's placed in your heart.
So as we overcome fear, encourage, and build one another up, we'll play our role and do our part!

'Cause fear is a liar from the pit of hell, so we can't give it the time of day.
And as we walk in unity towards our purpose, NOTHING can stand in our way!

Author and speaker, Bob Goff, would eloquently sum it up like this:

"We won't be distracted by comparison if we are captivated with purpose."[3]

In other words, when you are so focused on who you are and the plans God has for you, comparison will no longer be a factor in your life. You will then see others as your biggest supporters, not competitors, and you will be unstoppable in your pursuit of purpose!

We truly are encouraging and cheering each other on in this awesome adventure we call life. What a privilege it is to be surrounded by others on the same mission!

End today by watching this video. We aren't in competition with others; we all just want to point the world to Jesus! Be blessed daughter of the almighty God!

"Casting Crowns - Nobody (Official Music Video) ft. Matthew West" (3:52 mins):
https://www.youtube.com/watch?v=1yBzIt_z8oY

Day **36** REACH for Your Purpose

"WHO I AM" INSTEAD OF "WHO AM I?"

"God said to Moses, 'I AM WHO I AM. This is what you are to say to the Israelites: I AM has sent me to you.' "

Exodus 3:14

Once, I asked a little 2-year-old girl, "What's your name?" She simply replied, "Princess". What a beautiful example of what we all should think! She didn't have the world asking her - "Who are you, to be a princess?" Instead, she truly believed it regardless of the world around her.

I think we all start out with a child-like faith that we can do or be anything! Unfortunately, as we grow up, we begin to listen to the voices of the world and question ourselves.

We say, "Who am I to be _____?" (talented, a princess, beautiful, worthy of love, etc.)

The inspiring story of Christopher Maloney from Britain's X-Factor TV show is an example of the world causing a person to question himself.

His first audition is quite moving:

"Christopher Maloney's audition - Bette Midler's The Rose - The X Factor UK 2012" (9:01 mins): https://www.youtube.com/watch?v=k1T9-l3wx8l -

The cynicism of the world questions who God created you to be.

Instead, ask yourself, "Who am I NOT, to be all things God has called me to be?"

By realizing your fears and speaking victory over them because of your identity as a daughter of the King of Kings, you will be able to make use of the light and power God has placed in you.

Listen to this woman speak to the "light" you shed on the world! She is so passionate!

"How To Let Your Light Shine Bright | Lisa Nichols | Goalcast" (3:48 mins): https://www.youtube.com/watch?v=CWpiCOmbVuY

When you shine your light to the world, knowing that God is the source, your life can truly cause others to live in freedom and liberation as well! Memorize the following passage from Day 13 and get it in your heart!

LIGHT

Our deepest fear is not that we are inadequate. Our deepest fear is that we are powerful beyond measure. It is our light, not our darkness that most frightens us. We ask ourselves, who am I to be brilliant, gorgeous, talented, and fabulous? Actually, who are you *not* to be? You are a child of God. Your playing small does not serve the world. There is nothing enlightened about shrinking so that other people will not feel insecure around you. We are all meant to shine, as children do. We were born to make manifest the glory of God that is within us. It is not just in some of us; it is in everyone and as we let our own light shine, we unconsciously give others permission to do the same. As we are liberated from our own fear, our presence automatically liberates others.

Marianne Williamson (*A Return to Love*, 1992)

Many people doubt their calling and allow their fear to override what God has placed in them.

Moses doubted his calling when God was asking him to lead the Israelites out of Egypt. He said, "Who am I, that I should go to Pharaoh and bring the Israelites out of Egypt?" And God said, "'I will be with you.'" (Exodus 3:11-12a) In other words, when you fail to have confidence in what you can do, God comes alongside, and helps you to do what you cannot.

Alvin Law's story is an excellent example of God helping us do what we cannot. He is the God of the impossible. As Alvin so eloquently puts it, "I AM WHO I AM."

"You're Not Your Label | Alvin Law | Goalcast" (7:33 mins): https://www.youtube.com/watch?v=fp5ju7_2uDM

God also refers to himself as "I AM" in the third chapter of Exodus, which shows by example that you need to see yourself like this, because you are formed in his image.

Moses said to God, "Suppose I go to the Israelites and say to them, 'The God of your fathers has sent me to you,' and they ask me, 'What is his name?' Then what shall I tell them?"

God said to Moses, "**I AM WHO I AM**. This is what you are to say to the Israelites: '**I AM** has sent me to you.'" (Exodus 3:13-14)

God knew who Moses was, and he gave him the power to overcome. When he says "**I AM**" this means that "**HE WILL**" deliver you, prosper you, heal you and protect you. He is whatever you need, whenever you need it! The Great **I AM** will use his power to show his glory in and through your life!

Therefore, instead of starting a sentence with "Who am I?" begin your sentences with "I am..."and allow God to show his power in and through you!

Steven Furtick drives this point home when he preaches about the great I AM.

"Don't Miss Your Purpose | Pastor Steven Furtick" (19:06 mins):
https://www.youtube.com/watch?v=zJDJ7Jvrn0I

God is so good! When we are talking ourselves out of things, God is reminding us of our strengths!

This is illustrated in Exodus chapter 4, shown again is Moses focussing on his weaknesses and fears, "'O Lord, I have never been eloquent, neither in the past nor since you have spoken to your servant. I am slow of speech and tongue.' " (Exodus 4:10)

Moreover, God answers, " 'Who gave man his mouth? Who makes him deaf or mute? Who gives him sight or makes him blind? Is it not I, the Lord? Now go; I will help you speak and will teach you what to say.' " (Exodus 4:11-12)

Once again, God is showing us to trust him; he will help you do what you don't have faith in yourself to do.

Finally, in Exodus 17, we see another illustration of God's power and might, "So Joshua fought the Amalekites as Moses had ordered, and Moses, Aaron, and Hur went to the top of the hill. As long as Moses held up his hands, the Israelites were winning, but whenever he lowered his hands, the Amalekites were winning." (Exodus 17:10-11)

As long as Moses' hands were up, the Israelites were winning and God did indeed give them victory in this battle. In their own strength, it wouldn't have been enough for them to win. This is an excellent analogy for our own lives! As long as we raise our hands and lift our praises to God, he can show his mighty power through us. However, when we lower our hands and take our eyes off God, doing things in our own strength, we will lose the battle.

Your purpose relies on you surrendering your life to God and allowing him to walk alongside you as he did with Moses.

The book of Exodus is a great reminder that God uses his power to rescue people that are helpless or in bondage. Like the Israelites, so many people are in bondage. It is part of your purpose to use your testimony to reach those that are lost and helpless, whereby overcoming satan and thwarting his wicked plans.

They will see hope through your story, and thus God will continue to use you as you remain in your purpose and on the path he has laid out for you. With his love and support, you can fully become who you are called to be!

We know that God loves us exactly as we are. Then, he watches us transform into the greatest, truest version of ourselves because of his unconditional, unfailing, unwavering love. When we feel loved for who we ARE, without any conditions attached, we are instantly empowered.

When empowered, you reach for the things God has placed in your heart, and you can find success and significance in your life.

The following chart really helps you see the difference[1]:

Successful People	**Unsuccessful People**
1-Read every day	1-Watch TV everyday
2-Compliment	2-Criticize
3-Embrace change	3-Fear change
4-Forgive others	4-Hold a grudge
5-Talk about ideas	5-Talk about people
6-Continuously learn	6-Think they know it all
7-Accept responsibility for failures	7-Blame others for failures
8-Have a sense of gratitude	8-Have a sense of entitlement
9-Set goals and develop life plans-know what they want and know their purpose	9-Never set goals- no direction in life
10-Value their time	10-Procrastinate
11-Know things take time and hard work	11-Want instant gratification, depend on luck
12-Are positive and optimistic	12-Are negative and pessimistic
13-Use fear as a motivator	13-Use fear as an obstacle or excuse

At the end of the day, let your success be defined by how you live for the kingdom of God. By overcoming obstacles, incorporating healthy habits, and allowing God to transform you from the inside out, you are well on your way!

Mentioned earlier in the book, if you haven't already watched it, the movie *Overcomer* (2019), is about a runner (Hannah Scott) who pushes herself to the limit. Watch it if you want to be challenged to overcome!

Victorious Verse
"They overcame him by the blood of the Lamb, and by the word of their testimony." Revelation 12:11

Mighty Melody
"Remind Me Who I Am" by <u>Jason Gray</u>, "Who Am I?" by <u>Casting Crowns</u>, and "Overcome" by <u>Jeremy Camp</u>

Armour in Action
As stated earlier, write out and memorize the quote titled "LIGHT" listed earlier in this day's devotion. Ask God to show you your worth in him. Thank him for walking with you and giving you the strength to carry out your purpose and be a successful, contributing member of the kingdom of God.

Notes:

_____

Day *37* REACH for Your Purpose

TO WHOM DO I BELONG?

"Long before he laid down earth's foundations, he had us in mind, had settled on us as the focus of his love, to be made whole and holy by his love. Long, long ago he decided to adopt us into his family through Jesus Christ."

Ephesians 1:5 (The Message)

God has adopted YOU as his child. Let that sink in. YOU are his daughter, which makes you a daughter of a king - Not just any king, the KING of KINGS! You are royalty, therefore walk boldly in your position!

When I am exercising in the morning, as I walk, I say to myself, "Shoulders back, walk confidently, you are an AMBASSADOR for Christ." It reminds me of WHO I am. The daughter of a MIGHTY king!

"On his robe and on his thigh he has this name written: King of kings, and Lord of lords." (Revelation 19:16)

You can have confidence in knowing "whose" child you are, and because of this confidence, you can truly know who you are according to God's standards, not the world's.

There is a song titled "Who I Am". Listen to it and be reminded who you are. Especially when the world wants to tell you otherwise!

"Blanca Who I Am with lyrics 2015" (3:11mins):
https://www.youtube.com/watch?v=mNXHEGCSg90

What powerful lyrics of truth! Because you know "whose" you are, you know "who" you are. This is quite a revelation for many women! No longer should you find your value in what others say, or the number on a scale, but instead, find your value in a Saviour who loved you so much he died for you. You are his child and he is jealous for your affection.

"For the LORD your God is a consuming fire, a jealous God." (Deuteronomy 4:24)

When the world tries to tell us we don't measure up, we know that "we are fearfully and wonderfully made" (Psalm 139:14) and we are "his masterpiece" (Ephesians 2:10, NLT).

Watch the following video about Les Brown. A depiction of a young man who was told a lie, but God put someone in his life that told him otherwise!

"Why it Pays to Be Hungry | Les Brown | Goalcast" (6:35mins):
https://www.youtube.com/watch?v=xFr0FKnaLDk

Les reminds you of the fact that greatness is within you and the responsibility is yours to manifest that greatness. You are "blessed and highly favoured" to reach your goals, and that's exactly how God created you. In fact, he created you specifically for his purposes even before you came to earth.

"Before I formed you in the womb I knew you, before you were born I set you apart." (Jeremiah 1:5)

Isn't that amazing that he knew you before you were even born? Moreover, he "set you apart", meaning he consecrated you or made you "sacred and holy". Anyone who is sacred or holy is special. That is EACH one of us! He bought us with his blood and paid for our sins on the cross.

"You were bought at a price...." (1st Corinthians 6:20a)

David eloquently writes in Psalm 139 that he thinks the world of us. He thinks about us ALL the time and there is no way we can run from him....he is all around us. He truly cares for each and every one of us, knows us better than we know ourselves, and he formed us all in the "secret place" while placing special gifts in us all.

Psalm 139:1-18 (TPT)

"Lord, you know everything there is to know about me.
You perceive every movement of my heart and soul,
and you understand my every thought before it even enters my mind.
You are so intimately aware of me, Lord.
You read my heart like an open book
and you know all the words I'm about to speak
before I even start a sentence!
You know every step I will take before my journey even begins.
You've gone into my future to prepare the way,
and in kindness you follow behind me
to spare me from the harm of my past.
With your hand of love upon my life,
you impart a blessing to me.

This is just too wonderful, deep, and incomprehensible!
Your understanding of me brings me wonder and strength.
Where could I go from your Spirit?
Where could I run and hide from your face?
If I go up to heaven, you're there!
If I go down to the realm of the dead, you're there too!
If I fly with wings into the shining dawn, you're there!
If I fly into the radiant sunset, you're there waiting!
Wherever I go, your hand will guide me;
your strength will empower me.
It's impossible to disappear from you
or to ask the darkness to hide me,
for your presence is everywhere, bringing light into my night.
There is no such thing as darkness with you.
The night, to you, is as bright as the day;
there's no difference between the two.
You formed my innermost being, shaping my delicate inside
and my intricate outside,
and wove them all together in my mother's womb.
I thank you, God, for making me so mysteriously complex!
Everything you do is marvellously breathtaking.
It simply amazes me to think about it!
How thoroughly you know me, Lord!
You even formed every bone in my body
when you created me in the secret place,
carefully, skillfully shaping me from nothing to something.
You saw who you created me to be before I became me!
Before I'd ever seen the light of day,
the number of days you planned for me
were already recorded in your book.
Every single moment you are thinking of me!
How precious and wonderful to consider
that you cherish me constantly in your every thought!
O God, your desires toward me are more
than the grains of sand on every shore!
When I awake each morning, you're still with me."

How comforting to know you have a God that knows how wonderful you are because he made you with a specific design in mind!

I heard a sermon where a pastor described us as "peculiar". At first, I didn't know what to think about being referred to as "peculiar"; I thought it meant weird or strange. But when he defined the word, it made me realize how God sees me. This is how he defined it:

Something "peculiar" is a **treasure** that is designed exclusively for the owner; something that transcends the average- special or one-of-a-kind; personally selected and elected by the owner.

Revelation 4:11 (KJV) says it like this: "Thou art worthy, O Lord, to receive glory and honour and power: for thou hast created all things, and for thy **pleasure** they are and were created."

To know that you are created for his **pleasure**, and that you are his valuable **treasure** should reassure you of your worth today! He carefully shaped and designed you specifically for his purposes and pleasure!

You are indeed blessed to have a Father in heaven that is a master potter carefully forming the clay. He sees the treasure inside your jar of clay and calls you to be a precious, antique, collectible vase displaying beautiful flowers for all to see!

Victorious Verse

"But we have this treasure in jars of clay to show that this all-surpassing power is from God and not from us." 2nd Corinthians 4:7

Mighty Melody

"Who I Am" by Blanca and "You're Worth More Than Gold" by Britt Nicole

Armour in Action

Read Psalm 139:1-18 over yourself every day for at least one week. Allow God to minister to your spirit and tell you how amazing and precious you really are! Let it sink in....he thinks you hung the moon!

Notes:

_____
_____
_____
_____
_____
_____
_____
_____
_____
_____
_____
_____
_____
_____
_____
_____
_____
_____
_____
_____
_____
_____
_____
_____
_____
_____
_____
_____
_____
_____

Day *38* REACH for Your Purpose

"WHO" OR "WHAT" IS LEADING YOU TO YOUR "WHY"?

"Because those who are led by the Spirit of God are sons (and daughters) of God."
Romans 8:14

There are so many things now-a-days vying for your attention. Friends, school, jobs, future spouses and children, or people pleasing in general can lead to distraction. Money and possessions can lead you too... all to a dead-end road.

Proverbs 4:11-12 says, "I guide you in the way of wisdom and lead you along straight paths. When you walk, your steps will not be hampered; when you run, you will not stumble."

Therefore, being led by God, and not by emotion, means that you will gain wisdom, you will be sure-footed in the process, and be blessed accordingly!

Be assured that you are, and will continue to be, blessed if the spirit leads you. Because with wisdom, comes blessing. However, how do you get there? How do you know the Spirit of God is leading you?

Psalm 128:1-2, "Blessed are all who fear the LORD, who walk in obedience to him. You will eat the fruit of your labour; blessings and prosperity will be yours."

Based on this Psalm, it really is plain and simple. Fear God and obey him, and you will be blessed! This "fear" of God is not a fear of intimidation or anything scary, as the world would define fear, but instead, godly fear is one of knowing just how powerful he really is and being in awe and wonder of his presence. The deep-rooted reverence for God and his laws is what governs your life. As you walk with him daily, this fear and awe of God never gets old.

"Because of the Lord's great love we are not consumed, for his compassions never fail. They are new every morning; great is your faithfulness." This scripture goes on to say, "'The Lord is my portion; therefore I will wait for him.' The Lord is good to those whose hope is in him, to the one who seeks him." (Lamentations 3:22b-25)

You can see that seeking him will lead to his goodness being poured out on you. The more you seek him, the more awe and wonder you have of the God of all creation, which is true "fear" of God!

Isaiah said "He will be the sure foundation for your times, a rich store of salvation and wisdom and knowledge; the fear of the LORD is the key to this treasure." (Isaiah 33:6)

This prophet also knew that fearing God was the key to blessings like wisdom, understanding, and knowledge.

In order to gain wisdom though, you need to learn the difference between the three. A great teacher of mine, Pastor Greg Fraser, taught on these very definitions, and this is what I want to pass on to you:

Knowledge- information or facts that one knows i.e. I know God loves me.

Understanding- knowing how to properly apply that knowledge i.e. Hearing that God loves me is important for my well-being and identity, and avoiding the opposite thoughts is important.

Wisdom- when we apply understood information i.e. Because of his love, I can speak his promises over my life.

Finally, you will come to a point where wisdom can be applied, and this is where true growth in your Christian walk can occur!

Application of this wisdom would look like this:

God loves me, therefore my identity is in his love. Because of his love and the power gained from speaking his promises over myself, I can have victory in all areas of my life. Therefore, if I rest in the knowledge of his love, my identity is secure, and His purposes and plans for me will be achieved.

God loves to see his children walk in the plans he has for them, because it leads them into abundance and blessings beyond what they could ever hope for or imagine!

As if blessings and prosperity weren't enough, the fear of God leads you to fall deeper and deeper in love with him, which allows you to have a much deeper father-daughter relationship. Army general and 34th President of the United States, William D. Eisenhower, put it like this,

"Fear of the Lord is the beginning of wisdom, but love from the Lord is its completion."[1]

This quote truly embodies the idea of correlation between fear of the Lord, wisdom, and God's love! When you have a healthy fear of God, you gain his wisdom, and therefore can rest in his love and stop trying to do things in your own strength.

God spoke this truth to the prophet Zechariah when he said, "'Not by might nor by power, but by my Spirit.'" (Zechariah 4:6b)

God was reinforcing this idea that you can only accomplish the things of God and walk in your purpose by his Spirit. That means when you are led by his Spirit, it's almost impossible to do things in your own strength because his power overrides yours. His word doesn't say you can do all things in your own strength, it says you can do everything "through Christ". He, and only he, can give you the strength to carry out all that he has for you, and the beginning of this is walking with him and being led by his Spirit.

When his Spirit leads you, you are not letting your emotions take control of your decisions and actions; therefore, your spirit is in tune with his. You are letting your heart be one with Christ and this is key to a being a mature Christian.

For example, this helps us as women to have godly boundaries in areas like relationships. When we guard our hearts and let God lead us, he then protects our hearts, and we not ruled by how we feel. God's Spirit will never lead us astray, we can be sure of that! Whether it is relationships at school, work, or with your future spouse, God's Spirit always leads you to bear beautiful, tasty fruit in each and every season!

"But the fruit of the Spirit is love, joy, peace, patience, kindness, goodness, faithfulness, gentleness and self-control." (Galatians 5:22-23a)

In our lives, we must be adamant about living by his Spirit. This is the only way we will fulfill our purpose here on earth.

"So I say, live by the Spirit, and you will not gratify the desires of the sinful nature. For the sinful nature desires what is contrary to the Spirit, and the Spirit what is contrary to the sinful nature." (Galatians 5:16-17a)

I remember a time when there was a young Mom murdered in our small town and instead of being defeated, my husband and I decided to make a small difference. We bought Christmas gifts for the kids and prayed for the family, because it would be their first Christmas without their Mom. Forgotten by many, a few months after the tragedy, we made a small difference.

This was one instance where we were spirit-led, and in turn, an act of kindness led to God's love being poured out on a hurting family. It brought glory to God instead of the spotlight being on the evil of the crime in the first place. Kindness always trumps evil!

Paul in the book of Romans (2:4b), says it like this, "God's kindness leads you toward repentance."

In other words, our relationships and the love and kindness we display in them will draw others to God. We don't need to bible thump them to death! As I stated before, our lives may be the only bible some people ever read, or you can preach louder with your life than with your lips!

Kindness won in the following circumstance as well. Bullied at school, a young man named Josh, decided to change things around, by simply showing kindness to his fellow students. After going through a particularly hard time when he lost his Dad to a brain tumour, he decided there was no time like the present to change his situation. Therefore, he began to hold the door open at school for people every day. This simple act of kindness made students appreciate his sincerity, and the bullying that he had endured started to decrease and eventually stopped! By using the fruit of kindness against the hurtful things he'd endured, he began to make a small difference, which turned into something bigger than he could ever imagine.

"Josh - opening doors and hearts | WestJet Above and Beyond Stories" (6:04mins):
https://www.youtube.com/watch?v=PIHtuKc3Gjg

This is the purpose of all Christians. By becoming more like Christ in our journey, we can make a small difference in this world, which at the end of the day, is something much bigger than we are, and gives God all the glory!

The previous two stories are examples of people stepping up and realizing that there is always a solution or an unseen benefit to every situation.

The only way we can be "solution-based" is to focus on why we are doing what we are doing.

There is always a "who" and a "what" to a situation, but if you can understand the "why", you will be able to continue walking towards your purpose as each circumstance prepares you for the next step.

In the words of Michael Jr., "Your 'what' is defined by your 'why' because when you know your 'why', your 'what' has more impact, because you're walking in or towards your purpose."

Before you end today's journey, watch this sermon by Michael Jr.:

"Know Your Why | Michael Jr." (3:49 mins):
https://www.youtube.com/watch?v=1ytFB8TrkTo

"WHEN YOU KNOW YOUR WHY, YOUR WHAT HAS MORE IMPACT, BECAUSE YOU ARE WALKING IN OR TOWARDS YOUR PURPOSE."

Now watch this video to remind you of your "why" as well! Your why will determine your destiny, but it will take a lot of hard work to get there!

"Rise and Grind - Greatest Motivational Video ᴴᴰ ft. Eric Thomas" (2:42 mins):
https://www.youtube.com/watch?v=_jHeqfZO69o&list=RD8QlvQC4MXxs

Victorious Verse
"Since we live by the Spirit, let us keep in step with the Spirit." Galatians 5:25

Mighty Melody
"Majesty (Here I Am)" by <u>Delirious</u> and "Hungry" by <u>Kathryn Scott</u>

Armour in Action
Like Josh, think of a way you can make a small difference in the world you live in. Maybe it is starting something small at your school or work place. Maybe it is showing kindness to your spouse or friend during a troubled time. Let the Spirit of God lead you in what you will do. When you are spirit-led, you will see God's hand move as your fear of the Lord leads to you loving him deeper, and letting the world see his love through you!

Notes:

_____
_____
_____
_____
_____
_____
_____
_____
_____
_____
_____
_____
_____
_____
_____
_____
_____
_____
_____
_____
_____
_____
_____
_____
_____
_____

Day *39* REACH for Your Purpose

TRUE WARRIORS ARE CALLED TO LEAD

"Your gifts are not about you, leadership is not about you, your purpose is not about you. A life of significance is about serving those who need your gifts, your leadership, and your purpose."

Kevin Hall- *Aspire* (2009)[1]

If you have been through some tough times in your life, take heart! God can use those difficult moments for his glory, and can help you lead others to victory!

"Good leaders came from people who have penetrated their own inner darkness and arrived at the place where we are at one with one another, people who can lead the rest of us to a place of 'hidden wholeness' because they have been there and know the way."

Parker J. Palmer- *Let Your Life Speak* (2000, pg. 80-81)[2]

I have a saying on my living room wall 'Only God can turn a mess into a message.'

With God walking beside you, you are more than a conqueror. You can overcome, and then help others be overcomers.

And inspirational author Palmer goes on to say, (2000, pg. 76), that "the power for authentic leadership is found in the heart."

In other words, people matter! You can't be a successful leader without truly caring about people. Most leaders want to be well known and make the biggest impact they can by reaching as many people as they can, which sometimes means foregoing relationship for popularity and being in the public eye. Yet, if we look at Jesus' example, his goal was to build relationships and leave a lasting legacy. He did not want to be popular, and actually discouraged publicity. In a piece of writing by Michael Hyatt called "The Leadership Strategy of Jesus" (2010), he confirms this[3]:

"On more than one occasion, after performing a jaw-dropping miracle, he told those who witnessed it, 'Tell no one what you have seen' (see e.g., Matthew 8:4; 16:20; 17:9; Mark 7:36; 8:30; 9:9; Luke 5:14; and 8:56)....instead of focusing on what the world says leaders should focus on, Jesus was focused on true depth and long-term impact."

Hyatt goes on to say that Jesus led himself well (which many leaders have trouble doing). He trained disciples that could carry on his work after he was gone, and he got on a very deep level with a handful of trusted people to guarantee an impact that would outlive him. Impact and getting deep with people is so important. The only way to get deep with people is to get into a relationship with them, which will in turn, cause them to carry on your legacy and continue carrying out your mission long after you are gone.

All of these things are valuable to learn as you come to realize the leadership qualities in yourself. While you study your own strengths and weaknesses when it comes to leadership, remember where your power and identity lie.

"A good leader has the knowledge that identity does not depend on the role we play or the power it gives us over others. It depends only on the simple fact that we are children of God, valued in and for ourselves.....a leader grounded in this knowledge....can be life-giving for all concerned."

Palmer, (2000, pg. 87)

This was a revelation to me about leadership. As a teacher, many times I would put my identity in my job itself, and pleasing people along the way. I think that is why I struggled so much with my identity when I left teaching, stayed home, and began to raise my own children. I had to ask myself some daunting questions about who I was.

Instead of carrying that 'identity crisis' into being a mother, I needed to see that my identity was in who God said I was, and realize that he gave me value and worth because I was HIS daughter. My identity did not come from my performance or how many people I pleased, but in WHO God created and called me to be. Identity in Christ is definitely a journey, but in order to be an inspiring leader, you must rest in your role in the kingdom of God.

We all want to leave our mark on this world. But if we truly want to lead others like Christ and transform the world, we must allow ourselves to be transformed from the inside out. As strong leaders, we must find opportunities for growth and capitalize on them. We must go through times of dying to ourselves, so that new life may spring up in and through us!

We must also take times of dormancy and rest and see them as essential to our growth both as a leader and as a follower of Christ.

Psalm 23:1-3 (RSV) reminds us of the rest that only God can provide:
"The Lord is my shepherd, I shall not want;
he makes me lie down in green pastures.
He leads me beside still waters;
he restores my soul.
He leads me in paths of righteousness
for his name's sake."

I don't think it is coincidence that this passage uses the word 'lead' twice within two verses. God is intentionally reminding you, in order to be an effective leader, and guide people with impact; you must rest, and be restored. These times bring about clarity and vision that we probably wouldn't get if we were distracted and busy trying to DO! In these times of rest, we are waiting on God. We are walking in obedience and continuing to have our confidence in Him.

In conclusion then, you are called to lead in different capacities during certain seasons of your life. Leading like Christ is definitely a challenge in the midst of many of these seasons. Something to help you in the midst of these times, is this acronym of the word LEAD. I pray that it will help you focus on what is important in God's eyes as you lead others to victory:

L **Listens and is a Life-long Learner**- truly listens to others while empowering themselves with knowledge

E **Example**- is a mentor or a good example of knowing when to rest

A **Authentic**- truly cares and is committed to deep lasting relationships with others

D **Dies to self**-knows his/her identity is in Christ, not in his/her position or power, embodies humility- which is strength in submission to God

As you meditate on this acronym, pray that God will help you lead well. Many times, it will involve humbling yourself and dying to your own selfish desires in order to fulfill his purposes and plans in your role as a leader.

When it comes to the last letter "D", remember Christ's sacrifice as he laid down his life for so many. His death on the cross allows us to model ourselves after his life and "die to self" as we live for him.

Before ending your journey today, watch the videos entitled "DESIRE" and "Don't Give Up". These videos drive home the idea again of the "why", or the "motive" behind what you are doing when you are walking towards your purpose.

"DESIRE- Motivational Video" (6:03mins):
https://www.youtube.com/watch?v=CMm6tDavSXg

"Don't Give Up // Christian Motivation - Troy Black" (6:19 mins):
https://www.youtube.com/watch?v=msmry_6V2gw

Remember that anything of value and meaning will not be easy, and that is how it should be! The road for Jesus was far from easy, and with him as our example, we need to submit to God's will and purse our purpose!

After watching these two videos, watch the actor Denzel Washington give a commencement speech where he outlines how to chase after your purpose. Some main points he makes are to put God first, fail big, set disciplined goals, don't put your hope in material things, be thankful, true desire is from God and aspire to make a difference!

"Put God First- Denzel Washington Motivational & Inspiring Commencement Speech" (8:36mins): https://www.youtube.com/watch?v=BxY_eJLBflk

Finally, I want to encourage you to follow the TRUE leader as you walk in purpose! Once again, I want to quote Stasi Eldredge in her phenomenal book *Captivating* (2005, pg. 217-218). Her message is so genuine in relaying what God's heart is for his daughters. Read it and be encouraged to step out and LEAD with confidence, humility, and grace because of his example of what a Christ-like LEADer should be!

> "You are a woman. An image bearer of God. The Crown of Creation. You were chosen before time and space, and you are wholly and dearly loved. You are sought after, pursued, romanced, the passionate desire of your Fiancé, Jesus. You are dangerous in your beauty and your life-giving power. You are needed.....the King is captivated by your beauty....we (the world) needs you. We need you to awaken to the desires of the heart that he placed within you so that you will come alive to him and to the role that is yours to play....
>
> Whatever your particular calling, you are meant to grace the world with your dance, to follow the LEAD of Jesus wherever he LEADS you. He will LEAD you first into the world that he loves and needs you to love. It is by *invitation*.

> [This *invitation* was illustrated in the movie "Anna and the King" (1999)]:

> When the feast is over and it comes time for the first dance, the king stands and extends his hand to Anna. He *invites* her to dance with him. He fixes his gaze upon her and is distracted by nothing and no one else. He waits for her response. She is clearly surprised, taken aback, but has the grace to respond and stand. As they walk past the long table, the king's eyes never stray from hers, a smile playing on his lips. Others are upset that he has chosen her. Some watch with contempt, others with pleasure. It is of no consequence to the king or to Anna.

> Anna came to the ball prepared. She was beautiful in a striking gown that shimmered like starlight. She spent hours getting herself ready- her hair, her dress, her heart. As they reach the dance floor, Anna expresses her fear of dancing with the King before

the eyes of others. 'We wouldn't want to end up in a heap,' she says. His answer to her questioning heart? 'I am King. I will LEAD.'

Jesus is extending his hand to you. He is inviting you to dance with him. He asks, 'May I have this dance...everyday of your life?' His gaze is fixed on you. He is captivated by your beauty. He is smiling. He cares nothing of the opinion of others. He is standing. He will LEAD. He, [and the world], waits for your response."

Victorious Verse
"And David shepherded them with integrity of heart; with skilful hands he led them." Psalm 78:72

Mighty Melody
"Lead Me to the Cross" by Hillsong and "Lead the Way" by Leeland

Armour in Action
Memorize this acronym for LEAD, or come up with your own. Memorize it so that it will be with you as you lead others in abundance and victory!

Another acronym I came up with is:

Listens and **L**ifelong **L**earner
Encourages
Acts (takes action)
Disciples and has discipline

Notes:

_____
_____
_____
_____
_____
_____
_____
_____
_____
_____
_____
_____
_____
_____
_____
_____
_____
_____
_____
_____
_____
_____
_____
_____
_____
_____

Day *40* REACH for Your Purpose

MAKING IT REAL & INTEGRATING IT INTO YOUR LIFE

Today we are going to build your Personal Mission Statement using a wonderful tool that I found online: http://msb.franklincovey.com/

Here is an example of my Personal Mission Statement that I built a few years ago:

I am at my best when:
   -I have structure and when I am proactive.

I will enjoy my work:
   -by finding employment where I can relate to kids and teens and speak life into them.

I will find enjoyment in my personal life through:
   -having balanced physical and spiritual time, and spending meaningful time with my spouse and children.

I will find opportunities:
   -to use my natural talents and gifts such as being an athlete, a good listener, a writer, a drummer, serving others, and working with youth.

I can do ANYTHING I set my mind to, through Christ who gives me strength. I aim to:
   -preach the gospel at all times, and use words when necessary- also let the youth know there is a purpose and plan for their lives.

My life's journey is to:
>
> -spread the gospel in any way, shape, or form by living like Christ did. I am doing it for the sake of my children and the lost- especially lost youth. My journey results in people living their lives on PURPOSE, following Christ's example, and inspiring others to do the same.

I am a person who is:
>
> -loved by God, the forgotten, my husband, biological and church family.

The tribute statement I would like them to make about my life would be:
>
> -"She lived her life on purpose and helped others to find theirs."

I will start working on:
>
> -becoming more organized and structured
>
> -being more assertive in certain situations instead of letting things slide and not having peace about it
>
> -being proactive instead of reactive

I will strive to incorporate the following attributes in my life:
>
> -unconditional love and acceptance
>
> -standing up for what is right, even when I'm standing alone
>
> -being humble and being a hard worker

I will renew myself and reflect on a regular basis:
>
> -physically- eat healthy, exercise with purpose, treating my body like a temple
>
> -spiritually- meet with God daily, have spiritual mentors
>
> -mentally- keep learning, growing, and discovering; be a life-long learner
>
> -emotionally- let emotions out, communicate effectively

Before starting your journey, please watch these videos:

"What's Your Purpose? Greatest Motivation ft. Les Brown & Eric Thomas" (8:38mins):
https://www.youtube.com/watch?v=8QlvQC4MXxs

"VISION - Motivational Video" (11:03 mins):
https://www.youtube.com/watch?v=ZOy0YgUDwDg

Step 1:

Get onto the website http://msb.franklincovey.com/ and click on the button "Personal". You can go back to this site at any point if you want to build a mission statement for your family or team that you are a part of.

Once you click on "Personal", follow the prompts and it will allow you to create your "Personal Mission Statement", which will help you define your purpose and help to guide your steps. Pray before and while you are writing this. Ask God's Spirit to direct your steps. You want his will to be done, not yours.

Step 2:
Once you have finished, print your "Personal <u>Mission</u> Statement" off, and keep a copy. Read it over a few times and begin to get it in your heart while listening to the song "Overcomer" by <u>Mandisa</u>! Get pumped for what God is going to do in you and through you!

Underneath your Personal Mission Statement, summarize your "WHAT" and your "WHY" in 2 simple headings. This will help you to stay focussed. Again, your "what" would be your gifts and talents that God has placed within you to make your "why" happen. And your "why" keeps you going.... it's what gets you out of bed in the morning...it is your PASSION! Also, reprint your strengths from the "notes" section in Day 1 and put them underneath your "what" and your "why".

For example, under my Personal Mission Statement, it reads:

> <u>MY WHAT</u>: Teaching, Writing, Drumming
>
> <u>MY WHY</u>: To disciple youth and inspire them to walk in purpose.
>
> <u>MY STRENGTHS</u>: I am a teacher, and an encourager, I am an excellent listener, I desire for others around me to succeed and reach their potential. The "StrengthsFinder" test tells me my strengths are that I'm a learner, I am consistent, I am unwavering in my beliefs, I am responsible, and I thrive on seeing people develop into all God is calling them to be.

To reiterate what Michael Jr. said in Day 38, **"When you know WHY you're doing what you're doing, your WHAT will have more impact, because you will be walking in or towards your purpose!"**

Step 3:
Write out your Personal Mission Statement, and put it in the front of your journal. Then, write your WHAT, WHY and STRENGTHS and put it in 3 places that you will see daily. Maybe in the front of a day timer or binder you use, maybe in a locker, maybe on your bathroom mirror or fridge. You need it to be somewhere where you will read it every day.

Steve Harvey illustrates the power of writing down your goals and vision. Very powerful!

"Write Your Vision | Motivated +" (8:44 mins):
https://www.youtube.com/watch?v=DIMAIYd7-J4

When you have your purpose or your "why" staring you in the face on a daily basis, it will cause you to walk with intensity towards your destiny. Fears will try to hinder you and tell you that you can't, but you need to use those fears to catapult you to the next level.

Famous speaker and author Tony Robbins states "Use fear as your ultimate motivator. Successful people don't let fear suck the life out of their dreams, they know that that the real fear is the price they'll pay if they don't give their goals their ultimate focus and energy, and end up compromising on what they really wanted."[1]

Step 4:
Ask God to lead you in ways that you can carry this out and begin to live your deepest desires, not just dream about it! THIS IS YOUR TIME TO SHINE, NOT TOMORROW, BUT TODAY!

"Life is found in the dance between your deepest desire and your greatest fear."[2] Tony Robbins

Listen to the song "Fearless" by Jasmine Murray and let God speak to your fears. They have no power OVER you as long as you have Christ's strength working IN you!

Listen also to "No Longer a Slave to Fear" by Zach Williams. Remind yourself of your identity in Christ as his precious daughter!

Step 5:
Think of someone who you look up to spiritually; someone who will be honest with you and help you to achieve your dreams. Pray about a spiritual mentor who can walk with you.

Tell them about your Personal Mission Statement and ask him or her to keep you accountable with staying on track and walking towards your God-given dreams and desires. Make sure your mentor or friend will follow through and support you. You are now well on your way to living your life on purpose!

Coming full circle, we come back to the scripture we started with on Day 1.

Like Queen Esther, we are called to do things on this earth that no one else can do in the season they were meant to be done.

"And who knows but that you have come to your royal position for such a time as this?"

Esther 4:14

Step 6:
Re-evaluate where you are in one month, six months, and one year from now. Make sure you write it on a calendar and set goals for where you want to be. If you have gone off course, re-calibrate and get back to what you were called to do! Time is of the essence!

Also, as a VIP, share your journey with others! Let them know about your growth and allow them to experience the joy of finding their mission and purpose in life!

In closing, RISE UP in your royal position mighty Warrior Princess and have the courage, strength, and determination to walk out what the "King of Kings" is calling you to do. Be fierce and fearless!

There is no one else on this earth that has what it takes to fulfill your specific plan. Be bold...take the first step and allow God to lead you on an adventure that you only dreamed possible!

YOU HAVE FOUGHT THE GOOD FIGHT, WARRIOR PRINCESS, AND HAVE FULFILLED THE FIRST THREE PARTS OF YOUR MISSION:

KNOW GOD

FIND FREEDOM

DISCOVER PURPOSE

NOW......GO OUT AND

MAKE AN IMPACT BY

MAKING A DIFFERENCE!!!

It isn't how LONG we live, but HOW we live that will determine the IMPACT we'll have on this world!! Watch and be amazed!

"The Most Inspiring Speech: The Wisdom of a Third Grade Dropout Will Change Your Life | Rick Rigsby" (10:21mins):
https://www.youtube.com/watch?v=Bg_Q7KYWG1g

GIRLS WITH DREAMS AND VISIONS BECOME WOMEN WITH PURPOSE.

REDEEM the Time

MAKE THE MOST OF EVERY OPPORTUNITY

"Redeeming the time, because the days are evil. Wherefore be ye not unwise, but understanding what the will of the Lord is."

Ephesians 5:16-17 (KJV)

The NIV version of this verse in Ephesians tells us in verse 16 to "make the most of every opportunity." Know that you are breaking new ground as you move forward in your purpose and calling.

The devil will want to thwart the plans God has for you. There will be pain, trials, fear....all kinds of ways to take you off task and distract you from what God's will is for your life.

The devil wants you to believe you are in a prison. That the things holding you back are too big to overcome, so you feel paralyzed. Watch the following video and feel free to rise above your challenges!

"BEFORE YOU OVERTHINK, WATCH THIS" (4:12 mins):
https://www.youtube.com/watch?v=_ICREZm9CtE

All of the "obstacles" in our lives should serve as "opportunities" to advance the kingdom. We shouldn't ask ourselves "Why is this happening to me?" but instead "God, what are you doing IN me as I walk through this?" or "How will this be used to further your kingdom?"

Know that when you are walking through trials, the Saviour of the world walks beside you. You are in a spiritual battle, and you have the King of Kings on your side!

Listen to "Surrounded (Fight My Battles)" by Michael W. Smith and "Raise a Hallelujah" by Bethel.

In the midst of your struggles as you fight to keep your eyes on Jesus, know that God is surrounding and protecting you. Praise HIM and worship HIM in the presence of the enemy, and beauty will rise from the ashes every time!

Those who make the biggest **IMPACT** in their earthly lives are not afraid to meet life "head on" and make a move when most people would stand by and watch.

Theodore Roosevelt put it like this in his speech "Citizenship in a Republic" speech (1910)[1]:

> "It is not the critic who counts; not the man who points out how the strong man stumbles, or where the doer of deeds could have done them better. The credit belongs to the man who is actually in the arena, whose face is marred by dust and sweat and blood; who strives valiantly; who errs, who comes short again and again, because there is no effort without error and shortcoming; but who does actually strive to do the deeds; who knows great enthusiasms, the great devotions; who spends himself in a worthy cause; who at the best knows in the end the triumph of high achievement, and who at the worst, if he fails, at least fails while daring greatly, so that his place shall never be with those cold and timid souls who neither know victory nor defeat."

Here is the video version to pump you up!

"The Man in the Arena - Boxing in 2010s" (2:19 mins):
https://www.youtube.com/watch?v=kd0SzDdZuoE

Watch Kyle Carpenter as he makes a life and death decision in the blink of an eye. He chooses to literally make an impact, and sacrifice himself for his comrade. What an unbelievable example of the love of Christ in action!

"A hand grenade suddenly lands between two American marines –Corporal Kyle Carpenter then" (3:41mins):
https://www.youtube.com/watch?v=L4z4gEel_3w

The sacrificial love of Jesus is something we find difficult to comprehend. Watch this reminder of our King laying down his life for us; so powerful and humbling!

"ABOVE ALL" (5:05 mins):
https://www.youtube.com/watch?v=RNKdnuw-eeE

This video moves me to tears to see that Christ put us above everything. He knew that he had to die to fulfill the scriptures. He had to die to advance the kingdom. Only in death, would he be able to live eternally in our hearts!

Like Christ, through his death, there is a young man by the name of Jesse Rotholz that also made an impact in the kingdom of God. He was a missionary on a YWAM team that contracted malaria and hepatitis in Uganda, and eventually succumbed to the illness in February of 2019.

In following his story, many people have been inspired by his zest for life and for the kingdom of God. He MOVED and unashamedly shared his faith with all the people he encountered. Even though he only lived a short time on earth, he made more of an **IMPACT** than many ever will.

Like Jesse, you can only make an **IMPACT** when you are advancing, or MOVING! Don't allow yourself to be stagnant or be paralyzed by your circumstances! Even in his hospital bed, Jesse was advancing the kingdom! He didn't let his situation, even in the face of death, hold him back! "Jesse" literally means "gift", and he truly was to this world!

Here is a video of him on the mission field:

"Deedee Jaurequi" (5:50 mins):
https://www.facebook.com/deedee.rafferty/videos/2350914904932672/UzpfSTgwMjAwMDE1NzoxMDE2MTYxMzc4NjQ0MDE1OA/

Thank you Jesse for the "gift" of your life and the legacy you have left through your undying commitment to your faith. Your favourite saying of "Today is the BEST day EVER!" reminds me that every day is indeed a "gift", and to live each day to the fullest as we make an **IMPACT** on this hurting world.

Watch the following video on making an **IMPACT**. Be encouraged that you already are making an **IMPACT**, and will continue to, in Jesus' mighty name!

"Make An Impact - Inspirational Video" (2:34 mins)
https://www.youtube.com/watch?v=pb7_YJp9bVA

Once you begin walking in your calling, you will cause others to do the same! Read this prophecy by Ebigale Wilson to ignite your passion all the more! You are a torch bearer! You are an overcomer, and will cause others to be overcomers! Be steadfast, warrior princess. This world is depending on you!

SURRENDER COMPLETELY

Many assignments from the pit of hell were sent to cage My daughters.
The enemy worked overtime to keep My daughters in bondage, only because he knows the yoke breaking assignments on their lives.
But to his dismay these daughters arose and broke free from the different cages they were in.

I saw thousands upon thousands of cages in what looked like a huge, dark warehouse.
Daughters sitting like they were in a trance in small cages, with despair written over their faces, while satan walked among these cages with a big smirk on his face.

Then without warning, daughters started opening cages and stepping out.
These daughters came to their senses and ran to cages to free daughters that are too scared to step out.
The enemy is furious, fuming, screaming, but no one is taking note of him.
They're all running in one direction, helping each other through a huge door where Light is pouring through and Love is calling them into a new season.

The Father is saying, some of My daughters are already free in their hearts and minds.
They surrendered to My processes, fought many personal battles and went through immense pain and training to become My vessels of honour.

281

It is time for My anointing to break the yokes placed on the downtrodden and hurting daughters. You will be My containers of love, healing, breakthrough and deliverance as you step out and take the wounded by the hand and transfer that which you have learned on your journeys to them.

Then there are the ones I saw in the vision, who are awakening to their identity in Me and breaking free from satan's identity over them.

They know that it is time for change, time to forgive and to step into a new season of healing, restoration, deep joy and My dreams for them.
I see these women completely broken, hurt beyond words, rejected to the core come before Papa, with tears streaming down their faces.
He starts to sing their new identity over them and as they drink in every word, claim it for them, they are transformed into His beautiful bride.

For I will do a quick work in my daughters when they surrender completely, so that they too will step out and bring other hurting daughters into My light.

Ebigale Wilson, <u>The Journey Heart Revelations</u> (2018, pg.118)[2]

Newsflash! Your purpose and your gifts have nothing to do with you. Instead, they are all about drawing others into the kingdom of God, and bringing God the glory! As Peter put it:

> "Each one should use whatever gift he has received to serve others, faithfully administering God's grace in its various forms. If anyone speaks, he/she should do it as one speaking the very words of God. If anyone serves, he/she should do it with the strength God provides, so that **in all things God may be praised through Jesus Christ. To HIM be the glory and power for ever and ever.**" (1 Peter 4:10-11)

When you realize this key concept of "your" gifts being about others, and God's glory, a true leader is born!

As Neale Walsh describes a leader in the introduction of his book, "Friendship With God" (1999)[3], you can see that when the focus comes off you, that is when we will truly make a difference!

> "God, it seems, is not looking for followers so much as leaders. We can follow God, or we can lead others to God. The first course will change us, the second course will change the world."

Finish your time with God today by being reminded of how your purpose is not about you. On day 9, we talked about success and significance and watched the following clip. Success and significance are two very different things; what is going to define your life?

"LIVE A LIFE OF FULFILLMENT - Live For Jesus | Tim Tebow - Motivational & Inspirational Speech" (4:43 mins):
https://www.youtube.com/watch?v=orj8KaD5JZo

REAFFIRM Your Calling

MAKE A DIFFERENCE

Conclusion- Three Important Questions

When carrying out your personal mission statement, ask yourself the following three questions to constantly evaluate where you are:

1. What does God desire from me? **When we are connected to his heart, our hands will know what to do!**

   "Whatever you do, work at it with all your heart, as working for the Lord, not for human masters." (Colossians 3:23)

2. What am I saying about Jesus? **How are you living your life? Are you a reflection of Christ?**

   "And we, who with unveiled faces all reflect the Lord's glory, are being transformed into his likeness with ever-increasing glory, which comes from the Lord, who is the Spirit." (2nd Corinthians 3:18)

3. Why am I holding back? **A lot of people are counting on you to take a stand, and make a difference! Mary, the mother of Jesus, said YES to God when she was told she would conceive a child by Immaculate Conception. Because she said yes, she shared Jesus to a hurting world.**

   "I am the Lord's servant," Mary answered. "May your word to me be fulfilled." Then the angel left her. (Luke 1:38)

<u>Courage to Make a Difference</u>

Did you know that Mary's courageous story is all about you and me?
We are all part of Christ's lineage, sons and daughters in God's family!

That magical night when Christ was born began with God choosing a very special girl,
She would bear a child that no one else could carry, one that would come to change the world.

Just a teen, not yet a woman, but God chose her just the same.
She said yes to what seemed like "the impossible", and Mary was her name.

She was told this would be heaven's perfect lamb, God's son who'd save this hurting world.
I'm sure she wondered, "Why me, Lord? I am just an average, Jewish girl."

Isaiah prophesied that when this child was born, this son given to us, the government would be on his shoulders.
He'd be known as our Wonderful Counselor, Mighty God, Everlasting Father, Prince of Peace; and he'd heal our sons and daughters.

So many things that his man would come to do that Mary could only imagine.
Walk on water, heal the sick, raise the dead.....beyond what she could fathom.

The plans for this man were supernatural, yet all she had to do,
was say yes to the plan and surrender her will, allowing God to move.

"I am the Lord's servant," Mary said in the book of Luke, "May your word to me be fulfilled."
Then the angel left her, she immaculately conceived, and with joy of the Lord she was filled.

In the face of shame and ridicule, she stood firm and embraced God's plan.
And because of her actions on that day, we have the precious son of man!

She left a legacy of hope in the form of a baby in a manger,
But she's not much different than me or you, we all have the power to be world changers!

She was just an average, humble girl, being obedient to God's perfect plan.
Obedience really is that simple for every woman, child, and man!

Like Mary, just take a step of faith and watch God work in your life.
Be amazed at how one person can **make a difference**- just by loving your children, husband, or wife.

For if we want to change the world, we need to start with those closest to us.
Placing our relationships in his hands, for it is in him we place our trust.

So when you feel like holding back, when the seeds he's given you seem so hard to sew,
Our prayer is that you would take a stand, as a young Jewish girl did, so very long ago.

May Mary's faith in the face of her own fear be a reminder to us all,
That God can use us mightily when we have the courage to answer his call.

Watch this video and be moved to go out and fulfill God's plan for YOUR life!

"God's Plan For Your Life- Nick Vujicic Inspirational and Motivational Videos" (6:46 mins): https://www.youtube.com/watch?v=beeaXdv_mGg

Meditate on the song "Legacy" by Nichole Nordeman. How will you be remembered? Be encouraged that when you walk in God's will for your life, your legacy will leave an impact long after you are gone. Just as Jesus left a legacy that still carries on to this day, may you leave a torch burning brightly for eternity!

"Nichole Nordeman Legacy" (3:46 mins): https://www.youtube.com/watch?v=7zf-2dKMt0Q

When Pontius Pilate stated that Jesus was a king, Jesus replied with passion and with purpose:

JOHN 18:37

"You are right in saying I am a king. In fact, for this reason I was born, and for this I came into the world, to testify to the truth."

Jesus knew that he was royalty. He knew who he was and what he was here to do. He was a true leader, as he rightfully took his place in his Father's kingdom. He left a legacy for us to follow; be brave enough to step into your purpose and be amazed at how God will change the world in and through you!

EPHESIANS 4:1

"Live a life worthy of the calling you have received."

Go and be commissioned in your Mission!

Lord, commission/empower this daughter of the King of Kings. Bless her hands; help her use them to reach out. Bless her feet; help her to take a stand, rise up, and **make a difference**! Bless her mouth; help her to share Jesus with others. Give her the strength to break records and new ground! There is no other person on this earth that was commissioned to do what she is meant to do. Help her to use all the gifts and strengths you have placed within her to make the mission and vision you have placed in her heart a reality. Amen!

You are the only VIP here to do what you've been called to do! Now go out and LIVE it!

"Dream Big, Princess – Live Your Story (Official Lyric Video) | Disney" (3:12 mins): https://www.youtube.com/watch?v=zRunkRiylvM

NOTES

Introduction- A Journey Like No Other

1. Sean R. Covey, *The 7 habits of highly effective people: Powerful lessons in personal change (25ᵗʰ anniversary edition.)* (New York, New York: Simon & Schuster, 2004), 46.
2. Bill Johnson (2015) *Quotefancy* Accessed July 6ᵗʰ, 2017, https://quotefancy.com/quote/ 1516277/Bill-Johnson-Royalty-is-my-identity-Servanthood-is-my-assignment-Intimacy-with-God-is-my.

Day 2

1. Kerry and Chris Shook, *One Month to Live.* (Colorado Springs, Colorado: Waterbrook Press, 2008), 14.

Day 3

1. John and Staci Eldridge, *Captivating.* (Nashville, Tennessee: Thomas Nelson, 2005), 196-197.

Day 4

1. Beau Taplin (n.d.) Accessed December 12ᵗʰ, 2020, https://afadthatlastsforever.tumblr. com/post/ 75881815418/perhaps-the-butterfly-is-proof-that-you-can-go.
2. Brennan Manning (n.d.) *AZ Quotes* Accessed January 31st, 2021, https:// www.azquotes.com/quote/715561.

Day 5

1. Jessica Rey (June, 2013) *The Evolution of the Swimsuit* Accessed March 4ᵗʰ, 2015, https:// www.youtube.com/watch?v=WJVHRJbgLz8.
2. Max Lucado, *Grace For The Moment Daily Bible.* (Nashville, Tennessee: Thomas Nelson, 2006).
3. D. Harper Online Etymology Dictionary. Accessed June 11, 2018, http://dictionary. reference.com /browse/perfect (definitions 4 &20).

Introduction to Pillar 2

1. Dale Carnegie (2001) *Brainyquote* Accessed October 4th, 2019, https://www. brainyquote.com/ quotes/ dale_carnegie_156627.
2. Marie Forleo (2019) Accessed November 5th, 2020, https://www.facebook.com/ marieforleo/posts/a-good-reminder-as-we-kick-off-another-week-spending-too-much-time-trying-to-def/10156929399383978/.
3. Definitions.net Accessed August 1st, 2015, https://www.definitions.net/definition/ atychiphobia.
4. Jennifer Lee (n.d.) *Pass It On* Accessed March 12th, 2020, https://www.passiton.com/inspirational-quotes/7773-be-fearless-in-the-pursuit-of-what-sets-your.

Day 8

1. Linda Ellis (1996) *The Dash* Accessed on February 6th, 2014, http://www.linda-ellis.com /the-dash-the-dash-poem-by-linda-ellis-.html.
2. Author unknown (n.d.) Accessed on July 7th, 2019, https://www.snopes.com/fact-check /steve-jobs-deathbed-speech/.

Day 9

1. Christopher Maricle, *The Jesus Priorities.* (Nashville, Tennessee: The Upper Room, 2007).

Day 10

1. D. Harper Online Etymology Dictionary. Accessed September 7th, 2018, http:// dictionary.reference.com/browse/ busyness?s=t (definitions 1 &2).
2. Kent Keith (1968), *Anyway: The Paradoxical Commandments.* (Inner Ocean Publishing, Maui, Hawaii; Revised by Mother Teresa, 2001). Accessed October 9th, 2016, http:// www.asa3.org/ASA/education/views/teresa.htm.
3. Teddy Roosevelt (1898) Accessed November 9th, 2015, https://www.biblestudytools. com/bible-study/topical-studies/who-said-comparison-is-the-thief-of-joy.html.
4. Helen Lemmel (1922) *Timeless Truths- Turn Your Eyes Upon Jesus* Accessed January 9th, 2016 http://library.timelesstruths.org/music/Turn_Your_Eyes_upon_Jesus/.

Day 11

1. Mary Stevenson (1936) *Footprints* (Revised by Carolyn Carty, 1963). Accessed March 3rd, 2016, http://www.wowzone.com/fprints.htm.
2. TD Jakes (2015) Accessed October 4th, 2018, https://www.arthurtoole.com/ 3-types-of-people-from-t-j-jakes/.

Day 12

1. Rachel Scott (1999), *My Ethics, My Codes of Life.* Accessed May 25th, 2015, http://www.clover.k12.sc.us/cms/lib02/SC01001948/Centricity/Domain/2243/Rachels%20Essay.pdf.
2. John Schlatter (1998), *A Simple Gesture.* Revised Version- Kyle's Friend. Accessed February 2nd, 2015, http://tahoeepiscopal.org/doc/insp_archive1.html.

Day 13

1. Marianne Williamson, *A Return to Love.* (New York, New York: HarperCollins, 1992), 190-191.

Day 14

1. Zig Ziglar (2013) Accessed April 10th, 2018, https://www.reddit.com/r/awesomelife/comments/ bvc6qq/your_value_doesnt_decrease_based_on_someones/.
2. Father Heart Communications (1999), *Father's Love Letter.* Accessed August 1st, 2014 http://www.fathersloveletter.com/text.html.
3. Constance D. Gordon (2020) *Queenly Me.* Accessed May 6th, 2019, https://www.queenlyme.com/post/joyce-meyers-7-secrets-of-a-confident-woman.

Introduction to Pillar 3

1. Jessica Harris (2012), *5 Reasons Purity Rings and Pledges Don't Work.* Accessed December 6th, 2015, http://www.covenanteyes.com/2012/09/12/5-reasons-purity-rings-and-pledges-dont-work/.

Day 15

1. Webster's American Dictionary of the English Language. *The King James Bible Page.* Accessed January 18th, 2017, http://av1611.com/kjbp/kjv-dictionary/consecrate.html.
2. Jordan Lee (Sept, 2016). *Dear Future Husband.* Accessed December 2nd, 2016, https://hellochristian.com/4586-dear-future-husband-bride-writes-letters-explaining-promise-to- save-herself-for-her-groom.

Day 16

1. Hana Ali, *More Than a Hero: Muhammed Ali's Life Lessons Through His Daughter's Eyes.* (New York, NY: Simon and Schuster, 2000).
2. Steve Maraboli, *Life, the Truth, and Being Free.* (Port Washington, NY: A Better Today Publishing, 2009).

Day 17

1. Steve Maraboli, *Unapologetically You: Reflections on Life and the Human Experience.* (Port Washington, NY: A Better Today Publishing, 2013).
2. Author Unknown (n.d.) *Premier Christianity* Accessed March 3rd, 2017, https://www.premierchristianity.com/Blog/Preach-the-gospel-at-all-times.-Of-necessity-use-words.
3. Robert Fulghum, "The Mirror." In *Chicken Soup for the Teenage Soul* by Jack Canfield, Mark Victor Hansen, & Kimberly Kirberger, 134-135. Deerfield Beach, Florida: Health Communications, 1997.

Day 18

1. Mother Teresa (n.d.) *Good Reads* Accessed October 18th, 2017, https://www.goodreads.com/quotes/2887-if-you-judge-people-you-have-no-time-to-love.
2. Max Lucado (n.d.) *Extravagant Hope* Accessed November 15th, 2020, https://extravaganthope.com/forgive-forgiven-mercy-grace-unforgiving-parable/_the-key-to-forgiving-others-is-to-stop-focusing-on-what-they-did-to-you-and-start-focusing-on-what-god-did-for-you-_/.

Day 19

1. Max Lucado (n.d.) *Christian Marriage Quotes* Accessed May 2nd, 2019, https://christianmarriagequotes.com/2333-a-womans-heart-should-be-so-hidden-in-god-that-a-man-has-to-seek-him-just-to-find-her/.
2. Unknown author (n.d.) *Quotespictures.com* Accessed March 22nd, 2020, http://quotespictures.com/we-need-to-teach-our-daughters-to-know-the-difference-between/.

Day 20

1. Anne Marie Drew, Joan Laney, Ellamarie Parkison, & Anne Wilcox, *365 Meditations for Teachers.* (Nashville, Tennessee: Abingdon Press, 1996).
2. John Simkin (1997-2020) *Spartacus Educational* Accessed September 1st, 2014, https://spartacus-educational.com/REnightingale.htm.
3. Lynn McDonald, PhD, Keynote Address, Department of Sociology and Anthropology University of Guelph for the 7th Annual Conference Canadian Association for Parish Nursing Ministry, Toronto (May 27, 2005). Accessed May 21st, 2018, https://cwfn.uoguelph.ca/spirituality/florence-nightingale-faith-and-work/.

Day 21

1. *ACE Homeschool Catalog- Character Traits of Jesus* (pg. 11-12). Accessed February 2nd, 2020, https://www.aceministries.com/media/pageimg/HomeschoolCatalog_web.pdf.
2. Terry Lige (2019). *The Character of Leadership* Accessed June 28th, 2015, https://www.terrylige.com/leadership/the-character-of-leadership/.

3. Abraham Lincoln (n.d.) *RXL* Accessed January 13th, 2019, http://www.reputationxl.com/quotes/character-is-like-a-tree-and-reputation-like-a-shadow-the-shadow-is-what-we-think-of-it-and-the-tree-is-the-real-thing/.

Day 24

1. Wayne Rice, "Table For Two." In *Still More Hot Illustrations For Youth Talks.* (Grand Rapids, Michigan: Zondervan Publishing House, 1999), 69.

Day 25

1. DJ Edwardson (n.d.) *The Tapestry Poem* Accessed October 6th, 2015, https://djedwardson.com/tapestry-poem/.

Day 28

1. WFMZ-TV (2011) *What Are the Doldrums?* Accessed May 16th, 2014, https://www.wfmz.com/weather/what-are-the-doldrums/article_60145144-bb25-540b-8a71-a86dfebd3f7f.html.
2. Stephen May (1997) *Carpe Diem: Seize the Day.* Alderson Press Corporation. Accessed March 22nd, 2019, http://www.christianstudy.com/data/nt/philippians_c3_v7a.html.
3. Albert Einstein (n.d.) *Brainy Quotes.* Accessed December 1st, 2020, https://www.brainyquote.com/quotes/albert_einstein_125368.

Day 29

1. Archbishop Desmond Tutu (n.d.) *Noble Research Institute.* Accessed November 17th, 2020, https://www.noble.org/blog/a-noble-journey/root-of-the-problem/.

Day 30

1. Katash Diakonia (2014) Accessed January 2nd, 2019, https://katashdiakoniadotcom.wordpress.com/2014/06/24/in-your-walk-with-christ-jesus-sons-of-thunder-katashing-the-nations-day-1/.

Day 32

1. Helen Mallicoat (1982) *Come Aside: Prayer Can Help.* Accessed July 22nd, 2017, https://www.comeaside.com/my-name-is-I-am.html.

Day 33

1. Mother Teresa (n.d.) *Goodreads*. Accessed May 30th, 2018, https://www.goodreads.com/quotes/288714-a-sacrifice-to-be-real-must-cost-must-hurt-and.
2. Max Lucado, *You Are Special*. (Wheaton, Illinois: Crossway Publishing, 1997).
3. Unknown author (n.d.) *Inspiration Peak: Twenty Dollars* Accessed January 12th, 2015, http://www.inspirationpeak.com/cgi-bin/stories.cgi?record=33#:~:text=It%20was%20still%20worth%20%2420,will%20never%20lose%20your%20value.&text=priceless%20to%20those%20who%20love%20you
4. Mac Anderson, "Someone Who Cares." In *Things That Grab Your Heart and Won't Let Go*. (Naperville, Illinois: Simple Truths, 2014), 63.

Day 34

1. Walter Wangerin, Jr., *Ragman- reissue: and other cries of faith*. (San Francisco, California: HarperOne, 2004), 3

Reach for Your Purpose- Erecting the Five Pillars and Putting the Palace Together

1. Tony Robbins (n.d.) *Quotes*. Accessed November 3rd, 2020, https://www.quotes.net/quote/51998.
2. Frederick Buechner, *Wishful Thinking: A Seeker's ABC*. (San Francisco, California: HarperOne, 1993), 118-119.
3. Bob Goff (n.d.) *Psychology Today: Living With Purpose Will Help You to Stop Comparing*. Accessed August 15th, 2020, https://www.psychologytoday.com/ca/blog/prescriptions-life/201805/living-purpose-will-help-you-stop-comparing.

Day 35

1. Google dictionary. Accessed May 17th, 2017, https://www.google.com/search?q=google%27s+ definition+of+humility&oq=google%27s+definition+of+humility&aqs=chrome..69i57j0i22i30i457j0i22i30l2.7476j1j15&sourceid=chrome&ie=UTF-8.

Day 36

1. Author Unknown (2014). *Business Insider: Here are the Major Differences Between Successful and Unsuccessful People*. Accessed March 28th, 2018, https://www.businessinsider.com/ differences-between-successful-and-unsuccessful-people-2014-3.

Day 38

1. William D. Eisenhower (n.d.) *Today's Christian Woman*. "Fearing God" by JoHannah Reardon (2012, March/April issue). Accessed April 29th, 2019, https://www.todayschristianwoman.com/ articles/2012/marchapril-issue/fearing-god.html.

Day 39

1. Kevin Hall, *Aspire*. (New York, NY: HarperCollins Publishers, 2009).
2. Palmer, J. Parker, *Let Your Life Speak: Listening for the Voice of Vocation*. (New York, NY: John Wiley and Sons, Inc., 2000), 80-81.
3. Michael Hyatt and Co. *The Leadership Strategy of Jesus*. Accessed on July 19th, 2018, https://michaelhyatt.com/the-leadership-strategy-of-jesus/.

Day 40

1. Tony Robbins (n.d.) *Success Resources: Your Learning Partners: Tony Robbins Explains Why and How to Face Your Deepest Fear*. Accessed February 9th, 2020, https://successresources.com/tony-robbins-face-deepest-fear-2/.
2. Tony Robbins (n.d.) *Quotefancy*. Accessed March 11th, 2020, https://quotefancy.com/ quote/ 922826/Tony-Robbins-Life-is-found-in-the-dance-between-your-deepest-desire-and-your-greatest.

Redeem the Time- Making the Most of Every Opportunity

1. Theodore Roosevelt , "Citizenship in a Republic," (speech at the Sorbonne, Paris, April 23, 1910 The Works of Theodore Roosevelt, Vol XIII, pp. 506-529) *Leadership Now* Accessed May 29th, 2019, https://www.leadershipnow.com/tr-citizenship.html.
2. Ebigale Wilson, *The Journey Heart Revelations: Discovering a Love that Transforms*. (Scotts Valley, California: CreateSpace Independent Publishing Platform, 2018), 118.
3. Neale Walsh, *Friendship with God*. (New York, NY: The Berkley Publishing Group, a division of Penguin Putnam Inc., 1999), Introduction.

ABOUT THE AUTHOR

Suzanne Gallagher and her husband, Sam, live in British Columbia, Canada.

They both understand that their powerful testimonies will be used to further God's kingdom. In the words of John in Revelation 12:11 "They triumphed over him (satan) by the blood of the Lamb, and by the word of their testimony."

They enjoy the outdoors and love spending time with their two children, Justice and Samuel. Like this book, they are raising them up to be mighty warriors for Christ.

Suzanne believes that every young person is a leader and a warrior for the kingdom. They just may not know it yet!

Suzanne is currently working on VIP (Very Important Prince), to remind young men of the calling God has on their lives as well. Her hope is that these books will inspire people to walk in purpose, and thus, fulfill their destiny!

If you feel led to correspond with Suzanne, she would absolutely love to hear your story! Please write to her at Box 688, Logan Lake, BC, V0K 1W0 or via email at sbourque6@gmail.com

CPSIA information can be obtained
at www.ICGtesting.com
Printed in the USA
BVHW011648160521
607399BV00002B/3